The Narrative Modes

Techniques of the Short Story

The Narrative Modes

Techniques of the Short Story

HELMUT BONHEIM

D. S. BREWER

© Helmut Bonheim 1982
Published by D. S. Brewer
240 Hills Road Cambridge
an imprint of Boydell & Brewer Ltd
PO Box 9 Woodbridge Suffolk IP12 3DF

Distributed in the United States
by Biblio Distribution Services
81 Adams Drive, Totowa NJ 07511

British Library Cataloguing in Publication Data
Bonheim, Helmut
The narrative modes: techniques of the short story.
1. Short stories, English—History and criticism
I. Title
820.9   PR829
ISBN 0 85991 086 5

Photoset in Great Britain by
Rowland Phototypesetting Limited, Bury St Edmunds, Suffolk
and printed by Nene Litho,
Wellingborough, Northants.

FOR JEAN

Table of Contents

Preface

It is with some diffidence that I offer this study to an English public. For although the language and the works discussed are both English, the approach is Teutonic. The very discipline to which the study belongs, *Literaturwissenschaft*, is untranslatable, and its nearest equivalent, "literary science", would set many English teeth on edge. On the other hand, systematic approaches to fiction have gained ground in the English speaking world in recent years, and there is a growing belief that some kind of "progress" in critical method is thinkable. The reader who agrees that such progress may result at least in part from a revival of positivist methods will excuse the lists, the tables and the statistics in what follows.

The statistics, in fact, are no more than percentages of the type "33% of these stories end in speech." To arrive at these statistics, I chose a set of 600 short stories and 300 novels. The representative nature of the stories may be shown by two separate findings. For one thing, most of the results were first obtained with 150 short stories, and since the results with 600 turned out to be almost the same, I conclude that the sample is quite large enough, and that a widening of the sample to a thousand works or more would have made little difference. For another, half the stories were chosen from anthologies like the Penguin or Everyman series, which represent a choice of the best pieces the editors could find in the writings of a century and more, whereas the other half were Canadian stories, most of which were only a few years old (indeed, some of them a few months) – in other words, the basis of selection was a different one. Yet the statistics which matter all ranged, with a single exception to be discussed, within two to three per cent of each other for both groups of three hundred works. The anthologies and collections which are listed in the bibliography were used in their entirety; that is, I made no further selection of my own except to weed out translations from other languages and pieces which were excerpts from longer works, not short stories in their own right. The works not used in their entirety were the collections of Nadine Gordimer and Leacock's *Sunshine Sketches*, each of which topped up the two groups of British-American and Canadian stories to the number of three hundred. The selection was therefore as objective as I could make it. As to the novels, these were drawn on where the short stories, by the nature of the form, could not yield enough material, as in Chapter V. The degree to which my findings are valid for both the short story and the novel is discussed briefly in the conclusion.

These findings, such as they are, involve nothing of the historical, political or sociological background of the works discussed, but rather the devices of narrative. It is the search for such devices which has been a common aim of structuralist approaches for some time now.[1] My argument is that the devices of narrative are more readily found when the reader bases his search on the model of narrative modes set forth in Chapter I. This model is offered as a "theory of structure" without which, as Bradbury puts it, we are not likely to find a "meaningful descriptive poetics" of narrative.[2]

An earlier version of the theory of narrative modes was published as an article in *Semiotica*, volume 14 (1975), parts of which I made use of in chapters one and two. Permission to use this article is hereby gratefully acknowledged. An earlier version of the section on mode-markers in Chapter II and a short section of Chapter III were published in the *Proceedings of the Fourth Congress of Applied Linguistics* (Stuttgart, 1976).

An expanded version of Chapter IV has appeared in *Kölner Anglistische Papiere*, ed. A. Wollmann, 1981 and most of Chapter VI is to be found in *Research in English and American Literature*, I (1982).

Special thanks are due to the students who helped with the statistics, to Manfred Pütz, who read the manuscript and made a number of suggestions for changes, to Mary Clegg for preparing the manuscript, and especially to my wife, who read through the manuscript and made countless cuts so that the reader would have less verbiage over which to stumble.

Cologne   *H.B.*

CHAPTER I

Theories of Narrative Modes

Even the shortest of story forms, the anecdote, tends to use all of the chief modes of narrative:

> Dr Johnson was well along in years when Boswell explained to him the solipsism of Bishop Berkeley, yet Johnson was still nimble enough to kick a pebble down the path and exclaim, "thus do I refute him, Sir!" His was the voice of common sense kicking logic out of the way.
>
> [All texts quoted as examples and not attributed to a specific writer are my own.]

As in most anecdotes, a scene is set, which includes a description ("well along in years"). Very quickly the narrator moves on to the report of an action, which is usually introduced by a time-marker (here it is "when"). He concludes with directly quoted speech and a comment. All the chief narrative modes are involved in our anecdote:

1. Description
2. Report
3. Speech
4. Comment

These four modes are the staple diet of the short story and the novel.

A Brief History of Modes

The attempt to identify narrative modes is as old as criticism itself. The distinction between *mimesis* and *diegesis* in Plato's *Republic* was taken over by Aristotle in the *Poetics* and has remained to this day a basis for discussion. Other opposed pairs and groups of modes have been suggested. Sir Walter Scott says at the beginning of chapter 19 of *Waverley*:

> Now, I protest to thee, gentle reader, that I entirely dissent from Francisco de Ubeda in this matter, and hold it the most useful quality of my pen, that it can speedily change from grave to gay, and from description and dialogue to narrative and character.

I

We can assume that Scott had something like our modes in mind – with his "description . . . dialogue . . . narrative . . . character" list – except that he thinks of the description of character as something rather different from the description of place (a distinction which we shall want to make use of later on). He also neglects to include a category like "comment" or "reflection" in his list. Perhaps it would have seemed to him a natural and inseparable aspect of each of the other modes mentioned. So if we interpret Scott's "narrative" as the equivalent of "report" and put in "comment" instead of "character", we have a complete set of narrative modes.

A more systematic list of modes is suggested by the traditional "five w's" of journalism: who, when, where, what, why. They can be roughly distributed between the four modes as follows:

1. who	(character)	
2. when	(time)	description
3. where	(place)	
4. what	(action)	report and speech
5. why	(motive)	comment

The anecdote about Dr Johnson at the beginning of this chapter follows this sequence and it seems a reasonable and sensible one for a conventional story, one which seeks to capture the reader's attention as quickly as possible. Thus people are introduced before places, action before abstract treatments of their motives.

Passing references to the chief elements of narrative are found in numerous critical studies of the nineteenth and twentieth centuries. But the matter has been pursued systematically only in the last fifty years, with an accelerated pace since the concept of structure came to the fore in linguistics and literary criticism. If structure is a relation of part to part, it becomes important to ask what the parts are and to try to make a list as valid for prose fiction as Aristotle's list of the six elements of drama had long seemed to be for that genre. A positive hunger for such a list is reflected in countless references in British and American criticism of the 1970's, the decade of structuralist literary criticism and metacriticism. As Hawkes puts it, one of the fundamental questions is: "what are the basic units of narrative?"[1] And contemporary criticism is full of attempts at an answer: usually a rather hazily conceived set of "kinds", "levels", "devices" or "functions" of narrative.

Thus we find six "kinds of utterances" mentioned by Suleiman in 1976,[2] and in a study of Faulkner in 1979 we find a differentiation between "those devices which penetrate human consciousness (commentary, omniscience, stream of consciousness) and those methods which present external reality (scenic description, dialogue)."[3] Needless to say, such a list mixes techniques like point of view with kinds of content and leaves out fundamental categories like report and description of character. In the same year Ross speaks of "levels" of discourse in "mimetic voice": dialogue, narrative and authorial discourse,[4] and in *The Story of the Novel* (1979) Watson briefly lists seven modes.[5] These correspond roughly to those presented here, except that some of the usual subdivisions (for instance, indirect as opposed to direct speech) are seen as independent modes.

What we find, then, is on the one hand an obvious need for an encompassing terminological framework and on the other a jungle of terms. Thus it is all too easy to write about these matters in one sense and be understood (or not) in another. But there have also been systematic attempts to locate the chief elements of narrative. There are three distinct streams of development: the oldest is the German one, the other two are the French and the Anglo-American. Since the latter two have come together in the last twenty years, quite uninfluenced by earlier German studies in the field, we can deal with the German tradition by itself and with the French and Anglo-American developments of the sixties and seventies after that. (The reader less interested in the shifting sands of earlier criticism is invited to skip on to the section on "Hierarchy of Modes", p. 8.)

German Studies

A thorough discussion which was highly influential for many years is that of Robert Petsch, who drafted a catalogue of what he called *epische Grundformen* (basic kinds of narrative prose).[6] His terms are the following:

1. Darstellung	roughly:	presentation
2. Bericht		report
3. Beschreibung		description
4. Betrachtung		discussion, reflection
5. Bild		picture, close-up view
6. Szene		scene
7. Dialog		dialogue

Petsch's model is particularly sensitive and detailed in his subdivisions of report, to which *Darstellung, Bericht, Bild* and *Szene* all belong in one way or another. The divisions between them may be debatable, but this is a problem which no system of modes can avoid. Koskimies takes up and elaborates upon this model in a theory of the novel[7] and the section on dialogue in particular encompasses more phenomena than did Petsch's discussion. To Petsch's list Koskimies added the *tableau*, which we will find useful in treating short story endings.

These basic forms are recapitulated by Kayser, who adds a mode he calls *Erörterung* (discussion);[8] by this he presumably means the sort of essayistic form we include under comment. Lämmert, in reviewing the question of basic narrative forms, argues that some of them differ in the degree to which they suggest the passing of time,[9] an observation which fits the reasoning behind our system of four narrative modes. Thus he claims that description is timeless, and Holdheim, following Lukács, speaks of description as "static blocks immune to the flow of time and action."[10] But taken seriously, this would mean that no depiction of something in motion, like clouds passing in front of the moon, could be termed description. Such a claim is hard to accept in critical practice, since even the longest catalogues of modes seem to include no other term to fill the gap. As Lämmert himself says, no satisfactory and systematic review of the basic forms has yet been achieved. If the model with four modes should prove more satisfactory than earlier ones, it is in part because it recognizes the overlapping and mutual embedding of modes, but above all because each mode allows a further division into subtypes, thus satisfying the need for a simple system which nevertheless allows for a wide diversity of narrative phenomena.

The most recent German attempt to attack the whole complex of narrative modes is that of Uffe Hansen, published in 1975.[11] Hansen includes such modes as indirect thought as well as indirect speech (*Gedankenreferat, Redereferat*), takes up the Lubbock distinction between scenic and panoramic description[12] and divides what I prefer to call comment up into the German equivalents of *commentary, analysis* and *reflection.* Hansen's is a clear and succinct collection of earlier work in the field. His set of twelve modes, although they constitute a list rather than a system, has the advantages of a comprehensive survey combined with a precision which makes his list potentially applicable in practical criticism.

Anglo-American and French Studies

The German studies were almost without exception ignored abroad and left untranslated, and the Anglo-American attempts to define the basic elements of discourse went a different way. In 1967 Thale, apparently without knowledge of the Petsch-Koskimies-Kayser development, suggested six modes of his own:[13]

> reportorial
> enumerative
> selective
> atmospheric
> metaphoric
> hyperbolic.

These terms, however, fail to meet all three conditions by which we judge a list of modes: balance, differentiating power and inclusivity.

Also in 1967, Bain named the four modes of discourse as *narration, exposition, argumentation* and *evaluation.*[14] We consider the first two as report and the other two as comment. An improvement on Bain's list was made by Kinneavy, who prefers the terms *narration, classification* and *evaluation.*[15] For obvious reasons, however, these suggestions are even less satisfactory than those suggested in 1934 by Petsch.

In an article appearing the same year as Kinneavy's book (1971), Chatman, using recent ideas of French narratologists, made an attempt to connect Plato's terms with the familiar contrast between *telling* and *showing,*[16] which goes back to Henry James and Percy Lubbock. He relates the *récit/discours* contrast of Benveniste to the terms of Plato's system, so that something like the following set of terms is posited:

Plato	Benveniste	sense
diegesis	*récit*	poet speaks in his own name
mimesis	*discours*	poet speaks through a character

But neither are the terms exactly parallel, nor is this an exact equivalent of the telling/showing dichotomy: James was capable of showing without necessarily making his characters speak. The further advocacy and use of the Benveniste terminology is complicated by the fact that *discours* means something else in the terminology of Todorov, namely the means by which the matter is communicated. In any case, subsequent discussions of the *récit/discours* dichotomy have failed to show that the distinction is very useful for coming to grips with a text. The distinction which Plato made is, in fact, incisive if we want to distinguish epic and drama, though even here quibbles are in order. But Chatman's distinction between mediated and unmediated narrative is questionable, in part because all narrative, including direct speech, is of course mediated, in part because there are many in-between stations, as I hope to show in Chapter IV. Chatman also discusses the dichotomy between "*existents*" (characters, atmosphere) and "*events*" (happenings, actions). These seem to correspond to the objects of description on the one hand and of report on the other. Neither speech nor comment seem to have a place of their own in this model.

In 1975 Chatman came back to the problem of what he calls "transmissional modes".[17] He suggests four: *enacts, recounts, presents, describes*. He also mentions a "process mode,"[18] but apparently with a different sense to the term *mode*. Although his four modes ignore comment, he recognizes its existence as well. Another improvement over the 1971 essay is the concern with "mediation": to what extent does a narrator seem to mediate between the fictive world and the reader? Does dialogue really represent a "mediated" reality, as critics often assume, whereas the report of an action is "direct" and "unmediated"? Chatman's formulation is more careful and tentative: "The bare description of physical action is felt to be essentially non-mediated."[19]

A close look at the narrative modes suggests that this is true of report, the "bare description of a physical action," and that "bare" means without an admixture of other modes:

> John opened the cupboard. It was empty,
> except for a dusty bar of soap.

On the other hand, more description and a touch of comment bring about a quite different effect:

> John, brushing his magnificent black curls behind his ears, opened the Louis XVI cupboard. Unfortunately it was quite empty, except for a dusty bar of soap which Jane had forgotten to take with her.

The sense of mediation is conveyed by the modifiers ("magnificent", "unfortunately") and by the information which a neutral, uninformed observer or camera eye would not register ("Louis XVI", "which Jane had forgotten to take with her.") The degree of mediation conveyed by a narrative text, in other words, is a matter of the choice and mixture of narrative modes, as Chatman seems to suggest in his later essay. Thus a point of view technique such as that of *The Camera*, as Norman Friedman calls it,[20] where no tinge of comment intrudes on the report, will seem less mediated than that of authorial omniscience, which will strongly betray the hand of the maker.

A third essay of 1971, one by Paul Hernadi, differentiates between sixteen modes, thematic, lyric, dramatic and narrative ones, with four specifically narrative modes called:

> *survey* (the authorial mode here called report)
> *directly quoted speech* (being the opposite to "survey" as far as distance
>   between the narrator and the character is concerned)
> *interior monologue* (private speech)
> *substitutionary narration*[21]

Hernadi's scheme has the great advantage of encompassing most of the standard genres, but has the disadvantage of all grand systems: it is so complex that it is practically impossible to apply it to a particular text.

The French views on narrative modes which are now in fashion ignore both the German school and the American ideas just surveyed, Bain, Kinneavy and Hernadi, but they do take account of the Jamesian tradition. The system of Todorov, which Chatman has interpreted for the Anglo-American critical audience,[22] includes the two modes of showing and telling (*representation* and *narration*). The showing-telling axis differentiates between the mode of least distance, speech, and that of greatest distance, report, but does not help us to place the in-between and vital submodes generally subsumed under *substitutionary narration*, including indirect speech, narrated monologue, and so forth. There is, however, no conflict between Todorov's system and the one outlined here. The distinction which Barthes, Brémond and Todorov insist on between *histoire* and *discours* is also compatible with my four-pronged system, especially since the term *discours* is further subdivided into *time, aspects* and *modes*.

More relevant to a system with four modes is the discussion of Genette (1969),[23] which appeared in English in 1976 and is made use of in his *Narrative Discourse* of 1980.[24]

Genette also goes back to Plato. He begins with the dichotomy:

logos   and   lexis
"that which is said"   "manner of speaking"

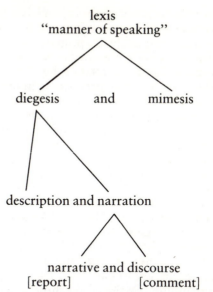

lexis
"manner of speaking"

diegesis   and   mimesis

description and narration

narrative and discourse
[report]   [comment]

Lexis is then split into:

Mimesis is perhaps similar to our ideas of speech, except that it ignores phenomena like interior monologue and *erlebte Rede.* *Diegesis*, in turn, is split between

and *narration* is divisible into

Benveniste had distinguished between this last pair, considering "narrative" as "objective narration" and "discourse" as "subjective discussion". Such a dichotomy is also the basis of the bimodal system of Weinrich, who distinguishes between "erzählte Welt" and "besprochene Welt" as fundamental categories of discourse (roughly: narration as opposed to discussion).[25]

The system of Genette is an attractive one, but it has a number of drawbacks, some of them due to the problems of translating a French system into English. For one thing, the terminology is confusing: it is hard to remember the difference between *narration* and *narrative*, and the term *discourse* is too well established in English for us to give it a new meaning. Second, the system still labours under the supposition that narrative is not mimetic if it takes a form other than speech. Then too, much of what nowadays can make up the bulk of a story, such as the tracing of a character's thought processes or what he sees and feels (substitutionary perception), has no place in the system nor can be conveniently made to fit into it. The problem is rooted in the binary oppositions at the head of the system: the mode of description is not only a "manner of speaking" but in fact also dictates the kind of thing that is said. The stark dichotomy between form and content leads to untenable distinctions. Thus Genette's "description" is supposedly a matter of *lexis* (manner of speaking), whereas in fact one can make a good case for it being inevitably a matter of *logos* (that which is said) as well. In other words, the system rests on a distinction between matter and manner which was thrown out of court by the new critics in the thirties and forties, and this weakness emerges when one tries to analyse a text using the system.

Nevertheless, it should be clear that our four narrative modes are related to the systems of the French structuralists; there are, however, differences. For one thing, the structuralist approach is largely deductive: it establishes an interrelated set of theories, and has been by and large little interested in applications to the explication of texts. Our system of four modes, by contrast, started life as a primarily inductive affair: from the examination of a great many texts it extracts a set of categories which, although they have a logical and systemic relationship to one another, are chosen because they can help us see and interpret details in literary texts which we might otherwise overlook. Then too, the four narrative modes can be seen as a categorization of the kinds of *referential* communication in narrative; but they also take into account what Jakobson calls the *emotive, phatic, conative, poetic* and *metalingual* functions of communication,[26] especially as these occur in the mode of speech (see Chapter IV).

The term *mode* often occurs in modern criticism, sometimes in the way it is used here (as in Watson's study of 1979), sometimes in the narrower sense of "style register" as in Page's essay, "Trollope's Conversational Mode."[27] In David Lodge's *The Modes of Modern Writing* (1977) the word "mode" is meant to suggest a general typology based on Jakobson's distinction between metaphor and metonymy.[28] Lodge uses it to help differentiate between fiction and non-fiction, realistic and non-realistic description as well as modernist and antimodernist narrative. Thus Lodge adds to the synchronic approach of structuralist criticism a diachronic consideration. This development seems inevitable when we consider that the status of the various modes is subject to historical change. That is, the hierarchy of modes is not a static one.

Hierarchy of Modes

Some modes are more popular in one age than another. In our own age, speech stands high in the esteem of most readers. Description is thought boring except in small doses; comment of a particular kind, namely moralistic generalizing, is almost taboo, even where imbedded in speech; and even report is preferred in the dress of, or at least heavily interlarded with, speech. The preference for speech shows clearly right up to and including the final sentence. Of 150 sixteenth to nineteenth century novels surveyed for the purpose (see Appendix B), 22 (14.6%) end with speech, and of the same number of twentieth century novels it is 48 (32%). Of the 600 short stories surveyed, the pre-nineteenth century ones often end with speech too (19%), but the twentieth century examples are twice as likely to do so (38%).

The belief that the author should intrude on the reader as little as he possibly can (this is the "exit author" thesis in modern criticism)[29] means that everything not in quotation marks is seen by some readers as an ugly signal: "Here I am, the author!" So speech in all its various forms is at the peak of our present hierarchy of modes. It seems most neutral, least authorial.

This has not always been so. In the nineteenth century novel, for instance, description plays a great role, especially in the exposition:

> It was about an hour before sunrise, on a fine spring morning, that the great gates of the celebrated Armenian monastery of Etch Miazin, or the Three Churches, situated at the foot of Mount Ararat, on the confines of

Persia and Turkey, were thrown open, preparatory to the departure of a company of travellers, who had enjoyed the hospitality of its venerable patriarch for the preceding night. A waning moon still shed sufficient light to exhibit the sublime form of the mountain, with its snow-capped summit, its undefined protuberance of crags and rocks, its mysterious and shadowy declivities of landscape, to those who stood within the court-yard; the arch of the gate forming, as it were, the frame of the picture. A covering of snow extended not only over all its great cone, . . .

J. Morier, *Ayesha, The Maid of Kars*

Speech is not essential here. The reader is kept waiting for an event, let alone a scrap of dialogue. Many a nineteenth century short story has hardly a word spoken in it, or only one sentence, as for instance Ichabod Crane's "Who are you?" in Irving's "Legend of Sleepy Hollow". This story consists of some report, a fair amount of comment, and much description, partly of persons, but mostly of scenes, and the "Who are you?" Such a hierarchy of modes is not, clearly, the normal one today.

Before the advent of the gothic novel and romanticism, scene played practically no role in the novel; this is true even of the "realistic" work of Defoe and Fielding. People are described, places only rarely. At the top of the hierarchy is report (action). There are some notable exceptions, like *Tristram Shandy*, but most novels of the eighteenth century are crowded chronicles of event. In earlier fiction, on the other hand, especially in many 16th century narratives, moralizing comment is an essential part of story-telling. Comment begins or ends the narrative, or both:

The ancient philosophers are of this minde, that there is nothing that doth more argue and shew a base mind, than covetous desire of coin and riches, and nothing more sign of a noble heart, than not to desire wealth if one want it, and liberally to bestow it if he have it. But I am of this mind, that nothing doth more argue a mad mind, than to desire goods which never did good. . . .

George Pettie, "Amphiaraus and Eriphile"

Pettie wrote in an age when writers of fiction often felt called upon to pretend to instruct rather than to entertain the reader. Such comment as would now be thought wholly unfit for inclusion in fiction was at that time an essential passport to respectability. This was not a simple matter of "primitive" technique, but a matter of what kinds of art were thought superior.

Each of our four modes may be seen as essential to a separate art:

Description: the domain of the painter
Speech: the domain of the dramatist
Comment: the domain of the preacher, scholar, philosopher, philologist, psychologist, critic, journalist

Report remains. It is the essential mode of fiction, although even here the

9

honours must be shared with the journalist and the historian. Report is the staple mode of narration in all ages. This is true however much the novelist may have a weakness for the art of the painter, the dramatist or the preacher. Each mode has been favoured at one time or another. Perhaps it is the sense of immediacy which we appreciate in speech nowadays. But in an age in which, say, moral value is the decisive yardstick by which an action is measured, moralistic comment has a higher status and great appeal for the reader – that is, it has more immediacy – than in our age, where tasting the widest possible range of what John Dewey called "direct modes of experience"[30] is thought to be a primary goal of man's life.

Such changes of taste are reflected in the narrative technique of modal facades. Pettie, for instance, begins his "Amphiaraus and Eriphile," quoted from above, with a moralizing disquisition, but what follows could just as well belong to an action-centered story in one of the collections of Boccaccio or Bandello. The opening with a block of comment is a tribute to the taste of the time. In many a 19th century story, on the other hand, the first paragraph describes at length a landscape which the reader (at least, today's reader) is likely to forget almost immediately and to which the writer himself may, perhaps, not return. In the 20th century, many a story opens with a short speech, after which several pages follow in which no character speaks for himself at all. Even report can be suggested in a first sentence, as in Mavis Gallant's story, "Irina", and then be followed by seven pages of almost unadulterated exposition.

The modal façade is a device of narrative which has no apparent organic relationship to the structure behind it, and so it often looks like an obeisance to the reader, or at least to the taste which the author imputes to the reader: the kind of narrative which the age considers most popular is that with which the narrative begins, although the sentences and paragraphs that follow show the opening to have been a false front. The modal façade is apparently a phenomenon of the short story, which strives for an immediate effect – the novel indulges in it only rarely.

The Articulation of Modes

Not only has the hierarchy of modes changed from age to age, but also the manner in which the modes are separated from one another – that is, their articulation. In earlier narrative it is often easy to say to what mode a particular sentence belongs. In our age this is not so. Whereas description in the Victorian novel tends to have an expository function, in our age description tends to be fused with other modes. In a Hemingway short story, for instance, there may be much of the painter's art, and yet hardly a sentence which is wholly descriptive. In many a modern story, then, speech and report may be easy to sort out, while description and comment tend to crop up only piecemeal and in imbedded forms. That is to say, in many a modern story we have the greatest difficulty in labelling the parts, as Leisi has noted:

Perception, reflection, speech and action, which appeared in the earlier novel neatly separate and in pure form at paragraph length, are now broken up and interwoven, as is made apparent by the division of long paragraphs into single and truncated lines.[31]

This tendency to fuse the modes is an essential quality of modern narrative technique, just as it has become increasingly difficult to separate the narrator's perceptions and comments from those of the characters. Doležel speaks of the "neutralization of oppositions in the stylistic structure of narrative prose."[32]

Nevertheless, the idea of narrative modes would be of little use if the four modes did not constitute distinct semantic baskets; otherwise we could not sort segments of narrative out between them. In practical textual analysis we must demand that our categories meet at least three conditions:

1. *Balance.* They must be large enough that, given a wide range of stories of several historical periods, the sorting process fills each basket at a more or less equal rate. Certainly, if one basket hardly gets used at all, or nothing of importance seems to go into it, it has proved to be of little use.

2. *Differentiating power.* On the other hand, if the four baskets all fill up at the same rate, no matter what text we try to segment and distribute between them, the system has no differentiating power.

3. *Inclusivity.* When the sorting is done, we want no left-overs. In other words, the four categories together must be as nearly exhaustive as possible: the narrower the compass of the model, the less it will reveal, and the harder it will be to link results up with those of neighbouring models and heuristic procedures.

A model with only two modes is easier to handle. Theoreticians have suggested such models, and some of them have been highly suggestive ones from which to start investigations, like Plato's division into *mimesis* and *diegesis.* Our division into four modes, by contrast, has a different basis. It assumes that most of what a narrative contains can be sorted out between the two hemispheres, the physical and the metaphysical. The physical hemisphere in fiction involves the showing of material worlds, real or imagined. The metaphysical, by contrast, involves reflections on such showing, or the discursive treatment of the places, people and things represented. This is essentially the division suggested by Mas'ud Zavarzadeh into concrete and abstract realms, or what he calls the "phenomenalistic" as opposed to the "noumenalistic."[33]

The physical world has two dimensions of its own, those of space and of time:

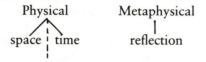

Physical   Metaphysical

space ┆ time   reflection

Fiction, then, is a representation of matters in space and time as well as the reflection on matters in space and time. We call the representation

- of things in space: *description*
- of things moving in time: *action*
- and the reflection on these: *comment*

These three modes, in other words, are not unrelated forms of narrative. They are generated by fundamental categories of thought. No concepts such as *plot* or *character* can exist beside them at the same hierarchical level.

The main ingredient of narrative, then, which no narrative can do without, is action. It is a concept that meets our demand for inclusivity, but it is too large a block to leave undivided if our model is also to achieve balance and differentiating power. Since action is either verbal or non-verbal, it is necessarily presented in fiction either in speech or in report. Thus our four basic modes are derived from the initial division into physical and meta-physical:

Each of the four modes has its peculiar characteristics and special ways of mixing with the others. Thus comment addressed to the world of description makes predominantly aesthetic judgements, addressed to the world of action it makes predominantly ethical ones. Speech is a very special narrative mode which demands further dissection (Chapter IV).

The model achieves a certain symmetry because each mode is distinguished by a different combination of the presence or absence of the two ingredients time and space:

	time	space
report	+	+
speech	+	−
description	−	+
comment	−	−

This is another way of saying that the first three modes are kinds of *mimesis* (though no longer in Plato's sense, who, as we saw, reserves the term for speech and for action directly presented rather than narrated); comment, by contrast, is ideational. But this is a division not to be upheld absolutely in practical criticism. True, report inevitably has a time dimension, the space dimension is normal but not obligatory. Speech generally suggests the passage of time, but it will often refer to things in space as well, although such references are incidental to the mode as such. Description is generally applied to physical things, but also includes the bare location of actions in time. And comment, although its essence is the application of a judgement (usually an abstract term) to something, often has embedded in it references to the thing being judged, like a landscape, a person or an action. The time and space affinities of the four modes thus represent essential tendencies but not absolute and inevitable parameters.

Nor is the model quite absolute in the claim that everything in narrative must belong to one of the four modes. For works of literature contain some elements outside the space/time continuum of the fictional world, including titles, mottoes, prefaces, postscripts, reflections of the author or narrator concerning his literary endeavours, and addresses to the reader. I shall call such elements *metanarrative*. They make up a small collection, but they deserve separate attention. One could argue that they are not a proper part of the fictional world at all. But metanarrative elements, even though they fail to fit neatly into the framework of the four chief modes, are too interesting and important to be ignored – interesting in part because they have often excited critical attention, important because their presence is a phenomenon which distinguishes earlier, conventional narrative techniques; and their increasing absence, at least up to the advent of postmodern fiction in the 1960s and 70s, seemed to distinguish the contemporary mainstream of sophisticated literary development from the seemingly primitive approaches that went before, even suggesting the illusion that storytelling is an art, perhaps a science, in which a measurable amount of progress is possible: away from metanarrative, away from authorial comment, away from the description of landscape.

It is probably significant that this development is not the same in all national literatures; American short stories tend to more landscape description than do their British cousins, and the Canadian short story, judging alone by its techniques of exposition, is even more firmly attached to this convention: 42% of Canadian stories begin with description, as opposed to 34% for the average of British and American ones.[34] In the Anglo-American novel since 1940, the rate has dropped to 18% (see the table in Appendix B). It is a question whether such differences represent "progress" in the art of narrative. We can, at any rate, measure developments, and see where the text before us at the moment makes use of the conventions in favour in one region or age as opposed to another.

The development of the American short story can possibly be seen as making a kind of progress in the use of the narrative modes. The short story genre itself may be thought of as the result of a confluence of earlier genres: the *essay*, the *sketch* and the *tale*.[35] Each of these tends to be a monomodal genre: the essay, especially the formal essay, is mostly comment; the sketch is description; the tale is report. Missing is the component of speech, the province of the drama. Indeed, some of the early short stories, notably those by Washington Irving, as we have noted, contain practically no speech at all.

The short story as we know it, then, tends to be an amalgam, usually an unbalanced one, of the four modes: whereas Irving's story consists of description and comment, these modes may be absent from stories written about a century later, such as Katherine Mansfield's "Theft", which contains the other two modes almost exclusively: there is report and speech, and practically nothing else. Nor are the metanarrative elements frequently found in Irving and Hawthorne in fashion any longer. All these differences, then, are symptomatic of the long-term development.

Probably the fashion that dictates which of the modes is in favour has to do with the purposes to which a writer puts his story, or at least with his assumptions about its functions. Such purposes and assumptions will vary from work to work as well as writer to writer and age to age. A piece of fiction meant to function as moral uplift demands comment, as does fiction seen as the sugar-coating on pills of philosophy or theology. Fiction as history, on the other hand, demands the mode of report. Fiction demands more description, however, if it seeks to convey information from certain other academic disciplines – geography has been popular since the early Victorian period, medicine and archeology became contenders in our age. There is some justice, then in the attempt of Charles Morris to connect the chief academic disciplines to a set of (albeit not narrative) modes of discourse: what he calls the *designative, appraisive, prescriptive* and *formative*.[36] The narrative modes, too, are presumably fundamental categories with a relevance beyond fiction. Where one mode dominates a work, this is sometimes because the fiction has been led into the channel of non-literary purpose. Indeed, literature has been considered a vehicle for economic change or for purveying otherwise indigestible historical facts; it has been seen as an adjunct to the social sciences, as a free-floating art (or even a kind of music), as a sub-discipline of philosophy, and so forth. Its role is still a matter of contention between warring schools of political ideologies. Thus the variety of ways in which one mode or another is preferred or suppressed suggests divergent concepts of what literature is and can do.

Imbedded Modes

From time to time the predominant mix and also the extent to which one mode includes another will change. Some of the modes tend to be harder to identify in a contemporary text than in one of a century ago because both description and comment now tend to appear in smaller blocks (usually less than a paragraph) and tend to be mixed or included in passages of the other two, more predominant modes.

Of our four modes, speech is the easiest to identify, but also that mode which most naturally includes elements of the other three. Speech is first of all a set of words which a person has supposedly spoken: primarily it is anything within quotation marks. Exceptions occur – the dash in French prose, the indirectly reported speech, etc; nevertheless, speech is that mode of prose narrative easiest to spot and label. This is valid even for renaissance texts, which use no quotation marks, for there are other linguistic markers which signal the shift into and out of directly reported speech.

But Dr Johnson's "Thus do I refute him, Sir!" also comments on Berkeley's philosophy. That is, speech can also contain comment (Com), as well as description (Des) and report (Rep) and other speech (Sp):

$$Sp \cap \{Com, Des, Rep, Sp\}$$

The other three modes include one another more rarely; on the other hand, they also amalgamate more easily with one another, and are therefore not always easy to separate.

Description can also have other modes imbedded in it. In its narrowest sense description tells how something looks: a landscape, a room, a face. We tend to think of a set of adjectives applied to a person as description, but as soon as that person begins to move, description turns into report. That is, one normally makes a rather arbitrary distinction: the depiction of things at rest is description, of things in motion, especially if they move by someone's volition, report. A description of a tree swaying in the wind, in other words, is description despite the motion of the tree. If the tree is cut down and falls onto a house, however, we would probably regard a description of the event as report.

Description, then, flows readily into report and the borderlines between them are often hard to draw with precision:

> Oh, heavens! What a scene did I behold at my first coming into the room! The good creature was lying behind the bolster, supporting at once both his child and his wife. He had nothing on but a thin waistcoat; for his coat was spread over the bed to supply the want of blankets. When he rose up at my entrance. . . .
>
> Fielding, *Tom Jones*, XIII, viii

Whereas "coming into the room" is report, "lying" and "supporting" suggest so little action that we must identify this part of the paragraph as description, which, however, goes over into report once more when we reach the time-marker "when" and a verb in the simple past, "rose up". So we can usually, if necessary, distinguish between description and report – though not easily. In the above quotation from *Tom Jones*, both are in turn imbedded in a speech.

Whether description also includes comment and speech is a matter of definition and convenience. A description can be so tendentious, can point so clearly in one particular direction, that it becomes comment:

> It was in their faces, the blankness, the deep intellectual repose of the twenty years of country-house visiting that had given them pleasant intonations.
>
> Henry James, "The Real Thing"

Description does not usually include speech. But it may do so:

> He was the difficult sort of person who always said "no thanks", whatever you offered him to eat, and then would fill up later on expensive after-dinner liqueurs.

The word "difficult" contains the kind of judgment we think of as comment, the "no thanks" is certainly speech. So description can contain not only report but comment and speech as well.

Des∩ {Rep, Com, Sp}

It is even conceivable that description be imbedded in a speech which in turn is imbedded in a description:

He was a sententious old man with a favourite phrase: "no Comanche is handsome until he's dead!"

Certainly this sentence is description to the very end, including the portion of quoted speech. Our formula will be more useful, on the other hand, if it reflects not what is just conceivable but rather what tends repeatedly to occur in narrative. For that reason too, the modes in the brackets are listed in the order of their likelihood, report tending to occur imbedded in description much more often than do the other two modes.

Report, in turn, tends to include snatches of description and comment:

Upon my entrance, Usher arose from the sofa on which he had been lying at full length, and greeted me with a vivacious warmth which had much in it, I at first thought, of an overdone cordiality. . . .

E. A. Poe, "The Fall of the House of Usher"

"At full length" and "vivacious" are clearly descriptive; "overdone" is comment. But when these two modes extend beyond a word or two we are likely to see them as independent, no longer as imbedded in report. This phenomenon is even more true of speech. Speech rears its head quite obviously from any context. Report, then, although in some narratives the predominant if not almost exclusive mode, tends to include the other modes only at the word-level, hardly at that of the phrase, clause or sentence. Nevertheless, we must conclude that

Rep∩ {Des, Com, Sp}

The fourth mode, comment, can also contain bits of the other modes; but, especially in twentieth-century English narrative, it does so only rarely. We may conclude, therefore, that all modes can be imbedded in all the others, but that some imbeddings are almost conventional, others occasional, others quite rare. In general, speech is most likely to contain one or more of the other modes, report less so; description and comment are the most autonomous or "pure" of the four.

Conclusion

What all this means to demonstrate is that our model of narrative modes, like modern linguistics, begins with synchronic considerations, but can also be used in a diachronic analysis of texts. But the most important justification of yet another model of narrative modes is that it meets the essential demands one makes of any model:[37]

1. The model has a *cognitive* value insofar as it brings the chief modes of narrative into a logical relationship with one another, as the simple lists of Kayser, Hansen, Ross and others do not.
2. The model has an *integrative* value insofar as it ties up with related concepts and can be applied to a wide range of literature, including the novel, the short story and to some extent the lyric.
3. The model has an *economic* value insofar as it sets out from a few easily grasped terms and gradually expands their applications and implications (law of parsimony).
4. The model has a *heuristic* value in that it will help generate new hypotheses and theories – for instance, concerning the submodes of speech or the nature of open and closed forms.
5. The model is *practical* in that it can be applied by the average student of literature.

CHAPTER II

Mode Chopping

Dividing up a narrative text according to the four narrative modes forces us to look at the text closely – a healthy preparation for the critical act. At the start, then, we regard the text as a cadaver to be dissected. This procedure presupposes that we can discern the difference between a nerve and a muscle, a sinew and a bone. Mode-chopping[1] presupposes an exact knowledge of the narrative modes, both in solo and in concert.

Linguistically based text models such as those of Todorov, Barthes, Brémond and Wienold,[2] postulate modes as their constituent parts, and some of these models are sophisticated, elegant, and seemingly precise and objective. But the complexities of these systems make it practically impossible to apply them to all but the shortest of texts: a poem or a very short story.[3] Some of the models, such as that of Todorov, have been demonstrated not with the original text at all but with a summary version, the preparation of which was undertaken according to a set of rules so far neither formulated nor apparently seriously reflected upon.[4] Such models have therefore aroused a widespread skepticism as to their applicability in practical criticism. David Lodge has gone so far as to condemn most structuralist poetics as "incomprehensible", although he has gone on to collect those of his own critical essays which make very plausible use of structuralist principles, and to publish them under the appropriate title, *Working with Structuralism.*[5]

Compared to many structuralist analytical procedures, mode-chopping is easy, though it too is neither wholly mechanical nor 100% objective. Many texts are so easily analysed that an investigation of, for instance, the different use of modes in representative short stories of the 19th as opposed to the 20th century, involving scores of stories, can be carried out within the limits imposed by a school or university term. Some passages, however, will cause difficulty. For one thing, the four modes overlap at certain points, especially at the borders between description and comment on the one hand and description and report on the other. This is especially so if we mean to dissect at the word and phrase level rather than the sentence and paragraph level. If someone in a story is called in passing "a nice boy", we might decide that this is description, comment or both. But the mode-chopper does not and need not chop as fine as all that: it is not our purpose to reach agreement on how many grams of this or that mode belong to this or that category. Such statistics are sometimes of interest, but they are of limited relevance in criticism, and where they do occur they must be taken with a grain of salt. Even a rough kind of mode-chopping will reveal that some 19th century stories, such as Poe's "The Fall of the House of Usher", contain mostly description, less report, some comment and almost no speech, whereas many stories of our century contain little description and practically no comment whatsoever. So violent a reversal allows us to draw conclusions about the art of the short story without worrying whether a story is 27% or 29% in a particular mode.

The other problems which may arise are the result of our model failing to represent the world of fiction perfectly; but this is a disadvantage that every model, not only in literary studies, necessarily has.[6] This lack of congruence will show up in two distinct areas: one is that of metanarrative, statistically speaking a minor but nevertheless important phenomenon; the other is in the area of non-representational segments, such as outcries and greetings, which also constitute a statistically negligible portion of our text but again an interesting one which will be dealt with in Chapter VI.

The Definition of Modes

For some purposes an exact description and definition of each mode will be useful, but for determining something as simple as the sequence of modes in a short narrative, common sense will probably suffice:

> Professor Nickle of Yale was a hale and handsome man, polite as a courtier and learned as a library, but rather absent-minded. [description] One day he came rushing out of the library and bumped into a cow that was being driven past. [report] He raised his hat in confusion and exclaimed, [more report] "I beg your pardon my girl!" [speech] Professors are cleverer at West Coast universities, at least they can generally tell the difference between a girl-cow and a cow-girl. [comment]

We could perhaps argue that the word "polite" is really a kind of comment and that the phrase "in confusion" is description. If we wished to analyse the passage at word and phrase level, we would call these imbedded forms; but if we are interested in the general sequence of modes in a typical anecdote, such precision is unnecessary. The rough mode-chopping of the anecdote reveals that the scene is set with a description of the character, then an action is reported and pointed up with a speech, whereupon a comment in the form of a general statement rounds the anecdote out. The introductory description and the concluding comment are the areas where the narrator is free to show off with stylistic acrobatics, whereas report and speech are likely to be comparatively sober. The anecdote reveals the traditional sequence of modes rather than that of the modern short story, which tends to use the more dramatic and dynamic modes, speech and report, as soon as possible:

> "I'll exquisite day *you* buddy, if you don't get down off that bag this minute. And I mean it," Mr McArdle said.

This is the beginning of J. D. Salinger's story, "Teddy". It is a direct speech followed by a report, here a speech tag or *inquit*. Without a closer examination of the exact nature of the modes involved, we can suggest at this point that the mid-twentieth century short story generally gives preference to speech and report in both the sequence and the general hierarchy of modes: that is, these two modes are normally introduced sooner and come up oftener. Whereas O. Henry could begin his stories with a generalization, and continue to pepper the story with authorial intrusions, Hemingway, Bellow and Updike have a quite different hierarchy of modes:

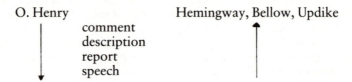

O. Henry   Hemingway, Bellow, Updike

comment
description
report
speech

If we examine two earlier stories, Edgar Allan Poe's "The Fall of the House of Usher" (1839) and Bret Harte's "The Luck of Roaring Camp" (1868), a detailed analysis shows them to be of the DRC type – that is, they rely most heavily on description, second on report, third on comment. As to speech, fewer words occur in that mode than in the other three. By contrast, Hemingway's "The Battler" (1925) and Bellow's "Looking for Mr Green" (1951) are of the SRD type, with no comment to speak of at all. In not much over 100 years, the hierarchy of narrative modes has been by and large reversed.

Nevertheless, for the purposes of more exact analysis, such as we shall require for the discussion of how narrative texts open and close, we need clear definitions of the four modes and a proper catalogue of the signals in the text which will help us to determine doubtful cases. The question therefore becomes important: how exactly do we know one mode from another? What linguistic markers or aspects of content tell us when a shift from one mode to another takes place?[7]

Speech

The beginning of the modern novel is often dated from Richardson's *Pamela*, in good part because one finds there a new interest in the psychology rather than the actions of the characters, in motivation rather than in plot. A process of internalization seems to have taken place. This thesis ignores the fact that the major works of prose fiction written in Shakespeare's day by Gascoigne, Lyly, Green and Forde are no less intensely devoted to an analysis of the inner workings of people than are the novels of Richardson and his followers. The development called *internalization* is not, as is often assumed, a matter of an increasing interest in human psychology. Rather it is a successive shift of techniques, away from an at-arm's-length authorial depiction (description) and authorial discussion (comment) to a use of the more dynamic modes, especially the submodes of speech. This development goes hand in hand with that of dramatization,[8] which conquers the short story in the epoch beginning with Edgar Allan Poe and culminating with Henry James and James Joyce. In our own century a number of submodes of speech have become increasingly popular: interior monologue, free indirect speech and others. The various ways in which speech can be represented has been the subject of a number of specialized studies.[9]

The easiest mode of all to identify is speech. It is usually marked by one or more of the following:

1. The *verba dicendi*, followed by
2. Quotation marks
3. The present or continuous tenses
4. The use of the first or second person
5. Incidental mode-switching indicators: new paragraphs, the use of capital letters, italics, dialect, expletives
6. Shift of perspective, tone or style register. In the Salinger quotation above, for instance, ". . . *you*, buddy", a quotational compound ("exquisite day") serves as a nonce-verb – an expression which Mr McArdle's son has presumably used just before the story opens.

A little more difficult is indirect speech and what is sometimes called "substitutionary speech", including stream of consciousness, narrated monologue, and so forth. Here, too, we often find the *verba dicendi*, but also verbs of thinking, feeling, supposing. Indirect speech tends to be in the past rather than in the present tense. It may be marked by contractions and by conversational tags, such as "didn't he?", or "isn't it?" Expletives such as *well*, *oh*, *ah*, *no* and *alas* belong to the modemarkers of indirect speech as well as of direct speech.

Sometimes the fact that the words are thought to be said is indicated in the course of the text: " 'It grew louder, I say, louder every moment' " (E. A. Poe). Important for our argument is the fact that indirect speech suggests a *selection* from what was supposedly said, with the extraneous details left out:

> . . . when the creamery agent came to the Rosickys to persuade them to sell their cream, he told them how much money the Fasslers, their nearest neighbours, had made on their cream last year.
> Willa Cather, "Neighbour Rosicky"

Indirect speech tends to be embedded in report ("when the . . . agent came") and to include explanatory material obviously intended to fill in gaps in the reader's knowledge ("their nearest neighbours"), and thus fulfill one of the functions of comment. It uses locutions to be expected of direct speech ("last year") rather than straight report in the past tense ("the year before"). Direct speech is now one of the most popular of the narrative modes, but it has not always been thought to be an essential ingredient of fiction at all, and some 19th century narratives do almost wholly without it. This is not true for report, which is the one mode which presents the fictional world both in its time and its space aspects, as our model has shown. Probably a work of fiction which contains little report will tend to slip off into another genre: if description predominates, it will be a sketch, and if comment predominates, we will consider the work an essay. What does not apparently exist is fiction consisting exclusively of alternating passages of description and dialogue. Although such a work has probably never been written, this mode-mix is a conceivable mutant of experiments in narrative.

Report

Report is chiefly marked by its use of action verbs, usually by the past tense and by the introduction of time-markers, especially where preceded by description:

> *After* groping, aimless, with his right hand for a time, he made an ineffectual attempt to release his left. *Then* he tried to disengage his head, the fixity of which was the more annoying from his ignorance of what held it. *Next* he tried to free his feet, but *while* exerting the powerful muscles of his legs for that purpose it occurred to him that a disturbance of the rubbish which held them might discharge the rifle . . .
>
> Ambrose Bierce, "One of the Missing"
> [my italics]

This passage might also be called a description of a man in a particular situation, and indeed, the borderline between report and description is not always easy to fix. Some of the verbs do suggest action (*groping, disengage, to free, exerting*) and the time markers, italicized in the passage, suggest a sequence of events. But certain adjectives embedded in the report (*aimless, ineffectual, powerful*) belong to the descriptive mode, and in fact, the lack of action and concentration on mental as well as physical processes suggests description. There is often little difference between report and description: the depiction of a person at rest is, as we have seen, considered description, the depiction continued when that person begins to move is report. The element of volition is also important: the depiction of waves on the seashore is probably thought to be descriptive; the waves move, but they do not will to move. The same phenomenon, seen as the wrath of Neptune, will strike us as report.

The problem of differentiating between report on the one hand and description on the other is considered in some detail by Stempel and van Dijk.[10] The former, however, does not provide an operational definition, and the latter provides a questionable formula:

> A simple test to identify action sequences is the impossibility to add the adverb *unintentionally* or the clause "He/she didn't want to."

One could simplify van Dijk's test by removing the double negation, yielding:

an action sequence can have added to it the adverb "intentionally".

Unfortunately, the matter is not as simple as that in practice. "The car careened around the corner and crashed into the brick wall (intentionally)" (or with van Dijk, "but didn't want to"). Here we have a report of an action, but the fact that we can add neither "intentionally" nor "unintentionally" to it seems irrelevant to its modal nature. One could also take a clear example of description like "the weather was beautifully sunny and clear" and although it would be impossible to add the adverb "unintentionally" this does not make the description an "action sequence".

Nor is it quite just to call any depiction of an event in time report, in contrast to the supposed timelessness of description.[11] If this finding were universally valid, it would support the basic divisions of our model very nicely; but although report always has an element of time connected with it, description may or may not. No matter how one defines these terms some phenomena remain in a gray area between them, and cannot be clearly assigned to the one side or the other.

There is even one view which regards both report and description as belonging to the same mode; they are both included in Kroeber's "seven regular categories of action".[12] For according to Kroeber these categories are *narration, description, exposition, interiorized dialogue, quoted letter, poem,* etc., *narrative within narrative* – a mixture of overlapping terms with which it is almost impossible to work.

In some of the forms of French structuralist theory a division is posited between report and description, but a practicable set of directions which a mode sorter could apply is not given. Todorov, for instance, distinguishes between *integrative sentences*, which use forms of the verb *to be*, and *functions*, which use the verb *to do*,[13] where the first seems to be description and the second report. But of course there are many verbs used in narrative which are not of the one kind or the other, so that the distinction is suggestive but not sufficiently helpful. There is also a division of stories into two elements: the *existents* (the characters and the atmosphere) and the class of *events* (happenings and actions).[14] *Existents* include what is in our system comment, and dialogue would be considered a kind of action. Chatman has claimed that in Saussurian terms, "the event-chain is syntagmatic and the existent-set paradigmatic".[15] But this too is not a distinction usable in practical criticism.

In the system of Genette[16] the two basic modes *diegesis* and *mimesis* allow of subdivisions which will yield the modes of description and report as well. For *diegesis* is divided into the subheadings or, as I would call them, *submodes* of *description* and *narration*, the latter in turn containing on the one hand *narrative* (report) and on the other *discourse* (comment). But this, too, is a model which includes no directions as to what we do when we are confronted with a difficult or borderline case.

The mode sorter is probably helped most by being told that report is usually characterized by the use of special verb tenses and time markers:

... On a fine autumnal afternoon (Irving)
... at sunset (Hawthorne)
... one morning (Melville)
... at last ... at last (Twain)
As Mr John Oakhurst, gambler, stepped into the main street of Poker Flat on the morning of the twenty-third of November, 1850 ... (Harte)
Jerome Searing, a private soldier of General Sherman's army, *then* confronting the enemy at or about Kenesaw ... (Bierce)
When Dr Burleigh ... (Cather)
Day had broken ... *when* ... (London)
Soon now they would enter the Delta. (Faulkner)

[italics mine]

In each example, a section of report is introduced by a marker, and that marker shows that a particular time sequence is thought to begin. This observation will often allow us to pinpoint that place in the exposition of a story where a passage of expository description gives way to the beginning of the story proper, that is, the point where description gives way to report.

Description

Description presents something which can be seen, heard, touched, smelled, tasted, weighed or measured. The category includes the mere assertion that an object or condition exists,[17] as well as a naming of its qualities. Generally the object is at rest, or at least not moving in a purposeful way or under its own volition. More careful attempts to say what exactly description is, however, have proved curiously unsuccessful[18] and of little help to the critic.

Of more relevance to the critical process is the attempt to divide the kinds of description according to their form and their objects. The kind of description for which Thomas Hardy is known and which is no longer in fashion may be called "expository", whereas the kind of description which may give difficulty to the mode sorter analysing contemporary literature is "fused"; that is, it is worked into passages of other modes at the word or phrase level. This is a useful distinction, although it does not say much more than that passages of description may be either long or short. When description is mentioned in manuals of writing, it is inevitably expository description which is meant. The favour in which expository description was once held both by writers and critics has been explained by Liddell as follows:

> In a descriptive passage in which a novelist is not getting on with his story [in other words, in which the narrated time as opposed to narrative time seems to come to a halt], it is thought his "style" has freer play, and can better be displayed – unhappily many novelists have thought this too.[19]

Liddell goes so far as to refuse the label *novel* to Lawrence's *The Plumed Serpent* because of its long passages of description.

One reason why the distinction between expository and fused description is useful, as we shall see, is that expository description has a different appearance in the modern novel or short story than it did earlier. It is used less at the beginning of the work. Probably it is felt that it will arouse less interest than the dynamic modes, and so it is rather tucked away at later stages to convey a kind of information which in the 19th century would normally have been given in a separate block at the beginning.

The division found in recent French criticism between decorative description on the one hand and *explicative* or *symbolic* description on the other[20] is hard to apply, and, it opens doors to subjective evaluations. The term *indexical*[21] is also used for such descriptions as are thought especially functional in a work of fiction. But the distinction is equally questionable. If we assume when confronted with a modern work of fiction that everything about the work is functional, "organic", then the distinction between *ornamental* on the one hand and *explicative* or *indexical* on the other serves primarily to reject the kind of description that was once in favour and to praise that kind which has taken its place. The distinction suggested by Mas'ud Zavarzadeh between noumenalistic and phenomenalistic fiction[22] says essentially the same thing: noumenalistic description has the function of revealing the general truth in things; phenomenalistic description registers phenomena for their own sakes only. Such a distinction is problematical. It asks not what a particular example of description is or does but what the author intended it to be. In other words, it is a thinly disguised invitation to the "intentional fallacy".

Description can be subdivided not only in relation to form, but also in relation to its objects. Extended descriptions in fiction are almost inevitably either of place or of person, whereby the expository description of places is nowadays considered to be particularly old-fashioned. Description can also have as its object a thing, but this plays no important role in most modern fiction, and practically none at all in fictional exposition.

Aside from the description of place, person and thing the location of an action in time often seems to be part of an expository description ("on the morning of the 23rd of November, 1850"). Very often such passages appear as bridges between expository description on the one hand and report on the other, just as inquit phrases act as bridges leading to passages of dialogue. Although it is hard to say what sense such a phrase as "early one morning" appeals to, no doubt there is some organ of the body responsible for our sense of time, and we cannot be very far wrong by sorting references to time into the basket labelled "description".

The way time is referred to in narrative reflects the subgenre: "once upon a time" fits a different kind of narration than does "on the 23rd of November, 1850". With "once upon a time" we would also expect a specification of place like "in a palace all of gold", whereas the calendar date draws to it something like "on the corner of 6th Avenue and 14th Street". Exact and seemingly mimetic description fulfills the function of what in rhetoric is called a "figure of testimony":[23] a turn of phrase (like "I saw it with my own eyes" or "the great Avicenna teaches us the following") meant to inspire confidence in the truth or validity of what the author then goes on to say. Exact specifications of time and place also constitute figures of testimony, especially if the reader thinks them (rightly or wrongly) historically accurate.

Such specifications necessarily have a special ontological status, especially in contrast to report and speech. We do not assume that someone "really" used the words quoted, but we know that certain times and places do exist in the nonfictional world. It is a general practice that authors take great pains to make their descriptions absolutely accurate. If necessary, they write to their friends to check on details they are unsure about, as we know from the letters of Thomas Mann to friends in Lübeck or those of Joyce to his relatives in Dublin. Onto this backdrop of topographical accuracy is then projected a set of fictive characters. These may show resemblances to the author's friends and relations, but they probably act out scenes which never took place, speaking sentences that were never caught with a tape recorder. Thus we have a gradual progression from a painstaking mimeticism to the fairly unfettered imagination which produces fictional dialogue and interior monologue:

1. description of place
2. specification of time
3. description of persons
4. report of actions
5. dialogue
6. interior monologue

Except for the final level of interior monologue, this progression is probably as valid for Homer as for a short story writer in our time. If Homer's description of Troy had been as freely imagined as the speech of Eurylochos to Odysseus before they disembark on the island of Helios, Schliemann would not have known to locate his dig at Hussarlik and succeed in excavating Mycenean Troy.

The current sense of *mimetic*, it should be clear, is not that of Plato, according to whom only speech can be mimetic. As we see, speech is one of the least mimetic of the narrative modes, in that it is the least likely to represent an accurate transcript from reality. Mimetic now means practically the opposite of what it once did.

In any case it follows that if we are interested in the nature of fictivity,[24] we cannot treat all of narrative as though it were an undifferentiated lump of material rather than consisting of various modes and submodes, some of which may be fictive, some factual, some a mixture of the two ("fictual" in the terminology of Zavarzadeh[25]), others fantastic. As we see, however, fictivity can vary according to narrative mode, and the relative fictivity of description varies according to the kind and object of the description.

The classification of description in terms of its objects is traditional in classical rhetoric, which distinguished between the description

of time: *chronographia*
of place: *topographia*
and of person: *prosopographia*.

The three together in a sentence produce a time-honoured and familiar formulaic effect:

> At nightfall once, in the olden time, [time] on the rugged side of one of the Crystal Hills, [place] a party of adventurers were refreshing themselves . . . [person]
>
> Nathaniel Hawthorne, "The Great Carbuncle"

In our day such compact mixtures are less likely to occur. Common is the mixture of a time-indicator with that of place *or* person. The object of description often indicates the subgenre to which the story or novel belong, and suggests what Karl Mannheim, Robert Jauss and others[26] call the reader's "horizon of expectation":

> *Time*: saga, historical novel, political novel, muckraking exposé, *roman à these*, utopia, science fiction.
> *Place*: the Western, the prairie novel, urban, rural tale, romance. In German criticism of narrative, there is such a thing as a *Raumroman*, a novel in which place is of central importance.
> *Person*: children's story, woman's novel, heroic fiction, story of initiation, novel of adolescence, detective fiction, ghost story, spy novel.

It is curious that most of these labels for narrative subgenres are usually applied to novels rather than short stories. Probably the reason is that the novel is a more highly valued and older genre, and novel criticism a much practised art; the short story, by comparison, has been a stepchild in the family of narrative forms.

The chronographia – topographia – prosopographia distinction, then, quite nicely divides up a number of major narrative types, though not by any means all of them. Each type, one should add, carries with it a set of conventions connected with the other categories: science fiction usually contains a certain kind of person living in a certain kind of place (such as a pilot in a spaceship), the Western requires a hero, a villain and a girl, and so forth. But by and large the chief subgenres are identifiable by their link to one of the three major objects of description. (The conclusion to this study contains a table of the 29 traditional subgenres of fiction categorized according to their usual objects of description.)

By contrast, no subgenres are indicated by the description of a *thing*; in fact, it plays a minor role in most modern fiction, and practically none in fictional exposition. The only examples in my selection of hundreds of works are the beginnings of Virginia Woolf's "Kew Gardens" (flowers) and Jean Stafford's "A Country Love Story" (a derelict sleigh in the yard). In each story the object described occurs again in the conclusion; it is of central importance to the story and not merely an adjunct of expository decor.

Not only the objects of description but also the degree to which it is used helps us define a number of genres and subgenres of fiction. Where description dominates, the piece will generally be called a *sketch*, or, if it is very short, a *vignette*. If it can be identified as a separable and self-contained block, it may be called a *Bild*,[27] and where a number of figures are shown simultaneously against a background, a *tableau*.[28] There is also the subgenre called the *Bildeinsatz* in German, which consists of the artful description of a picture or work of art. The oldest example is Homer's description of the shield of Achilles.[29] Such classical "novels" as the *Aethiopica* of Heliodorus and the Greek novel *Clitophon and Leucippe* make use of this subgenre, which occasionally occurs in modern fiction as well (for instance, Cary's *The Horse's Mouth*). In every one of these examples, from Homer to the present, it would be most difficult to say whether the description is explicative or merely decorative, phenomenalistic or noumenalistic.

A special submode of description which occurs with particular frequency in first-person narratives, interior monologues and narratives employing a central intelligence is that of *apperception*. This is a mental process "in which a presentation is brought in connection with already existent and systematized ideas".[30] That is, that which is at first merely sensed and registered (perception) is then interpreted and thus – from the point of view of the perceiver – understood. The distinction goes back to Leibniz:

> One should distinguish between *perception*, which is an inner state of the monad reflecting the outer world, and *apperception*, which is our conscious reflection of the inner state of the monad.[31] [italics in original]

Kant divides these terms a little differently: he sees apperception as including both the primary perception (he calls it *apprehension*) and the secondary reflection on what has been perceived.[32] His concept that apperception involves the mere consciousness of the perceiver *that* he is perceiving, is not usable in text analysis; for we can analyse only what is recorded in a fictive consciousness, not the fact of that consciousness itself. But the garden-variety of the distinction between perception and apperception is usable for us. This differentiation is also used in psychology. Wilhelm Wundt speaks of active apperception, inherent to which are *will* and *attention*.[33] Writers using interior monologue are not so sure that the will is operative when a character muses on what he has perceived. The character may decide to think about something he has seen or heard, but he may also make unspoken judgements and comments, he may undergo inchoate visions, memories and chance associations, until he receives through one of his senses a new stimulus from the outside. Whether the will is involved one cannot usually say.

Sometimes fiction will contain a character's perception hardly linked to or followed by one or more of these kinds of apperception. But this is unusual. Thus the descriptions in Robbe-Grillet's novels are famous for their bare, apparently phenomenalistic quality. On the surface, at least, his descriptions are empty of connotations. That is, they convey the observer's perceptions but not his apperceptions. Hemingway, too, prefers to convey perceptions rather than apperceptions:

> Outside it was getting dark. The streetlight came on outside the window.

The two men at the counter read the menu. From the other end of the counter Nick Adams watched them.

Ernest Hemingway, "The Killers"

On the other hand, Henry James allows almost no perception to take place without a great deal of apperception:

Mr Moreen had a white moustache, a confiding manner and, in his buttonhole, the ribbon of a foreign order – bestowed, as Pemberton eventually learned, for services. For what services he never clearly ascertained: this was a point – one of a large number – that Mr Moreen's manner never confided. What it emphatically did confide was that he was even more of a man of the world than you might first make out.

Henry James, "The Pupil"

The difference of balance between perception and apperception is not a peripheral quality which the critic can ignore when he considers the narrative art of Hemingway or James. It is a difference of characteristic tone (in the narrow sense of the attitude toward the world depicted) and characteristic texture.

A particular ratio of perception to apperception is also an essential and central quality of the stream-of-consciousness passages in Joyce and Woolf: there is a steady alternation between the impinging of an impression on a character's consciousness and a train of private associations and interpretations; the oscillations are usually slow and wide in *To the Lighthouse*, quick and brief in *Ulysses*:

A procession of whitesmocked men marched slowly towards him along the gutter, scarlet sashes across their boards [perception]. Bargains [apperception]. Like that priest they are this morning: we have sinned: we have suffered [apperception]. He read the scarlet letters on their five tall white hats [report with *verbum sentiendi*]: H. E. L. Y. S. [perception]. Wisdom Hely's [apperception]. Y lagging behind drew a chunk of bread from under his foreboard, crammed it into his mouth and munched as he walked [perception]. Our staple food [apperception].

Here the oscillation between the two techniques has been elevated to an artistic principle and becomes a distinguishing quality of Joyce's narrative method.

Too much apperception is considered a fault in third-person narration. George Eliot, for instance, has been accused by critics of too much "interference" in the depiction of her fictional world. Such "interference" is by nature couched in the static modes, in description of the apperceptive kind, which shades off into and is often indistinguishable from comment.

A number of subcategories for description, then, have been or can be suggested. Which division into submodes a critic chooses ought to depend not so much on theoretical considerations as on the work to be interpreted. For

George Eliot's *Middlemarch* the term *explicative* as opposed to *decorative* description makes sense, and in Virginia Woolf's novels description is surely *noumenalistic* rather than *phenomenalistic*, subjective though this distinction may be. For Joyce, however, as the passage from the "Lestrygonians" chapter quoted above should suggest, the perception/apperception contrast is more relevant (how can we say whether Bloom's observations are genuinely explicative – explicative of what? – or noumenalistic?) and has the great advantage of being both more objectively verifiable and of central relevance to his art.

Comment

The fourth mode, comment, is usually easy to identify at sentence and paragraph level, but it poses problems of sorting at the word and phrase level. We expect this mode to use evaluative modifiers, generalizations not imputed to one of the fictional characters or judgments using a fairly high level of abstraction. If we wished to make the inconvenient non-mode of metanarrative fit into our system, we could argue that it too belongs with the mode of comment:

> Begin with an individual, and before you know it you find that you have created a type; begin with a type, and you find that you have created – nothing.
>
> F. Scott Fitzgerald, "The Rich Boy"

The context (the opening words of a short story) makes clear that the narrator is discussing the difficulties which an author has in the writing of a short story. The level of generalization allows us to label it as comment; but the use or avoidance of *metanarrative* in modern fiction is of such importance that it seems better to allow it a category of its own and to deal with it separately. More difficult to categorize is the following:

> . . . but Mapuhi's mother and wife, and Ngakura, Mapuhi's daughter, bolstered him in his resolve for the house.
>
> (Jack London)

"Mapuhi's daughter" is a bit of explanation directed at the reader, who has not been told who Ngakura is. Such furnishing of "inside information" has some of the quality of authorial comment: the narrator seems to intrude in order to provide background information. But no judgment of an aesthetic or ethical kind, nor of the psychology of a character nor the motivation of an action, is involved. So it seems more sensible to speak of a fragment of description which has been imbedded in a passage of report, and not of an example of comment. Markers which also suggest comment are the logical connectors, mostly conjunctions used at the phrase and sentence level: *in spite of*, *after all*, *nevertheless*, *moreover*, and adverbials such as *possibly* and *it might be that*. Here observations and connections are made which we would not expect of a casual spectator.

Comment is avoided in much modern literature, and when it occurs it tends to be imbedded in other modes:

"It's an awful thing," Nick said . . . "I can't stand to think about him waiting in the room and knowing he's going to get it. It's too damned awful."

Ernest Hemingway, "The Killers"

The story from which this quotation is drawn is known for its lack of descriptive and evaluative elements, but in fact these are present in imbedded form.

Just as the other modes have their special affinities to particular genres, comment in fiction is normally a fragmentary form of essay, philosophical discourse, sermon, or newspaper editorial. It is related to the aside in drama. Like description, it is generally avoided by writers of fiction in our age, especially in its pure forms, that is, unalloyed with other modes, at sentence and paragraph length and in the present tense. More often it appears as an integral part of passages in the other three modes, or not at all. Although fiction is thinkable without direct speech and without description, these modes always seem to be made use of at least in small measure. Comment, by contrast, can be dispensed with almost altogether. It has become a commonplace of modern criticism, but surely one of no eternal validity, that too much comment spoils a work of art.

The affinity of comment to the sermon suggests that the submodes of that genre will also apply to comment. One system of submodes was suggested by Melanchthon,[34] the German protestant reformer and professor of Greek at the University of Wittenberg in the first half of the 16th century. He differentiates between a *literal* kind of didactic preaching on the one hand and the so-called *epitreptic* and *paraenetic* forms on the other. Epitreptic preaching is devoted to inducing belief. Paraenetic preaching is devoted to persuading the hearer to a course of conduct. Thus the didactic, epitreptic and paraenetic forms are parallel to three of the four literary modes current in the Middle Ages and discussed by Dante in his *Vita Nuova*, the *literal*, the *allegorical* and the *moral*. The fourth of these modes would be the *anagogical*, that is, the reflection in literature of a paradisiacal state, a blessed state beyond this life. This is a function which modern fiction rarely takes upon itself. One could, however, point to the short story by E. M. Forster, "The Other Side of the Hedge" or the passages in Aldous Huxley's *Time Must Have A Stop* in which the sensations of Uncle Eustace in the process of dying (and afterwards) are described. The *anagogical*, however, is not conveyed there in the mode of comment, and therefore need not be pursued here.

A Marxist version of Dante's four senses is presented in Fredric Jameson's *The Political Unconscious* of 1981.[35] Here the medieval view of an anagogical interpretation, that is, the way in which a text reflects a view of the heavenly kingdom, is transformed into a view of a political utopia, a paradise in which the class struggle has been finally won.

Certainly many of the most generally respected writers of fiction since the eighteenth century, Marxist or not, insofar as they have a strongly didactic intention at all, make this penchant as little obvious as possible. But there are exceptions. One thinks of the historical background Hawthorne sometimes supplies his reader. In Slater's story, "Adrift", the death of the mother is set against the following statistical background:

> In the summer and early fall of 1847, 863 poor Irish died in Toronto, and of the 97,933 emigrants who sailed from Irish ports for Canada in the spring and summer of that year, 18,625 souls did not live to feel the frosts of a Canadian winter.
>
> Patrick Slater, "Adrift"

Who shall issue an edict saying that this kind of thing shall not be allowed in fiction? Some stories have a how-to-do-it strain, which is also a little foreign to the chiefly undidactic development of the modern form:

> It might be of interest to the reader to follow a simple job from start to finish. First came the problem of getting the old cement up and out, which could be managed in several ways, depending on its age and hardness. If there happened to be grass or mud at the edge of the sidewalk, we took a long bevelled bar and worked it under the concrete, placing a rock under the bar for leverage. Then . . .
>
> Hugh Hood, "Recollections of the Works Department"

This is an unadulterated form of *literal* comment which, considering the usual balance of narrative modes in the contemporary short story, strikes one as curiously out of character. This is in part because literal comment, where it occurs, tends to concern the psychological rather than the physical world. Again, Hardy's disquisitions on rural life are exceptions to the convention.

As to epitreptic (belief-inducing) comment, there is a vigorous strain of it in Hemingway's novels and stories. He advances a set of beliefs which his commentators have dubbed "the Hemingway code". This code, however, tends to be conveyed in the three modes other than comment, and where comment intrudes it is of the integral rather than the pure kind. Hawthorne, by contrast, lets many a story conclude with a block of comment so massive that it almost reduces the preceding story to the level of an exemplum. But even Hawthorne is rarely as outspokenly paraenetic (behaviour-inducing) as is Allen Cunningham in his story "The Haunted Ships", who concludes this story with "bless all bold men, say I, and obedient wives!" Such a sentence, both in its form and its content, is not likely to grace the conclusion of a short story today. In the nineteenth century the short story was apparently thought the better for containing an explicit block of comment (in the latter part of the eighteenth century it would have been termed a *sentiment*) to direct the reader's perceptions. Its most "pointed" form, as Williamson[36] called it, is the epigram, still popular for bringing a narrative to a resounding close. *Epitreptic* (belief-inducing) comment may still crop up in subtle ways, but out-and-out *paraenetic comment* is altogether out of fashion.

Borderline cases

Having looked at the four modes in detail, it will be clear that a brief definition of each cannot do its varieties of form and function justice. Yet we need a summary definition of each of the four, if only to grapple with some typical borderline cases.

1. In speech the fictional character rather than the narrator or author expresses himself. Thus not only direct speech but also thought and perception (see Chapter IV) may fall under this heading.

In first-person narration, however, the narrator must be excepted from this rule. Otherwise the whole work would consist of speech; this would blur and weaken the differentiating power of the four modes.

Sometimes, especially in narrated monologue, one can hardly decide whether the emphasis is on the narrator's or on the character's consciousness:

A. Wasn't that ugly old Mr Roedutton coming over? (speech in the form of narrated monologue)

B. Dorothea saw that Mr Roedutton was approaching her. (description and report)

In sentence A the expression is at least in part that of the character, in B rather that of the narrator.

2. Report is the depiction of actions, usually human.

A. Birds were singing in the trees. (description)

B. Children were singing in the classroom. (report)

The assumption is that in sentence B there is an element of volition or at least of consciousness on the actor's part. Therefore report.

3. Description is primarily the naming and orientation of things in space but also the naming of the time or season: "It was noon of a fine spring day." Description usually tells the looks or the attributes of places, persons and things as well as the naming of relationships between them.

A. A weathered look-out stood at the edge of the clearing. (description)

B. Martha was John's daughter by an earlier marriage. (description)

C. Martha stood in the doorway. (description)

D. Martha got up and stood in the doorway. (report)

In sentence D the focus is on a motion *in time*. Therefore report. Sentences A, B and C, however, count as description.

Whether description can include evaluation or not has been debated in recent years.[37] Certainly description in fiction often includes a judgement, covertly if not overtly, and therefore the borderline with comment is easily reached.

4. Comment is the explanation or interpretation of persons, places, objects and actions. Its chief functions are to define their nature by the application of abstract terms, especially by ethical and aesthetic judgements, but also political, social and economic ones. Comment assigns purposes, causes, motivations. The language of comment is distinguished by a lack of space and time references, although these may be embedded:

A. He was in an ugly mood in the spring of that year. (comment? description?)

B. Ledoux always wore a supercilious and skeptical smile on his lips. (description)

C. Ledoux had a supercilious and skeptical attitude toward others. (comment)

Sentence B emphasizes the look of the person, registering qualities to be perceived directly by the senses, whereas in C the emphasis is on the general nature and psychological attitude of the person being analysed.

Problems in Mode-Chopping

Fictional texts sometimes contain passages which are hard to ascribe to one mode or another, not because they are borderline cases but because at first glance none of the definitions given above seems to fit. Usually this is because the passage contains a "transformation" or a "virtual" mode. The "transformations" are those familiar from transformational-generative grammar: the passive, the question, the negation. Thus we can take a statement like "he was taken to the station" to be the equivalent of "X took him to the station." "Did he go to the station?" seems even less a clear example of any mode, unless it is a speech; but it seems legitimate to read this as "he went to the station" and classify it as report. The negated form "he did not go to the station" can be seen, modally speaking, as a variant of "he went to the station" as well.

The "virtual" form is one which any of the modes except for comment may take. It consists of imagined speech, of report conceivable rather than actual, or of imaginary description. The phenomenon is very common in modern fiction.

In *virtual speech* what a character says is only imagined by another character, or by the narrator in a first-person narrative:

> There's something I have to tell you, I thought of saying during the commercial.
>
> Margaret Atwood, *Lady Oracle*

The unspoken speech may also be a narrator's way of interpreting a scene or an action:

> I said to him: "It's lucky that I'm an old hand. If I were a raw recruit, I might be disillusioned by your attitude." He gave me a long, cool, shrewd look which said: Well, of course I wouldn't have made the remark if you hadn't been an old hand . . .
>
> Doris Lessing, *The Golden Notebook*

> He wore a look of great sincerity most of the time, as if he wanted to say, Please tell me what you are thinking. I so much want to know.
>
> Mavis Gallant, "An Unmarried Man's Summer"

Here virtual speech is not marked in the way direct speech usually is, but the same author also uses the technique with quotation marks or with italics:

I thought he would say, "Oh, I'm sorry," and I had my next answer ready about not begrudging a cent of it. But my father closed his eyes, smiling, saving up more breath to talk about nothing.
                                    Mavis Gallant, "The End of the World"

His stupid, friendly face wore its habitual expression of deep attention: *I am so interested in you. I am trying to get the point of every thing you say.*
                                    Mavis Gallant, "An Unmarried Man's Summer"

Virtual report is the statement that an action *might* have occurred or been undertaken:

. . . I had thought, for some hours, of excerpting the lines of Gray's — the ones that still ring in my head. But, on reflection, though they suit well enough, they yet seem too cruel to the dust.
                                    Stephen Vincent Benet, "The Curfew Tolls"

Virtual description, again, is the presentation of that which cannot be or would not have been seen:

Even farther out, somewhere beyond Cape Spear lies Dublin and the Irish coast; far away but still the nearest land and closer now than is Toronto or Detroit to say nothing of North America's more western cities; seeming almost hazily visible now in imagination's mist.
                                    Alistair MacLeod, "The Lost Salt Gift of Blood"

Often it occurs together with virtual report:

In her mind's eye she is always advancing, she is walking between lanes of trees on a June day. She is small and slight in her dreams, as she is in life. She advances toward herself, as if half of her were a mirror. In the vision she carries Ruth, her prettiest baby, newly born, or a glass goblet, or a bunch of roses.
                                    Mavis Gallant, "Malcolm and Bea"

The increasing use of the virtual modes may be connected with the turn toward internalization in modern fiction, with the increasing focus on consciousness rather than plot, or with the penchant for fabulation: the inclusion in fiction of further fictions imagined by fictional characters or presented by the narrator himself as alternative versions of events.[38] In classical rhetoric this is called *hypotyposis*: the description of people and events that exist in the imagination only. The phenomenon has been recognized by the linguist van Dijk,[39] who speaks of "seminarratives". It usually occurs at sentence-length or a paragraph at a time, as the examples above show. Rarely does it extend over major blocks of narrative: in Ambrose Bierce's "An Occurrence at Owl Creek Bridge" most of the events turn out to have occurred only in the imagination of the protagonist in the seconds before he dies by hanging, and in William Golding's *Pincher Martin* we also find in the last chapter that we have followed no "real" events but the visions of a drowning man. In Bierce and Golding the technique is a trick which cannot be pulled off again and again. But at the sentence and paragraph level the virtual modes can be of repeated service. The virtual modes tend to appear with particular frequency in the final paragraph of a work of fiction. We find 106 examples in the final sentences of our 300 novels (35%) and 186 in our 600 short stories (31%), with a steady rise from the sixteenth century to the post-WW II period. In Mavis Gallant's collection, *The End of the World and Other Stories* there are dozens of examples. In practice they do not pose any great problem when we set about chopping modes.

CHAPTER III

The Modes in Concert

Once we are able to identify the narrative modes in solo, we can move on to consider them in concert. As I have noted, the sequence of modes in the modern story tends to be different from that in the nineteenth century. There the story may begin with report, but the exposition with description and comment is more common. This is probably even more true of the novel than of the short story. If there is speech in the story, it follows later. Certain sequences seem to be common, others are rare, although all sequences are conceivable. Certainly the style of a narrative is in part dependent on the kinds of sequences and the frequency of a shift from one mode to another. This matter has been examined in a number of Victorian novels by Kroeber, who argues that fiction is distinguished by its "interaction between narrative and dialogue."[1] He shows that some novels are characterized by passages of *stichomythia*, the alternation of short speeches in a dialogue, whereas others tend to advance in blocks of report interrupted by dialogue containing a series of longer speeches.

The sequence and balance of modes is of course easier to survey in a short story, easier yet in the anecdote. Here there seem to be three basic types of sequence, a division also applicable to short story expositions. First there is the simple or anecdotal, illustrated at the opening of Chapter I in the story about Dr Johnson and Berkeley's solipsism: the sequence Des→Re→Sp→Com. The traditionally didactic exposition, by contrast, begins with a comment, usually including a statement of intentions:

$$Com \rightarrow Des \rightarrow Rep \rightarrow Sp.$$

The third type, the dramatic, is almost the reverse of this, either beginning with speech or moving to it as quickly as possible. It is illustrated by an anecdote which J. F. Wallwork tells about his own son in *Language and Linguistics*:

"Adam," we asked, "which is right, 'two shoes' or 'two shoe'?" His answer on that occasion, produced with explosive enthusiasm, was "Pop goes the weasel!" The two-year-old child does not make a perfectly docile experimental subject.[2]

37

In contrast to the anecdote about Dr Johnson kicking the stone, this one starts with speech, has almost no report or description, and concludes with a comment.

Whether simple, didactic, or dramatic, the "transitional probabilities", as a linguist would call them, remain similar. Description tends to be followed by report rather than speech, and speech tends to be preceded, and less often, followed by report. On the whole, speech and report, the more dynamic modes, tend to come together, and the static modes, comment and description, also tend to pair off.

Modal Deficits

We can characterize some authors by showing that they use the static modes almost exclusively, like Irving, or prefer the dynamic modes, like Hemingway. But we cannot get at essential qualities of many works in this way: fiction generally uses both static and dynamic modes, especially description and report. Mode chopping becomes a more sensitive instrument if we ask not only which particular modes are preferred but also which modes are in deficit. For in the detailed analysis of texts we often find that one of the modes is underrepresented. Many passages, indeed, whole works, have a special texture and effect because they contain very little comment, speech or description. This finding also applies to some authors in general. Thus we would not expect a critic to write a study of Irving's dialogues, of Hemingway's moralizing, or of Salinger's description of landscape. One might as well attempt to study the function of the telephone conversation in Jane Austen. Even report, the staple of narrative, is sometimes underrepresented in a striking way, a phenomenon by no means rare in modern fiction.

Modal deficits also occur at the submode level. Some works of fiction contain exclusively scenic as opposed to panoramic report, description in the form of a character's perception but not of apperception, or exclusively direct as opposed to indirect or reported speech. In the novel, occasionally in the short story too, a whole chapter or section will be radically distinguished in this respect. A modal deficit is often a function of what a particular passage or work is about, but it may also reflect special interests of the author which persist from one work to another, or it may reflect the taste of the period.

Changing Tastes in Narrative Modes

Much of what has been said above concerning the nature of the four modes, how they function separately and in combination, is objectively verifiable. But why one age prefers a different sequence and balance of modes or sets more store by the one than the other is harder to explain. I should like to suggest that four concepts help explain why writers have come to prefer the dynamic to the static modes. They are the concepts of *mediation*, of *narrative pace*, of *selectivity* and of *reader participation*. Each of these concepts is based on assumptions which must remain in part subjective and unverifiable.

Modes and Mediation

According to Plato, the *mimetic* mode is that of drama, in which words and actions are presented directly, whereas a work of fiction like the *Odyssey* belongs to the *diegetic* mode: the poet mediates between the fictional world and the reader/listener/spectator, in that he speaks *for* his characters. It is a basic distinction which has given rise to over two millenia of discussion. On closer scrutiny, as we have seen, it is not unproblematical. For some plays have *diegetic* portions (characters tell stories, comment on the action, etc.); and epic works are in parts more *mimetic* than in others. Telling is less mimetic than showing, a distinction at odds with Plato's, where by definition an undramatized work of literature cannot in the original sense be *mimetic*. Yet the distinction has continued to prove fruitful for the criticism of prose narrative: it has come to be accepted that an author who too obviously meddles with his fiction is being somehow unartful. This standard has surely helped lead to the demise of metanarrative and comment, since they seem to be kinds of *unmimetic* or even *antimimetic* art.

The domain of description too has come to be thought dangerous ground, since it seduces the writer into calling attention to his own craft, that is, to the fact that the fictional world is being mediated. This is especially true where the description reveals the guiding hand of the narrator by means of telltale rhetorical touches:

> The last of light was gone now save the thin stain of it snared somewhere between the river's surface and the rain.
>
> William Faulkner, "Delta Autumn"

The metaphor "snared" is a poetic device which the reader may find unusual. The reader can ask himself whether he, as a chance observer of the scene depicted, would have registered with his camera the evening light as a "stain" that has been "snared". Whether we choose to classify "snared" as description or as a kind of comment, it reveals the mediating hand of the narrator, his apperception as well as his perception. The problem will generally occur when a rhetorical figure occurs at phrase or clause level, as in this passage from a Benet story:

> The stranger came in — very dark and tall he looked in the firelight. He was carrying a box under his arm — a black japanned box with little air holes in the lid. At the sight of the box Jabez Stone gave a low cry and shrank into a corner of the room. "Mr Webster, I presume," said the stranger, very polite, but with his eyes glowing like a fox's deep in the woods.
>
> Stephen Vincent Benet, "The Devil and Daniel Webster"

The passage begins with report and proceeds to a description of the devil come to fetch the soul of Jabez Stone. There is a slight break in perspective at "air holes", since a camera might register the holes in the laquered box, but it would not tell us that they are meant to let air into the box. One might also inquire into the perspective of "at the sight of the box". The words "very polite" are another borderline case: let us call them description rather than comment, since "polite" might be thought an objectively observable phenomenon. But "glowing like a fox's deep in the woods" is a simile which strongly suggests the artist's guiding hand. Thus description which is given the high polish of rhetoric becomes less mimetic: it suggests mediation. The effect is increased by blocks of expository description, minimal in fragments of fused description.

It follows that, whereas metanarrative and comment are usually grossly *diegetic*, description is in a middle position, suggesting more or less mediation according to how it is handled. The writer who wants to be safe in this regard had best restrict himself to report and speech as much as possible, for these convey about as weak a sense of mediation as can be achieved this side of the theatre performance:

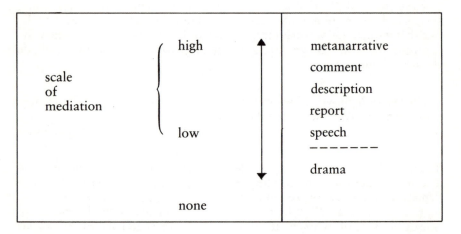

Report and speech, in fact, are just as subject to variations in mediating quality as is description. In the domain of speech, as I want to show in the next chapter, we can find a whole range of phenomena reaching from direct speech on the one hand to reported speech on the other.

It should be clear that the "scale of mediation" both simplifies and makes pseudo-objective what is by nature a wide range of subjective impressions. Understandably enough, critics are likely to hedge in statements about degrees of mediation with reservations and modifications. Chatman says of report: "The bare description of physical action is felt to be essentially non-mediated."[3] Of course we know that nothing in fiction is non-mediated. Every word a fictional character utters is just as much a product of the author or narrator as is an authorial comment in the style of Fielding or Thackeray. But we like to forget this fact and enjoy the illusion which fiction can convey. The taste for seemingly unmediated fiction has led to a strong preference for report and speech, a preference which has survived and perhaps grown through all the vicissitudes of modern and postmodern literature.

The Submodes Reviewed: Narrative Pace

I have already, bit by bit, introduced the most common submodes; I should like at this point to review them briefly and to show how each is the vehicle for a narrative pace peculiar to itself.

We have seen that description can occur at the word rather than the sentence-level, and thus seem so imbedded in one of the other modes that we might well overlook it. I have called this kind of description *fused*, and the extended kind, that which occurs in a block, *expository*. Within this subclass, again, there are sub-types: the expository descriptions of Irving, for instance, may be thought *ornamental* or *phenomenalistic*; those of Edgar Allan Poe tend to be *integral*. That is, Poe's descriptions tend to set a scene within which events develop, and develop as they do in part *because* of the scene which has been set, such as a dungeon or a mansion on insecure foundations. As I have said earlier on, description in the major twentieth century writers tends to be of the fused rather than of the expository type. If it is the latter, it is integral rather than ornamental, or at least critics hope for and prefer the integral kind: it gives them more scope for interpretation.

Report can hardly be ornamental, unless we choose to call the digression of the eighteenth century novels so. But the distinction between panoramic and scenic report, that is, between the close-up and the telescopic lens, has been suggested by Lubbock,[4] and it is a useful one, since one can localize the two kinds in most pieces of fiction. Again, there is a historical development: scenic is the kind of report preferred since Fielding and Sterne, although narratives have always used both types. The kinds of narrative report, especially the variation in point-of-view which it allows, have been examined in great detail by such contemporary theorists of fiction as Franz Stanzel,[5] Wayne Booth,[6] and the modern structuralists.

When we come to speech, a subdivision into *direct* and *indirect* is conventional and useful in everyday textual analysis. As to comment, it can be subdivided into *pure* and *integral*. Nowadays one prefers comment which is integral or fused with other modes, or at least confined to short passages imbedded in speech. An opinion attributed to a fictional character can arouse a reaction, start a discussion, help to characterize the speaker, or motivate an action. That is, it is likely to be multifunctional. Pure comment, by contrast, even where hardly intrusive, is in the eyes of many critics material which an author has failed to integrate by means of his narrative art. This is especially true of comment in present tense ("It is a truth universally acknowledged, that . . .").

The submodes reviewed here differ from one another not only in that they arouse in the reader different illusions of mediation but also of narrative pace. Some modes are slow, some are fast, some make the clock of fictional time seem to stop altogether. That is to say, the reader feels a story to be making "progress" when speech is quoted or action is presented scenically. On the other hand, the sense of fictional time passing is absent where the author philosophizes or where he describes a landscape at great length. The modes and their subclasses can be arranged in a table to show the range of possibilities for conveying the illusion of time passing.

1		2		3		4	
comment		description		speech		report	
pure	integral	exposi tory	fused	direct	indirect	scenic	pano ramic
stopped	slow	stopped	slow	fairly fast	fast	fairly fast	fast

Although our chart cuts out all the transitional phenomena, it does allow us to make a number of convenient generalizations:

1 each of the chief narrative modes has at least two submodes;
2 each submode suggests a slow, medium or quick passage of time;
3 the static modes, naturally enough, give less sense of time-flow than do the dynamic;
4 the illusion of pace is caused by narrated time being telescoped, stretched, or balanced with narrative time, and two of the submodes allow such a balance: direct speech and scenic report. These are the two submodes which English writers in our time most favour;
5 the submodes most difficult to separate from one another in a text are in part those which treat time in the same or in a similar way: integral comment and fused description, where the sense of time passing is slow if not altogether stopped.

Like his sense of mediation, the reader's sense of time passing is in fact only an illusion, not an absolute and constant function of the narrative submode. When fictional characters speak, a sense of time passing is conveyed, of something happening. In fact, usually nothing *happens* when a character speaks in a story. Indeed, talk stops when the character fights or runs. Or talk may be interspersed with a depiction of sword thrusts, pistol shots and shouts: but these things can occur simultaneously only in the drama, not in conventional fiction. Then too, a character may speak for three minutes, and the reader, who takes half that time to read the passage, may have the impression that three minutes have elapsed. Again, the reader's feeling that narrative and narrated time coincide is an illusion. Thus such labels as "slow" and "fairly fast" in our chart denote subjective judgements, and the lines between them are fuzzy. Nevertheless, critics who have commented on this matter show a large measure of agreement. German criticism in particular has devoted considerable attention to how a sense of time is conveyed in narrative.[7] The term for telescoping time is *Raffung*, literally the taking of an area of cloth, like a window curtain, and folding it so that it covers less area. A rough English equivalent is the *pleat* or the *ruffle*. Lämmert, for instance, lists a number of ways in which narrative ruffles are made.[8] At least one critic has seen that such ruffles are achieved by a certain choice of narrative modes,[9] that some are slow and others fast. The writer who sticks to report at the expense of description and speech[10] can telescope the "real" time of the fiction – at the expense of the more balanced relation of narrated to narrative time which has become an essential quality of modern realism. The highest degree of ruffling, then, is to be achieved by report at the expense of the other modes, and most of all by the "fastest" mode of all, panoramic as opposed to scenic report, which can encompass the chief events of several years in a sentence.

Different representations of how the submodes affect the illusion of time are possible. We might, for instance, choose to represent the relationship between narrative time (the time taken by the author to tell his story) and narrated time (the reader's sense of the time which is passing in the story) as two parallel lines:

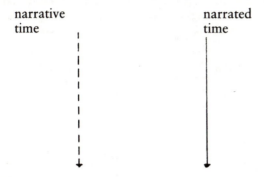

narrative time

narrated time

In direct speech the two lines are parallel. What, however, happens when the events of several weeks are related in a few sentences? Then more fictive reality is represented per minute of narration, and a kind of time cave interrupts the surface of the fiction conveyed:

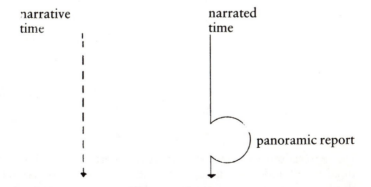

narrative time

narrated time

panoramic report

On the other hand, the sense of fictive time passing may be interrupted when the author stops to describe a landscape or to comment at length on what has occurred. Here the narration continues while the movement of narrated time stops. In other words, a time pouch results:

43

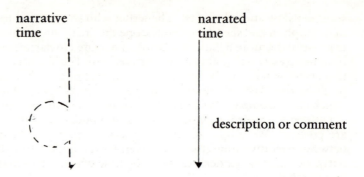

narrative
time

narrated
time

description or comment

Thus the relationship between narrative time and the time structure within the fiction varies according to the narrative modes and submodes; this variation can be represented with a series of time pouches and time caves:

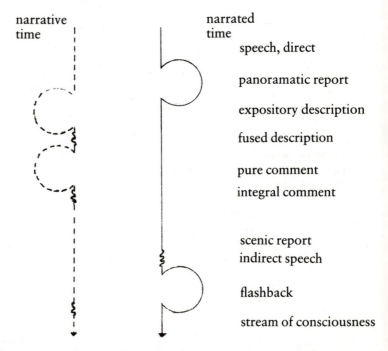

narrative
time

narrated
time

speech, direct

panoramatic report

expository description

fused description

pure comment
integral comment

scenic report
indirect speech

flashback

stream of consciousness

The representation of a particular piece of narrative in this way is a laborious and difficult undertaking, especially because, as we have seen, the modes are all mutually inclusive. A simpler system has been suggested by Cwik.[11] He assumes that the narrative time proceeds at a constant pace, and so needs no graphic representation. There remains only one line for narrated time, which is interrupted by dots or horizontal dashes where it seems to be slowed down or stopped:

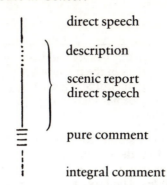

direct speech

description

scenic report
direct speech

pure comment

integral comment

On the other hand, the line is given arrows where it seems to be speeded up:

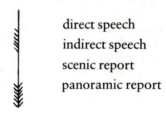

direct speech

indirect speech

scenic report

panoramic report

The following text, taken from D. H. Lawrence's short story, "The Horse Dealer's Daughter", is segmented and the segments are roughly labelled with the appropriate mode or submode:

pace	text	mode
	"Well, Mabel, and what are you going to do with yourself?"	direct speech
	asked Joe,	report
slow	with foolish flippancy.	comment
	He felt quite safe himself.	description
slower	Without listening for an answer,	
	he turned aside,	
	worked a grain of tobacco	
	to the tip of his tongue,	scenic report
	and spat it out.	
stopped	He did not care about anything,	comment
	since he felt safe himself.	description
fairly	The three brothers and the	description
fast	sister sat round the desolate	leading into
	breakfast table,	report
	attempting some sort of	
	desultory conversation . . .	

45

pace	text	mode
very fast	↓ For months, Mabel had been ↓ servantless in the big house, ↓ keeping the home together in ↓ penury for her ineffectual ↓ brothers.	panoramic report; some embedded description

The method is suited to the lecture hall, for it displays graphically the relation of submode and narrative pace. It has the disadvantage that most texts contain not only the clear modal sounds but much "noise" in the way of imbedded modes. Then too, the danger is that the focus narrows too much to the single word or phrase. One can of course consider the grammatical status of individual words such as "without", "anything", "servantless" or "penury", but at the clause or sentence level they become part of a narrative, and thus of a narrative mode. The critic gains little by labelling each word separately. Rarely does a single word (adverbs like "later" and "suddenly" are exceptions) very much affect narrative pace.

If narrative pace is greatest in panoramic report, one might think that this would be the writer's favourite mode. But the optimum relationship between narrative and narrated time seems to be about 1:1. Extended passages of the modes which seem either very fast or altogether stopped are not nowadays in favour. Popular are the middle-paced modes, above all scenic report and direct speech, which yield the most balanced relationship of narrative to narrated time.

The Selectivity Principle

The technical level of much modern writing is high: the writer today is generally aware of the possibilities of his craft in a way that his predecessors were not. He is more careful in the choice of his ingredients and techniques: more self-conscious, more efficient, more attuned to an elite audience which assumes his command of narrative strategies and artifices. The short story in particular has been thought to have been born of Poe's demand that every detail in a story must be telling. Selectiveness is also the principle of the "wellmade novel": inserted stories, irrelevant episodes, exotic settings described in detail — these are jettisoned in favour of a concentration of novelistic effects.

Yet we demand of the narrative of our time that it *seem* to be slapdash and apparently *un*selective, that no materials, whether ways of life, actions or views, be thought taboo. Craftsmanship must remain concealed. The artist should be realistic, should hold a mirror up to society, should give us the truth but should not obtrude on his audience with his craftsmanship: his prose should be "transparent", should reveal the objects to which it refers without the interference of a rhetorical veil.

It is not surprising, therefore, that the kinds of narrative which are patently selective of content are less in favour. Indirect speech, for instance, in contrast to direct speech, is characterized by an apparent selectivity among words which a character may be supposed to have spoken.[12] This is equally true where direct and indirect speech are mixed:

> He undertook as he called it, to "nose 'round" and see if anything could be made of our questionable but possible show.
>
> Henry James, "A Passionate Pilgrim"

The reader has the sense here that he has been given the summary of a speech which must have taken much longer to deliver. By suggesting that more had been said and done than is reported to us, the author confesses to having made a *selection* from the "reality" before his mind's eye. Few writers would dare be so provocative about admitting their selectiveness as was O. Henry in "A Municipal Report":

> Azalea Adair and I had conversation, a little of which will be repeated to you.

Block description, on the other hand, especially if richly ornamented with "flowers" of rhetoric, seems equally unnatural to today's reader.

We have the paradox, then, that as the writer becomes more sophisticated, he must try to seem less so. His selecting and manipulating hand must become as invisible as possible. He chooses a narrow rather than an omniscient point of view; he avoids unimbedded comment; of the four modes he finds those more aesthetically pleasing, namely speech and report, which are most mimetic and which suggest as little as possible the guiding hand of the artist. The two static modes, description and comment, are either avoided or restricted to embedded forms, preferably at the word or phrase level; expository description, "poetic" settings and obvious authorial comment are avoided. The writer prefers scenic to panoramic report, he consistently prefers direct to indirect speech, unless he moves to stream of consciousness or narrated monologue. He conceals that manipulating hand of which earlier writers were proud, and tends to that mode or submode which will make it seem as though he were holding the mirror up to nature once again.

Reader Participation

One last reason for the increasing popularity of scenic report and direct speech: in the terminology of Marshall McLuhan, they are *hot* as opposed to *cool* modes.[13] The *hot* media, so McLuhan, require little participation. Television is an example. The *cool* media, by contrast, invite participation.

Recent critics have assumed that literature in general is, in McLuhan's sense, a *cool* medium, in that it leaves gaps for the reader to fill in. The idea of gaps which the narrative seems to invite the reader to fill has been developed especially by Wolfgang Iser.[14] Stanzel speaks of the "complementary narrative"[15] which the reader conceives so as to complete the one which the writer presents.

I believe, however, that although readers apply their imagination to narratives, they do so in a selective way. I found on questioning a number of readers that almost nobody spun an incompleted story out in his own mind, or fitted the characters out with further speeches. The answer was clearest in a discussion of Shakespeare: the reader is aware of his inability to produce in his fantasy so much as one additional Shakespearean couplet to complete Juliet's answer to Romeo or Polonius' advice to Laertes. Only in a discussion in which one of the texts was a detective story did one reader think he might have tried to imagine how, exactly, the murder had been committed. But that was an exception. On the whole, no "complementary narratives" were imagined in the mimetic modes of speech and report.

On the other hand, most readers make judgements on the actions they read about in stories, and they imagine roughly how the characters look. Most stories are perfectly senseless if the reader does not bring to them his own standards of what is normal as opposed to abnormal behaviour, of what is right and wrong. So the reader is induced to supply some sort of comment of his own, though it may not be wholly conscious or in any sense formulated. And the fact that description is normally supplemented by the reader seems to be suggested by the common reaction when a familiar story is seen as a film: then, having to readjust our conception of the heroine's face or the look of the farmyard, we realize that we had a set of well-defined and yet perhaps subliminal images of the fictive world, images which the film forced us to erase or readjust.

In recent years both the theory of how meaning is constituted in a reader's mind and empirical research in the field of "reader response studies" have been pursued with energy and in a variety of directions.[16] I believe that both such research as has been published and my own questioning of readers indicate that an empirical investigation of the hot/cool division between the modes is a questionable undertaking: the methods which might be used are still insufficiently developed and may in fact never do the matter justice.

As to the theory: the theory can only state how readers will probably tend to react, but that this response will necessarily depend on the particular work that the readers have in mind. So-called analytic works (that is, those which present a series of puzzles or building blocks the answers to which or the functions of which are revealed gradually in the course of the work) will invite to more filling in of blank spaces, including report. The synthetic work, that is, that which introduces the reader to the fictional world step by step, may invite to no filling in with report at all. In other words, the response of the reader necessarily will depend on the work which he has in mind at the moment that he is answering our questions. This also suggests that the reader's response will vary, depending on whether a synthetic or analytic kind of narrative is put before him.

As to the method: the reader responses I have elicited show that readers are very uncertain about their own responses. Introspection is an unreliable measure, and the introspectors are usually aware of this fact and diffident about their own answers. Often the reader cannot say with certainty how or what he thinks, even at that very moment. The difficulty is much greater when he tries to determine in retrospect what he thought. He is likely to think he thought that which he thought he ought to have thought. The reader who believes it is the function of literature "to make you think" is more likely to draw on his fantasy to say what impression the work made on him and what was the content of his complementary narrative than is the more hedonist reader, who is happy to swim along on the top of the waves of his narrator's impulses and feels little impelled to participate in the construction or deconstruction of his author's intentions.

Therefore a number of factors make empirical research into the coolness or hotness of the various modes a difficult undertaking – above all the fact that questionnaires which the subject can answer only on the basis of his introspection cannot yield reliable data. Most empirical studies confine themselves to finding out what and how much a given sector of the population reads, what is bought and what is borrowed in the way of reading matter, or how positively or negatively a certain text strikes the reader.[17] Relevant here, however, may be Norman Holland's study, *5 Readers Reading*,[18] since he gives extensive transcripts of what his subjects had to say about some short story texts. Their comments are confined almost exclusively to the modes of description and comment. The evidence also suggests that the dynamic narrative modes are cool: although they require little reader response in the same mode, they elicit it in the other, i.e. complementary narrative modes.

The complementary sets of modal pairs that have been the focus of this discussion are always the same ones: the static ones on the one hand, the dynamic ones on the other. This is the case whether it is a matter of mediation, of narrative pace, of selectivity or of reader participation. Always the preference is for the two more dynamic modes. In the last century apparently all these various pressures have united and worked in the one direction, toward a more generous use of report and speech. Why writers in earlier ages did not have the same preferences remains to be explained. We can perhaps link the change to related phenomena in the history of taste: to explain *why* it occurred is beyond the scope and power of our theory.

CHAPTER IV

The Submodes of Speech

Speech occurs in narrative in a variety of ways. Critics distinguish between direct and indirect discourse, inner speech and narrated monologue, and a number of half-way stations difficult to identify. In English alone there are some two dozen terms in current use, including various attempts to translate the French *monologue interieur* and the German *erlebte Rede*. A systematic treatment can show us how to differentiate between this confusing set of terms.

Most of the terms in use can be located on two axes:
– the degree to which the speech is "direct", that is, reported in the exact words which a fictional character is supposed to have used, and
– the degree to which the words are supposed to be spoken to someone and are therefore heard, rather than merely being spoken by the character to himself – a mode which has been called "inner speech" as opposed to "outer speech":

	direct	indirect
	a	b
outer:	1 direct speech	indirect speech
inner:	2 thought	substitutionary thought

According to this scheme, there would be only four kinds of speech, two of which are not speech in the narrower sense at all, but ways in which thoughts of a fictional character may be expressed – as if they had been spoken. Recent work on narrative technique, however, has broken out of the bounds of this simple model and suggested, in effect, extensions on both the vertical and the horizontal axis:

Fehr saw that a character's consciousness (this is the area in which the twentieth century has seen a veritable explosion of narrative techniques, including stream of consciousness, *style indirect libre* and so forth) may take the form of perception as well as thought.[1] That is, a character may describe scenes and people on behalf of the author as well as merely reflecting on them. This third plane beyond speech and thought Fehr called "substitutionary perception", a concept taken over by Hernadi[2] and others.

50

2. In a detailed analysis of speech in several English novels, Page[3] has shown that a number of stages exist between direct and indirect speech, and a number of ways in which authors indicate these stages, and that some novelists, especially Dickens, shift between them with a virtuosity which cannot be described by a critic who confines himself to the two poles of direct and indirect.

3. The modes of comment, description and report can be used both by people in stories and by their narrator. We call them *speech* or *thought* when they stem from the fictional character. On one side of our expanded model, then, we find a kind of fence: on its right side lie the areas of narrative unfiltered through the consciousness of the *dramatis personae*; on the left lie the submodes of speech:

		Submodes of speech				
1	Speech	direct	free	indirect		
2	Thought	direct	substitutionary thought		comment	
3	Perception	direct	substitutionary perception		description and report	

In the wider sense, speech is everything which shows the consciousness of a character from inside; it includes not only direct speech. As Espinola puts it, the term *speech* is used "to indicate non-verbal perception and sensory processes" and Genette argues that "the novelistic convention ... is that thoughts and feelings are no different from speech ..."[4]

The narrative mode *speech*, then, includes not only speech in the narrower sense of words supposedly spoken aloud but also a variety of ways in which thoughts and perceptions can be conveyed – that is, those kinds of *substitutionary narration* often represented as though they had been spoken. The term *substitutionary* is to suggest that narration is accomplished in the first instance by a narrator, but that he may use a substitute (i.e. a character) to do the job for him. A character may also function as a substitute for the reader, for whom he may seem to listen (audition by proxy) or provide whatever sense organs may be required to take in the fictional world.

On the vertical axis of our model we find the chief submodes of speech, including speech itself as well as the submodes *thought* and *perception*. On the horizontal axis is represented the degree of mediation, that is, the degree to which the author seems to speak in his own voice (the right end) or allows his characters to speak for themselves (the left end), or in mixtures of the two extremes. We note that the top right square is unoccupied. This is so because speech is a mode reserved exclusively to the character. If the author speaks, that is his private affair. The reader cannot hear him: only the written words register. If the author wants to represent his own speech, he must step into the novel as a narrator or character or reflector figure.

Distance

The horizontal axis represents the degree of what Wayne Booth calls "distance".[5] *Speech* and *thought* in quotation marks allow the reader to experience the character directly, at least in contrast to the stronger sense of a narrator's mediation in *reported speech*.

This, however, is only one kind of distance. We can diagram the obvious kinds as follows:

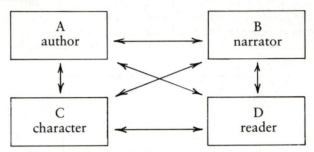

Each of the six arrowed lines represents a kind of distance; the line A–B is that with which Booth is chiefly concerned: for him the narrator is a fictional construct of an age, sex, time, social class, political persuasion or linguistic competence which may be at variance with that of the author. For Uspensky[6] the interesting kind of distance is the line B–C, especially insofar as the narrator may occupy psychological or ideological positions at variance with those of his character. For the purposes of defining the submodes of speech, however, the C–D distance is the interesting and relevant one. For *direct speech* suggests the closest possible nexus between character and reader, as the term *direct* suggests. *Indirect* and *reported speech*, by contrast, blur the impression and distance us from the character. For our purposes here, the complications of author-narrator relationships are not relevant, nor the fact that there is a variety of characters and of readers (fictive, virtual, actual). Interesting at the moment is only the distance of the actual reader to the fictive character. A number of intermediate stages between no distance and great distance may occur.

> direct speech: Paul said, "I'm going this minute. Good-bye."
> indirect speech: He was going that minute.
> reported speech: Paul announced that he was going to leave immediately and bade the others good-bye.
> report: Paul said good-bye and left immediately.

The same stages of distance can be differentiated in the ways a character's thought can be expressed. No distance at all means that the character conveys his idea quite directly, that is, in his own words:

> Johnson thought, "Inglis peple here, dey be too happy togeder, dey sing every day, make play."

Thought, however, is not always "coloured" by the speech of the character like this.

At very little distance from the character is the same impression expressed in interior monologue:

Inglis peple there, they were too happy togeder dey sing every day, make play.

Although no quotation marks are used, we are supposed to be overhearing the *thoughts* of the character. Since he is not supposed to be speaking, however, all the terms for this phenomenon which suggest speech are a little misleading:

> free indirect speech (Page)[7]
> erlebte Rede (Lorck)[8]
> substitutionary speech (B. Fehr)[9]
> represented speech (Jespersen)[10]
> narrated speech (Vickery and Lethcoe)[11]

Dujardin had also called interior monologue a kind of speech, but as Humphrey points out, it is a representation of thought, "partly or entirely unuttered".[12] Other scholars have suggested terms which get around the difficulty:

> style indirect libre (Bally)[13]
> narrated monologue (D. Cohn)[14]
> dual voice (Pascal)[15]

There is a consensus that the technique is near to but not the same as direct thought, even though it may occasionally appear in quotation marks. Among other things, it does not use the same tense as direct speech and direct thought. Important, too, is that the deictic "here" and "now" are usually changed to "there" and "then". The technique, in other words, is on both a different horizontal and a different vertical axis from direct speech: it is neither direct nor is it speech.

At a medium distance we would expect

English people there, they were too happy, they sing every day, they make play.

Here the expression is still "coloured", as Norman Page calls it,[16] but the language no longer carries the phonological idiosyncrasies of the character, only its lexical and grammatical ones.

Simple indirect thought is a so-called "free" form, that is, it is not bound into the grammar of the reporting phrase which introduces it. The bound form is called "reported thought" and is stylistically neutral. The special qualities of the speaker's or thinker's dialect, for instance, are "submerged":[17]

Johnson supposed English people to be happy, singing and playing every day.

In pure comment, finally, the idea is not that of the character but of the narrator himself:

English people are happy, singing and playing every day.

As in direct thought, the tense is often the present, the style on a level with that of the contiguous discourse.

The stages from no distance to maximum distance are not absolutely clear-cut and cannot be made so, because a number of factors suggest degrees of distance: the use of an inquit, quotation marks, personal pronouns, deictic signals, and the colouring in phonology, grammar, diction and rhetoric which suggests to a greater or lesser extent the "voice" of the character rather than that of the narrator or author. The minimal number of stages is probably three, if we want to make use of those distinctions the usefulness of which earlier critics have more or less agreed upon. The result, if we include the various stages of perception as well as of speech and thought, is the model on page 55.

If we now reduce the model by eliminating redundancies and aligning the terminology at levels one, two, and three, we come to the following structure:

a	b	c	d
1. direct speech	indirect speech	reported speech	
2. direct thought	narrated monologue	reported thought	comment
3. direct description	narrated perception	reported perception	report and description

A stronger alignment, such as calling "narrated monologue" what it usually is, namely "narrated thought", would mean a shifting of terminology in current use, and would probably fail to be adopted. A coarser mesh would miss distinctions which text analysts nowadays find necessary and illuminating. A finer mesh, on the other hand, though useful for speech, would be excessively confusing. The overlapping nature of some of our categories should be accepted in the interests of usability; but at the same time we must remind ourselves that our model is not to be mistaken for reality. It yields terms useful in textual analysis, categories for sorting operations, rather than phenomena which can be taken out of the model, measured, weighed and inspected. If we take such a model too literally we will be confronted by a set of paradoxes:

    1. Speech in a story is of course inaudible. It is a phenomenon to be seen

Direct Speech and its Substitutes ("substitutionary narration")

Distance → Submode ↓	none (a)	little (b)	great (c)	authorial or narratorial (d)
1. Speech	direct speech / free direct speech (Page)	parallel indirect speech (Page) / substituted direct discourse (Voloshinov)[18]	free indirect speech idiosyncratic ↔ neutral / coloured ↔ submerged / transposed speech (Genette)	✕
2. Thought	direct thought / interior monologue (Dujardin) / inner speech (Goldstein, Vygotsky, Page) / subvocal speech (J. Watson) / endophasy (Vygotsky, Cohn) / private speech (Hernadi)	free indirect speech / erlebte Rede / style indirect libre (Bally) / substitutionary speech (Fehr) / represented speech (Jespersen) / dual voice (Pascal) / narrated speech (Vickery) / narrated monologue (Cohn) / immediate speech (Genette)	reported thought coloured ↔ neutral / substitutionary thought (Hernadi) / psychonarration (Cohn) / narrated speech (Genette)	comment
3. Perception	description by fictive character / description in interior monologue	narrated perception / erlebte Wahrnehmung / vision avec (Pouillon)[19]	reported perception / substitutionary perception (Fehr)	report and description

from the viewpoint of a reader pretending that the fictional world is real, that words in quotation marks are being spoken. What the author has to say we cannot hear, only the written words register. What the characters he has invented have to say is conveyable in written form only.

2. The difference between direct speech and narrated monologue is a difference, redundantly expressed, between outer expression and inner impression, that is, between level one and level two – but on the part of the character only. As far as "directness" is concerned, there is no difference between what an author makes one of his puppets say or makes him think: the fictional utterance is no more or less a product of the author's imagination than is the fictive thought, direct, indirect or reported. Thus "outer" and "inner" are submodes within the fictional world only.

3. From the point of view of a narrator, he communicates with his reader directly (though we must not look at this adverb too closely) if he comments or describes in his own words rather than using the indirection of letting his characters describe or comment in their own words. That the comments he puts in their mouths should be called "direct speech" is a paradox of critical terminology, a leftover of the *oratio recta* of Latin grammar. What could be more indirect than direct speech? Direct speech, direct thought and direct perception are the ultimate in authorial indirection – methods of letting the puppets speak for the ventriloquist-narrator.

Finally, I have left out of consideration here the class of phenomena discussed in chapter II as *virtual* modes, of which a single example should suffice here:

"I want someone to whisper once in a while – 'Courage, courage; you'll come out all right.'"

Henry James, The Reverberator

As this example, since it is torn out of context, may serve to suggest, virtual speech may be spoken or only thought, and is thus hard to fit neatly into our model. It is a favourite trick of the later Henry James: at least fifteen instances of it occur in the second book of *The Golden Bowl*.

Applications

Direct speech (1a on the chart) should be the easiest sub-mode to identify, since it is usually set off by quotation marks, by a special use of personal pronouns, by a shift of tense and sometimes by the inquit which introduces, interrupts or follows it.

In fact, however, there are special cases, special manipulations and effects. One of them might be called "translated speech": the quotation is in one language, the supposed original in another:

"Yes," he said in Armenian.

William Saroyan, "The Summer of the
Beautiful White Horse"

The foreign language may be used only in a particular situation:

> "Bolt the door," Tom said to Jonathan. Then Tom said in Italian, "Any more of you?"
>
> Patricia Highsmith, *Ripley's Game*

Or we may be asked to imagine all the direct speech between particular persons as having been translated:

> "I'm not hungry, Ma. I had something in the hospital cafeteria." (We speak in Yiddish; as I mentioned before, Ma can't speak English.)
>
> Shirley Faessler, "A Basket of Apples"

Translated speech may also be "coloured" (a term Page uses for indirect speech which has traces of the speaker's dialect or other idiosyncrasies) or "irregular",[20] especially where some of it is left untranslated:

> "And look – inside." Heloise opened it. "Really str-rong," she said in English.
>
> Patricia Highsmith, *Ripley's Game*

> Yardley looked at the blacksmith and then he grinned. He began to talk fast in his bad French. "Now you listen, Alcide. You fellas around here are just trying to get me sore, talking thet way. You know goddam well we don't lost this war . . ."
>
> Hugh MacLennan, *The Two Solitudes*

In the Highsmith passage the term "direct speech" is applicable in the standard sense, at least to the second quotation. In the MacLennan passage, however, several elements are meant to suggest Yardley's insufficient French, both phonologically (*fellas, thet*) and grammatically (*we don't lost*). The representation of the faulty use of a foreign language is naturally a recurring problem for writers who use exotic backgrounds, like Conrad, or who live in or write about bilingual societies, like the French and English Canadians. The matter has been studied in detail by Russian scholars because it was a considerable problem for Puschkin and Tolstoy. The latter had included a wide variety of French elements in *War and Peace*, and was forced to eliminate them from his third edition of the work.[21]

In theory direct speech is a report of what a figure "really" said, whereas indirect and reported speech convey only a selection of what was said. But there are certain forms of direct speech in which the words quoted represent merely a summary – in other words, also a mere selection:

> The bishop crossed the floor soundlessly to ascend the four steps to the low pulpit. He laid his book carefully on the shelf before him, paused, and looked up.
>
> ". . . our beloved sister, Diana . . . her unfinished work which she now

can never finish . . . irony of fate not a proper term to apply to the will of the Lord . . . He giveth; He taketh away . . . if He takes away the olive tree He has given before its fruit has ripened, it is for us to accept His will . . . Vessel of His inspiration . . . Devotion to her aims . . . Fortitude . . . Change in the course of human history . . . The body of Thy servant, Diana . . .''

The eyes of the congregation, the several hundred women with a sprinkling of men, turned to the coffin.

John Wyndham, *Trouble with Lichen*
[ellipsis original]

This technique can be called "summary speech", if one will. But it does not occur so often that a further category is required. It is worth noting, however, because it illustrates once more that direct speech is not an unvarying, unified submode of speech, any more than are the other submodes yet to be discussed.

A further variant of direct speech appears in the following:

> The bliss of having a secret required, in short, the consummation of telling it, and she looked forward to the My-dear-I-had-no-idea's, the I-thought-you-and-Bill-were-so-happy-together's,   the   How-did-you-keep-it-so-dark's with which her intimates would greet her announcement.

Mary McCarthy, "Cruel and Barbarous Treatment"

The hyphenated expressions are "quotational compounds" which could also, though not as effectively, be marked like straight quotations. What signals direct speech here is not only the hyphenation but also the capitalization of the first quoted word and the syntactic break before it as well as the shift of style register. Salinger gains a similar effect by capitalizing the words presumably quoted:

> . . . what our mother called Unsanitary Food Made by Dirty Men That Never Even Wash Their Hands . . .

J. D. Salinger, *Seymour: An Introduction*

Another special case that comes up with increasing frequency in modern fiction is that a portion of direct speech is not heard "directly" by the reader. Instead, the words are filtered through the consciousness of one of the characters who is listening – yet we can still consider the words in quotation marks as a kind of direct speech:

> "Masses sung in English, you know," Tom was saying . . . ". . . Don't you agree? Sir John Stainer . . ." Jonathan woke up when the car stopped.

Patricia Highsmith, *Ripley's Game*
[ellipsis original]

Here the ellipsis indicates that we are overhearing those words which Jonathan hears Tom speak. When Jonathan falls asleep, the reader is no longer tuned in to Tom's speech. We can call this phenomenon "audition by proxy". It is usually indicated by the past progressive:

Scott was explaining something, but the Colonel hardly listened, contented to give himself up to the care of this shabby, tall, thin officer and be led by him across the burning airfield towards a snub-nosed fifteen-hundred-weight truck drawn up in the shade of some trees behind a sheltered bay.

". . . and of course," Scott was saying, "we only had your message about half an hour ago."

Paul Scott, Johnnie Sahib [ellipsis original]

As in the Highsmith passage, the point of view (or the point of audition) momentarily shifts: seemingly direct speech turns out to be not so direct.

Direct speech, then, is not all of one kind. Even the provision of the conventional markers is by no means universal. The way speech is indicated, in fact, has changed in the last two hundred years[22] and still takes a variety of forms, including not only double and single quotation marks, but also graphological markers such as italics, parentheses or, as in summary speech, no markers at all. The deviant forms usually serve special purposes:

> *Morag's Tale of Lazarus Tonnerre*
> . . .
> It was at the time of the fire.
> (I don't like that part. Don't tell it again.)
> Okay. I won't, then.
> (He was brave, though, wasn't he?)
> Yes. He was that.
>
> Margaret Laurence, The Diviners

Here Morag remembers how she told her daughter Pique a story about Pique's grandfather. She includes the answers of her daughter. The story is not given in quotation marks since it has a special heading to declare what it is, and Pique's words are apparently given in parenthesis to show that they are interruptions, not belonging to the genre of the tale being told. Nevertheless, they obviously constitute direct speech.

> Lazarus shambles over to the two men.
> "I'm going in," he says. "They're mine there, them."
> Dere mine dere, dem.
>
> same source

Here we have another kind of translation: the narrator repeats the old man's words to give us an idea of his dialect. This is still a kind of direct speech, despite the lack of inquit or quotation marks. It is just as much of the family of direct speech as those members already mentioned: translated speech, summary speech, quotational compounds, audition by proxy and the simply unmarked passages of direct speech which one finds in twentieth century narration with particular frequency since the time of Joyce. In Joyce's *Ulysses* and *Finnegans Wake* unmarked speech abounds, and, especially since Joyce's day, stories as well as novels will sometimes do without quotation marks altogether, like William Saroyan's "The Summer of the Beautiful White Horse". A not uncommon variant is an italicized passage of direct speech, often indented, which sometimes also serves to indicate a flashback or a flashforward.

Some critics will consider certain deviant kinds of direct speech to be "free direct speech". The adjective "free" is a useful but also a dangerous one, for it is used by different critics in different ways:

1. The "free" forms of speech are sometimes contrasted to the bound ones. Thus in the sentence, "John said, 'snow has fallen on the pass'", John's utterance is bound syntactically to the reporting phrase or inquit, "John said"; in indirect speech it might be linked by the optional "that". What critics often mean by "free", therefore, is that the quoted utterance is not introduced by an inquit. Thus Ross[23] argues that "in English the term 'free' seems to denote free of the need to keep saying who says it . . ." Chatman[24] speaks of "direct tagged speech" to differentiate the form with an inquit from that which is "free".

2. A more widespread view is that "free" can denote not only the lack of an inquit but also of the relative "that" and the standard graphological indications of speech, including separate paragraphing (though this does not apply to eighteenth century texts, as Mylne[25] has shown) and quotation marks. Thus Gregory,[26] who remarks that the "'free' categories have to cover . . . 'a multitude of sins'".[27]

3. This "multitude of sins" includes the use of "free" in the sense of "inaccurate" or "not exactly in the form in which the words would probably have been spoken". In this sense "free" suggests a step toward indirect speech, which conveys the words of the narrator, not necessarily those of the speaker; in other words, a step away from *mimesis* to *diegesis*. A source of difficulty in comparative studies is that the French *libre* does not have the same extension as does its English counterpart (thus Stephen Ullmann's use of the term in his *Style in the French Novel*[28] is at variance with all of the above), and in German one manages without the additional term. Then too, some of the submodes of speech are by nature (or by historical convention) only bound or only free. Thus "reported speech" generally means that an inquit is present. That is, this submode is always a bound form: critics do not speak of "free reported speech". The free, in the sense of unbound, version of reported speech is "indirect speech" in its "free" form. Finally, it must be added that these are distinctions often made in text analysis but not in the grammar books.[29] There "reported speech" is synonymous with "indirect speech". Both of these terms, then, and the adjective "free" as well, are used variously by different critics. No wonder that such variations in technical terms lead to uncertainty and confusion. But the term "free" is now so traditional and familiar and unduplicated by alternative terms that one has no choice but to use it, making clear, however, where doubt might arise, in what sense the term is meant.

Both reported and indirect speech are normally conveyed without quotation marks, and with shifts of verb tense, of pronouns and of deictic references:

> He replied to my remarks with readiness, and in well-chosen words. Had he much to do there? Yes; that was to say, he had enough responsibility to bear.
>
> Charles Dickens, "The Signalman"

Direct speech would demand "Have you much to do here?" – the verb would be present tense, the pronoun *you* instead of *he*, the deictic *there* would probably be *here*.

Indirect speech can also occur with quotation marks, but this is a rare and now archaic convention:

> . . . Elizabeth gave the invitation. "Would he give Robert the meeting, they should be very happy."
> "With the greatest pleasure," was his first reply.
>
> Jane Austen, *The Watsons*

As Norman Page has pointed out,[30] it was not uncommon in the 18th century to use quotation marks for indirect as well as direct speech.

Page has suggested a special category of indirect speech which has the phonetic colouring of the speaker: his dialect or ideolect. Agreed, phonetic colouring can occur with indirect speech, where it will suggest a minimal distance from direct speech. But colouring is only one of the qualities which we can use to help sort out the kinds of speech. If phonetic idiosyncrasies were an essential parameter for the categorizing of speech, we would also want to divide direct speech this way. Further subcategories might take into account whether it is only the speaker's pronunciation that is coloured or if the colouring is that of grammatical and semantic idiosyncrasies. Then there would need to be a third category of speech (certainly the most common) which has none of these markers. But that would elevate obvious differences in the representation of style register in speech to a useless and most cumbersome addition of categories.

Frequently the kinds of speech discussed so far occur in indirect and reported speech (category 1c):

> . . . he held brief disappointing conversations with emphatic butlers and maids. So-and-so was out, riding, swimming, playing golf, sailed to Europe last week. Who shall I say phoned?
>
> F. Scott Fitzgerald, "The Rich Boy"

The first sentence is in the mode of report; the second begins in free indirect speech, "free" because "so-and-so" cannot be a direct echo of what was said. Since the verbs which follow seem to be gathered from several telephone conversations, we also have here another example of "summary speech", but of the indirect kind. In indirect speech of the usual kind, however, "sailed to

Europe last week" would have to be "had sailed to Europe the week before" (the deixis of time as well as of place shifts from the one submode to the other, a phenomenon called "back-shifting" in grammar[31]). "So-and-so was out" seems to be indirect speech on the way to the direct speech of "Who shall I say phoned?" – which Fitzgerald does not, we may note, set in quotation marks, with "sailed to Europe last week" at a stage between. Contrast the following passage:

> At sixteen she'd left Stratford and come up to London as kitching-maid. Yes, she was born in Stratford-on-Avon. Shakespeare, sir? No, people were always arsking her about him.
>
> Katherine Mansfield, "Life of Ma Parker"

Here we have an example of horizontal "slipping" from indirect speech to coloured indirect speech (marked by the cockney "kitching-maid") and then on to direct speech: "Shakespeare, sir?" But the third sentence slips back from 1a to 1b, as we see from the verb tense and the pronoun *her* instead of *me*, and has the phonetic colouring of Ma Parker's "arsking".

A bolder set of shifts is accomplished in the following passage:

> Kathleen was the youngest in a family of four. In a three-storey house, they lived in the right half of the second floor. Below them was a family of Jews from Galicia and above them was a crazy Englishman who said he was the younger son of a bleeding earl and that it was a bleeding shaime, him having to live in a place like this.
>
> Hugh MacLennan, *Two Solitudes*

Kathleen is reminiscing here, telling her story to another, more important character, so that the whole passage may well be indirect speech rather than narratorial report. We cannot be sure. But "crazy Englishman" is not at all the author's style. It might well be Kathleen's. When we arrive at "bleeding earl" we have Kathleen's quotation of the Englishman, and in "bleeding shaime" an indication of the phonological qualities of the Englishman's speech as well, which cast a doubt on the truth of his claim to be an aristocrat. This configuration of elements might make us think that the passage combines several variants of indirect speech, except that then "in a place like this" would have to be, according to standard narrative conventions, "in a place like that". We conclude that the end of the sentence is in a form of direct speech, despite the absence of quotation marks. In other words: free direct speech. So we have "slipped" neatly from 1c (reported) through 1b (free indirect and indirect) to 1a (direct speech). It is, in fact, an elegant and effective slipping, which neatly accompanies the move from the panoramic report at the beginning to the close-up at the end, from the narrator's point of view to that of Kathleen, or, in the terms of Genette,[32] from the *voice* of the narrator to that of Kathleen to that of the crazy Englishman. An appreciative nod is due to the Fitzgerald and Mansfield excerpts (quoted before the MacLennan one) as well: here too the possibilities of slipping from more distance to less are put to excellent use.

The horizontal slip can also be inelegant, especially if the move from one end of the scale to the other is made within the boundaries of a phrase or clause:

> He reached the stairs. A man was shouting for the "Polizei!"
> Patricia Highsmith, Ripley's Game

This form may have the advantage of bringing in some local colour. But the move into direct speech is normally felt, apparently, to require an inquit or a break by way of spacing, punctuation or syntactical shift:

> Then Tom said he had changed his mind: both bodies were going into the Citroën.
> "... even though the Renault," Tom said between gasps, "is bigger."
> same source [ellipsis original]

Here "said he had changed" is reported speech, "both bodies were going" may be free indirect or free direct — we cannot tell how closely the wording follows what Tom would have said — and then direct speech follows (1c to 1b to 1a); the ellipsis dots suggest a gradual transition through 1b to 1a. Again, there is an efficient compromise between the pace of reported and the scenic impact of direct speech.

By "scenic" is usually meant a one to one ratio between narrative and narrated time. The panoramic view, by contrast, compresses into reported speech a narrated period many times as long as it takes us to read what was supposedly said:

> The ways and good Jokes of Osborne Castle were now added to his ordinary means of Entertainment; he repeated the smart sayings of one Lady, detailed the oversights of another, and indulged them even with a copy of Lord Osborne's style of overdrawing himself on both cards.
> Jane Austen, The Watsons

Here we move from report to an illustration of that report in catalogue form. The mode of reported speech allows us to read in ten seconds what would have taken minutes or hours, apparently on successive days, to happen. The image of the ruffle is appropriate here: the narrated time is set in deep folds, so that only an occasional edge of the material is allowed to surface at the level of narrative time.

A special form of such ruffling is achieved where direct and indirect speech alternate, as in Salinger's story, "For Esmé, with Love and Squalor", or in the following passage:

'He's got something up his sleeve, I'm sure," she said. "But what?"
I did not know. And:
"It isn't as if we were being asked to watch a particular person, is it?"
I agree that it was not. And:
"It wouldn't be really different in principle from what a Medical Officer of Health does, would it?"
Not very different, I thought. And:
"If we don't do it for him, he'd have to find someone else to do it. I don't really see who he'd get, in the village. It wouldn't be very nice, or efficient, if he did have to introduce a stranger, would it?"
I supposed not.

John Wyndham, *The Midwich Cuckoos*

This is a prose version of what would be termed *stychomythia* in the criticism of drama: a swift alternation of short speeches. The effect, however, is to contrast the sober brevity of the narrator to the volubility of his wife. It is achieved by the difference between the narrated time/narrative time ratio of direct and reported speech. This effect may seem but a subtle and unimportant difference, which the average reader will not notice. In terms of the classical theory of modes, however, which contains only the two terms *mimesis* and *diegesis*, direct speech is mimetic, whereas indirect speech is in the opposite camp: it is diegetic. It belongs to *récit* rather than *discours*. Whether this reading of the matter should influence the critic is hard to say. At all events it is clear that the writer intended the contrast. He must have felt that it would have an effect.

The Submodes of Thought

What is often called interior monologue is as often as not no monologue at all, but a representation of a character's thought. The convention of quotation marks may be followed:

He paused with one foot on the first step and drew the fresh morning air into his lungs, thinking, "How many weeks will I have to enjoy such mornings?" He remembered thinking the same thing last spring, however.

Patricia Highsmith, *Ripley's Game*

The passage which follows the quotation is hard to place, especially since one might expect "last spring" to take the form of "the previous spring" or "the spring before" to suggest the greater distance which is indicated both by the closing of the quotation and the reporting phrase, "he remembered".
Direct thought, as we have seen, can be put in quotation marks just like direct speech:

"The good man who did that," he thought, "must have been as blind as a bat."

H. G. Wells, "The Country of the Blind"

This is a convention not universally recognized. In his classic reading of Virginia Woolf's *To the Lighthouse*, for instance, Auerbach assumes that certain words of Mr Bankes might be spoken aloud rather than merely thought because these words are in quotation marks.[33] But this practice is not at all unusual in modern literature. True, thought is often set without quotation marks, but it need not be. It may or may not be introduced by an inquit; it usually has the same grammatical form as direct speech:

> He thought, I never realized how free I was before this fear came. Even if we get Cato out I'll be afraid for the rest of my life.
>
> Iris Murdoch, Henry and Cato

The reporting phrase alone is no sufficient signal of direct thought, but may indicate narrated monologue, although this does not usually appear in bound form:

> The factory had also been explained to the general several times. It was too bad, McQueen thought, how the old gentleman's memory was going. "One of Rupert Irons' subsidiaries took it over," he said.
>
> Hugh MacLennan, Two Solitudes

Direct thought would read "It is too bad" and "is going". There is also a tendency in both direct thought and narrated monologue to use the kind of syntactic fragments which are thought to go through one's head when one thinks. Fehr calls this the atactic nature of narrated monologue, and we find it as early as Jane Austen:

> . . . Anne left Westgate Buildings, her mind deeply busy in revolving what she had heard, feeling, thinking, recalling and foreseeing everything; shocked at Mr Elliot, sighing over future Kellynch, and pained for Lady Russell, whose confidence in him had been entire. The Embarrassment which must be felt from this hour in his presence! How to behave to him? how to get rid of him? what to do by any of the Party at home? where to be blind? where to be active?
>
> Jane Austen, cancelled chapter of Persuasion

This atactic quality is often one of the signs of "slipping" from 2c to 2b:

> Jonathan knew he was alone [reported thought], that even Georges was more than half cut off from him now, because surely Simone was going to keep Georges [indirect thought?] but Jonathan was aware that [back to reported thought] he didn't yet realize it fully. That would take days. Feelings were slower than thoughts [narrated monologue]. Sometimes.
>
> Patricia Highsmith, Ripley's Game

Up to the last two fragments, the passage consists of well-formed sentences, one of the signals that the presence of the author is stronger than that of the character. The atactic, that is, syntactically imperfect expression "sometimes" is a signal that we are either in narrated monologue (2b), in which, as critics seem to agree, the presence of narrator and character are of approximately equal force, or in direct thought (2a), where there should be *no* signs of a distance from the character – his thoughts are conveyed, as it were, without the perceptible mediation of the narrator.

The qualities of narrated monologue have been much discussed in studies of *erlebte Rede*.[34] They need be examined here only insofar as we are gradually gathering a list of the various signals which will help us arrive at a systematic catalogue or set of definitions. At this point it should be clear, however, that the number and kind of signals in a text can vary from several to practically none. The relevant signals include punctuation, the use of an inquit, the use of tenses, both in the inquit and the speech or thought, the choice of personal pronouns (first and second person in direct speech and direct thought, third person in the other submodes), the deixis of time and space, and the three possible kinds of idiosyncracy, phonological, grammatical and lexical. This makes nine parameters discovered so far – nine kinds of signal, in other words, which can occur singly or in any of several dozen combinations, and which suggest, apart from contextual clues, the degree of directness. The number of parameters makes clear the quandary of the model-maker: fewer categories would not differentiate sufficiently, but one or two further intermediary categories would not solve the problem either, both because there are too many parameters and because we have no firm basis for defining the effect of all the possible parameter combinations. The divisions between the categories of our model, in other words, are not absolute, except for the unmitigated directness of most direct speech and thought, and even here, as our last example from Highsmith showed, one cannot always be absolutely sure.

These considerations should be kept in mind when we consider "slipping" between more and less direct stages of speech or thought. The difficulty did not loom large when Schuelke first suggested the term "slipping" over twenty years ago,[35] since she focussed on phenomena we might wish to see rather as "skipping" than as slipping:

> They sent the firm a letter to the effect that "you are doing a fine job". (p. 91)
> His personal decision would be given as soon as "it is fixed in my mind". (p. 92)

Here there are obvious jumps from report or reported speech to direct quotation. Slipping between the stages of thought often occurs in a more gradual and less clearly marked way:

> Tom ran after Simone, thinking to get her keys from her, to remove the two corpses from her house, or do *something* with them, then he stopped abruptly and his shoes slid on the pavement.
>
> Patricia Highsmith, *Ripley's Game*
> [italics original]

We begin with report and move on to reported thought: "thinking to get her keys . . ." There is no clue to a lessening distance until we come to the italicized *something*, which suggests an emphasis in colloquial speech – whether in narrated monologue or direct thought we cannot tell. The emphasis, certainly, belongs to the rhetorical habits of the figure rather than to those of the narrator.

Of special interest in the Highsmith example is that the nine parameters discovered so far are not relevant here. One could say, in the terminology of Norman Page, that an italicized word suggests a "coloured" or "idiosyncratic" expression. But the difference between written and spoken (or thought) language is not a matter of idiosyncrasy but of other structures, of intonation, stress and of style register – that is, of rhetoric. Indeed, style is known to have three dimensions: a semantic, a syntactical and a rhetorical one. Thus our list of parameters is necessarily incomplete if it leaves out the parameter of rhetoric. For narrators are not only bound, by and large, by the norms of correctness in diction and syntax, but also by their initial choice of style register. Thus a noticeable difference between the register, usually formal or consultative, to which narrators tend to feel confined and the colloquial or otherwise deviant register of the fictive characters signals a distance between:

> I had often watched him under the meter, stretched out from his tip-toes at the top of a broken step-ladder, yelling at Grandma to lift the God-damned Holy Candle a little higher so he could see what the Christ he was doing.
> Ken Mitchell, "The Great Electrical Revolution"

In other terms: elements of reported speech are direct enough to allow us to hear the colouring of the character's voice. His style register being different from that of the narrator, the distance between reader and character is momentarily reduced. The effect can be more subtle:

> Jonathan had to wait in Dr Perrier's front room with its sickly, dusty rose laurel plant. The plant never flowered, it didn't die, and never grew, never changed. Jonathan identified himself with the plant.
> Patricia Highsmith, *Ripley's Game*

The artful asyndetic sequence "never grew, never changed" is not at all Jonathan's kind of rhetoric but that of the narrator. Certainly the final sentence is in 2c; but the asyndeton "never grew, never changed", suggests 2b. The rhetorical stance may force us to opt for the more filtered mode, since in 2b one is necessarily more fully inside the mind of the character and is aware of the language he uses. For narrated monologue corresponds to what Hough calls "free indirect style", which he neatly defines as "the actual quotation of the words of one of the characters, but in the syntactical forms of indirect speech".[36] Although "actual quotation" is, strictly speaking, meaningless with reference to fiction, which rarely copies "actual" dialogue, the essence of Hough's definition applies to the Highsmith passage: the rhetorical flourishes of the narrator could not be an "actual quotation" from

Jonathan's speech or thought. Despite the contraction of "didn't die", which suggests direct speech, we may opt for indirect thought: reported thought without an introductory verb and subordinated clause. But clearly it is a moot point.

The decision would go the other way for the following passage:

> Paul was happy now as they walked along, thinking about the *Odyssey*. He wanted to see the place where the salt water was azure blue the way pictures showed it, and the men had straight noses and the women wore flowing robes. He thought of Ulysses tied to the mast, and the sailors with wax in their ears rowing him past the island where beautiful women, white-skinned and black-haired like his mother, sang over a heap of bones. That was a very sensible thing Ulysses had done with the wax.
>
> Hugh MacLennan, *Two Solitudes*

We begin at the narrator's end of the scale and gradually move closer to the character. The fact that the rhetoric at the end of the passage is not at all MacLennan's but that of the young boy, Paul, proves this part of the text to be narrated monologue. The passage shows the gradual slipping from indirect to direct which we noted in an earlier quotation from MacLennan, ending within the consciousness of the character concerned, without, however, moving into direct thought.

More problematical is a passage in which some of the signals point to more distance, some to less:

> "Before they come to the door. They'll be suspicious if their chums don't come out." If the Italians saw the situation *here*, they'd blast the three of *them* with guns and make a getaway in their car, Tom was thinking.
>
> Patricia Highsmith, *Ripley's Game*
> [italics mine]

The first words are direct speech. The deixis of "the situation here" points to direct thought, but then we would need "If the Italians *see*" rather than "saw", so we must opt for narrated monologue rather than direct thought. The following clause also contains contradictory signals: "they'd blast" is rhetorically not Highsmith but Tom Ripley, and would not be out of place in direct speech or direct thought, but the deictic "three of them" instead of "three of us" indicates narrated monologue. So the "here" indicates Tom's view, whereas "them" suggests the narrator's. This is not so much a "slipping" from one submode to another as a wobble presumably unintended by the writer. Here is another example:

> Baxter tore off yesterday's date from the calendar and saw that it was exactly one week to Christmas day.
>
> Paul Scott, *Johnnie Sahib*

"Yesterday's date" would conventionally be "the date of the day before" in authorial discourse. It is a matter of "yesterday" for the figure, of course, not for the narrator.

The conventions of fictional discourse have perhaps grown more complex as the "inner view" has come to be increasingly favoured. Thus writers come more and more unwittingly to break the rules their own art has established. Where a writer forgets that the deixis of time and place experience a common shift between one stage of distance and another, the contravention of an unwritten law may take place. In theory the artist takes pleasure in breaking rules and balking our expectations. In practice, a certain grammaticality has to be observed in narrative modes as in syntax.

It should now be clear that the submodes of thought are by and large parallel to the submodes of speech, but that the problems of identification and categorization are sufficiently different to demand separate treatment,[37] quite aside from the consideration that speech and thought really are two different modes of expression and appear in modern fiction in a proliferation and variety which deserve attention. The range of intelligent comment on how thought is conveyed in fiction – especially in the matter of *erlebte Rede* – gives us many a pointer on what to watch out for in a text conveying a character's thought; on the other hand, the critics have often given easy definitions which turn out on closer inspection to be not only incomplete but positively misleading when one tries to apply them to a wide variety of texts.

The Submodes of Perception

It is now over 40 years ago that Fehr saw *erlebte Wahrnehmung* (narrated perception) as parallel to and separable from *erlebte Rede* (narrated monologue). He also called it "vision by proxy".[38] Bühler and Beyerle have used the term *erlebter Eindruck*[39] (narrated impression) and some recent critics writing in English have accepted Fehr's lead and differentiated between "substitutionary thought" on the one hand and "substitutionary perception" on the other. Hernadi calls the latter "represented perception".[40] Narrated perception is usually visual, but it may involve any of the senses: we have already noted examples of *audition by proxy*, one recent critic speaks of *olfaction by proxy*,[41] and the other senses are also as likely to be exercised by the puppets of the narrator as by himself. The variety of terms which have been used for such phenomena in narrative indicates a widely felt need to give the matter separate treatment.

The common denominator is the implicit or explicit recognition that most of the information which a narrator conveys to the reader can also be loaded onto the vehicle of the characters, who take over some of the jobs of conveying details of the fictional world. From the point of view of the reader, such characters judge for him, provide him with eyes, ears, and other sense organs. But there is also the recognition that what a fictional character thinks is one matter, what he sees, hears and feels is another. We can see the division in analogy to the narrator's *comments* on the one hand and the *description* of things and the *report* of events on the other. In modal terms, a character's thoughts constitute substitutionary comment, whether directly or indirectly conveyed. But his sensations and observations are substitutionary *description* and *report*. We shall treat the latter phenomena together.

In analogy to speech and thought, there is a phenomenon easily identifiable as *direct perception* (3a in the chart). It may occur in quotation marks, as in a Maugham story in which a husband tells his wife Doris how he had met his Malay mistress:

> ". . . He went to the door. She'd been waiting on the steps with her mother. They came in and sat down on the floor. I gave them some sweets [substitutionary report]. She was shy, of course, but cool enough, and when I said something to her she gave me a smile. She was very young, hardly more than a child, they said she was fifteen. She was awfully pretty, and she had her best clothes on . . ." [substitutionary description]
>
> W. Somerset Maugham, "The Force of Circumstance"

Direct perception may be given, as here, in quotation marks and in the past tense. It may also appear without quotation marks, both in first-person and third-person narration, occasionally in present tense as well:

> Oh, did you know they tried to get Tom to run for mayor? Tom is making faces at me to shut up, but I don't see any harm in telling it to his best friends.
>
> Ring Lardner, "Who Dealt?"

In both the Maugham passage and the Lardner passage it is hard to say at some points whether what is perceived constitutes description or report: both "she gave me a smile" and "Tom is making faces at me" contain enough action in time that we may call them report, but the distinction is not vital here.

Narrated perception (3b) has most of the qualities of narrated monologue, mixing the direct perception of a character with the grammatical constituents of indirect speech or indirect thought:

> How hot it was! So hot that even the thrush chose to hop, like a mechanical bird, in the shadow of the flowers, with long pauses . . .
>
> Virginia Woolf, "Kew Gardens"

It is not always possible to differentiate between narrated monologue (2b) and narrated perception (3b), except that perception is generally assumed to be nonverbal; thought may be, or at least in the conventions of narrative usually is represented as, a process which can be considered verbal. Often one cannot be sure about a particular text:

> Appleby turned round and gazed at the house. Quite a different impulse had been at work there. It looked uncompromisingly permanent, totally removed from the ravages of time.
>
> Michael Innes, *The Bloody Wood*

The first sentence is plain report (3d), the second is substitutionary thought (2c), the third conveys both the perception and the apperception of the character (3c), and is introduced by what Fehr[42] called a "perception indicator": "It looked . . ." The gradual shift from the narrator's report through *reported perception* to the more "inner" view of *narrated perception* and *apperception* is a common technique. The tinge of apperception in the following example is evident in the simile, "like a living thing", and in the metaphor of "brooded":

> As he passed each field he looked at it carefully (3d) and saw how the land was merging out of the snow like a living thing (3c). The lower fields were brown and wet, and crows pecked and brooded in the old furrows (3b).
>
> Hugh MacLennan, *Two Solitudes*

The perception indicator "saw how" makes the next clause reported perception; what follows is in the same submode, except that there is no further indicator, so we might wish to call it indirect description or perception (the "free" cousin of reported perception). But in most texts we have little reason to differentiate between reported and indirect modes: the first perception indicator is probably felt to govern any subsequent sentence of the same kind:

> Clarence was silent (3d). He stared at Morrissey until Morrissey's eyes flickered and looked down at the papers before him (3c?). Morrissey looked even a trifle frightened, Clarence noticed (3c), though there was a telephone and the usual box of buttons on the desk (still 3c) so Morrissey could summon a couple of strong men in a trice if he wished (indirect thought, so 2c). There was probably a gun somewhere, too, maybe in a drawer (2c).
>
> Patricia Highsmith, *A Dog's Ransom*

Important for an interpretation of the passage is the slipping from 3d to 3c and 2c, since Clarence's sizing up of the situation is not that of the narrator and proves to be mistaken. Morrissey is not "a trifle frightened", as his cold-blooded murder of Clarence soon after will show. Clarence turns out to have been an unreliable perceiver. In other words, fiction can have not only an unreliable narrator, but also unreliable speakers, unreliable thinkers and unreliable perceivers. The latter is a staple of detective fiction: the witness sees that the restaurant clock stands at 12:15 at the moment of the murder, and it is the detective's job to find out that the clock was seen in a mirror over the bar, so that it must really have been 11:45. The point is possible only because events were filtered through the substitutionary perception of a fictional figure.

The vertical slipping between thought and perception is a common phenomenon, and usually appears where narrated monologue is used:

> He watched [perception indicator] sleepily the flakes, silver and dark, falling obliquely against the lamplight [description]. The time had come for

him to set out on his journey westward [thought]. Yes, the newspapers were right: snow was general all over Ireland [both narrated monologue and narrated perception].

James Joyce, "The Dead"

In the interior monologue which Joyce exploited later in *Ulysses*, the slipping back and forth in the stream of consciousness between what the character perceives and the play of his thoughts, triggered off by these perceptions, constitutes the special charm of the technique. Here thought takes the form of apperception, the overlay of meaning with which the character endows that which he has seen and felt.

Sometimes indirect perception will alternate with narrated perception and direct perception, with more or less "colouring" according to the shift of viewpoint and distance:

> Cliffie read it. *Lucy G. Beckman* to *Wed Kenneth L. Forbes* . . . Cliffie had put on a faint, casual smile, and now he lit a cigarette, shaking. He was of course paying no further attention to the barman, who hadn't a glimmer of what the news meant to him, who couldn't care less, and anyway the guy was queer, so what the hell could he know about anything? Kenneth – something – Forbes. Was he some good-looking or rich swine who had been hanging around for some time, maybe the one Luce had had a quarrel with?

Patricia Highsmith, Edith's Diary
[italics in original]

The italicized words might be classified as narrated monologue, except that these words are not the thoughts of Cliffie but the words he reads in the newspaper, on which Cliffie then reflects. "Kenneth – something – Forbes" repeats the newpaper's words but filtered through Cliffie's consciousness: he does not remember the initial of Forbes' name. These words might be considered direct thought, except that the sentences before and after are in the past tense of narrated monologue ("what the hell could he know" and "was he some good-looking or rich swine") rather than in the present tense.

Another possibility is that we take the words in italics to be *free direct perception*, where "free" means that we are not given the words exactly in the format they presumably had in the original newspaper clipping, nor with the quotation marks one expects of a direct quotation. But the words *Lucy G. Beckman to Wed* could not as effectively have been rendered in quotation marks and set off as a separate paragraph. This form of presentation would have removed it from Cliffie's consciousness, and weakened the impact of the inner views which Highsmith apparently values.

A Review of the Submode Markers

We have seen that there are degrees of distance, degrees of innerness. Many a passage of narrative cannot be placed precisely in one box or another. At all three levels, however, a certain set of markers is operative, according to which, insofar as one or more of them are present in a particular text, we make our judgements. An awareness of these markers helps us to analyse texts of substitutionary narration, be it speech in the narrow sense or in the wider sense, including thought and perception:

1. Quotation marks (often missing in direct thought and direct perception), other graphological indicators (paragraphing, italics, exclamation marks, dashes, ellipsis dots)
2. Inquits (verba dicendi, reporting phrases, perception indicators)
3. Use and shift of tenses (with more distance, the present continuous, the present, the past and the future tend to turn into the continuous past, the past, the past perfect and the subjunctive)
4. Deixis of place and time
5. Personal pronouns (first vs. third person)
6. Relative pronouns (*that* as mark of distance)
7. Phonological
8. Grammatical
9. Lexical
10. Rhetorical differences (in more direct modes: lack of connectors, lack of explicit subordination, ellipsis, ataxis, alogical or associative linkages, colloquial repetition, intensives, emphasis to suggest the character's intonation, contractions, lexical fillers, register of speech rather than literary prose).

As we have seen, there can be no easy formula to define how these parameters apply. Quotation marks are mostly used at position a, but may be omitted there or used with position b. Inquits may or may not be in order at positions a and c, the use of the tenses does not always help us either; so it goes right through the list.

Let us assume that we are confronted by a large number of texts to be analysed, and that we can find in each text between one and ten of the above parameters. We would then try to categorize the texts according to type. The problem is that ten parameters yield $2^{10} - 1 = 1023$ possible combinations. But other parameters will be found from time to time: for instance, the use of explanatory information which the character is not likely to have had, but which is nevertheless directed at the reader. Then we would have $2^{11} - 1 = 2047$ categories. In fact, the text may contain several markers of one kind, and the clues of one kind may be mutually contradictory (we have seen in a Highsmith passage that deixis of place and time may diverge). Thus the number of possible combinations dizzies the imagination. No wonder that critics have differed as to the markers of such techniques as "free indirect speech". No wonder that such a regiment of terms for different types of substitutionary narration has been recruited in the last eighty years.

We can conclude then:

1. Our chart displaying the submodes of speech is a simplification of a myriad of possibilities, and must remain so.

2. No set of technical terms for the submodes of speech can avoid reductionism and overlapping.

3. As we find when we sort passages out between the chief narrative modes, the clear cases will predominate, but many texts elude certain categorization.

4. The chief submodes constitute a useful heuristic system, but the system cannot replace the intelligent reading of a sensitive critic.

CHAPTER V

Inquits

The "free" in "free indirect speech" is generally thought to mean that no *inquit* or reporting phrase, such as "she said that" or "answered the general", introduces the speech. With an inquit, the speech is said to be *bound* or *tagged* rather than free.

The inquit acts as a hinge between passages of speech and the adjacent narrative modes, and belongs properly to the mode of report. Such hinges were once thought more necessary than they are now. Thus, as with the modes in general, not only the immediate narrative context but also historical and stylistic considerations, not to speak of grammatical ones, govern its variations. These variations conform to a set of unwritten laws.

Both historical and stylistic considerations are relevant, for instance, when one looks at the position of the inquit relative to the speech to which it is attached. For the inquit sometimes precedes the speech, sometimes interrupts the speech, sometimes follows. That is, it occurs in initial, medial or final position:

1. Initial position: "The same steady voice answered him. 'Yes, keep it about two points off the port bow.'"

Stephen Crane

2. Medial position: "'I don't know,' the nigger said. 'I hurt bad.'"

Ernest Hemingway

3. Final position: "'What were you doing on the floor?' I asked."

Graham Greene

In modern prose the inquit tends to come in final position. Second in popularity is the medial position. The initial position was dominant in narratives of the renaissance, but today's writers, by and large, avoid it. In early narrative almost every speech was accompanied by some kind of inquit, whereas the modern tendency is to let speech follow speech, if possible without interruption. An inquit in medial position is one way of allowing speech to follow on speech. The more radical tendency is to do without the inquit altogether.

There are probably a number of reasons for this tendency. One is that the inquit is akin to the static modes in that it is a constant reminder of the

75

narrator's presence. This reminder is necessary when a story is told orally, but it becomes an embarrassment if the effect wanted is that the narrative seem to tell itself – effortlessly, without authorial intervention. The decrease in the use of inquits in the last half century has been traced to the influence of Joyce's *Ulysses*. It was Joyce who introduced a wealth of inquitless monologue in third-person narration, and this innovation did not remain unnoticed.[1] The growing preference for the free forms of speech is in fact a preference for inquitless narrative.[2]

An examination of inquits in fiction leads us to a number of interrelated questions:

1. The question of convention. Do authors in weaving inquits into their narratives follow conventions of which textual critics and the authors themselves have been unaware? Inevitably the answer will be *yes* when we come to look at the questions which follow in detail.

2. The question of essayistic versus dramatic narrative. Modern narrative is known to lean away from the essayistic stance, which favours comment and description as its staple narrative modes, and towards the dramatic, the staple of which is of course speech. Thus the inquit-formula becomes an unwelcome guest, which is to be either pushed into the left margin to get it out of the way, as in a dramatic text, or made as inconspicuous as possible, or eschewed altogether, that is, reduced to its zero stage.

3. The question of inquit style. According to systems theory,[3] any aspect of a system, such as a coherent narrative may be supposed to be, is necessarily linked to and affects other aspects of the system. If, for instance, an author is a foe to the inquit and prefers the zero stage, he will have to find other methods of letting the reader know who is speaking to whom – by the use, for instance, of concealed stage directions. If, on the other hand, he likes to interlard his inquits with extended descriptions of the speaker and his situation, he will prefer the inquit in initial position. For only an initial inquit normally allows a heavy admixture of material from the modes of description and comment.

4. The question of period style. The inquit in initial position is an essential ingredient of the period style of renaissance narrative, in contrast to the usage of contemporary writers, as a comparison will show – our examples are drawn from longer narratives rather than from the short story since only the longer work yields enough material for a statistical analysis:

Inquit distribution, 15th to 20th centuries

	Initial	Medial	Final	Ø-stage
1. William Caxton, *Paris and Vienne*, 1485	98%	2%	–	–
2. John Lyly, *Euphues*, 1578	76	18	8	4
3. Aphra Behn, *Oroonoko*, 1688	68	32	–	–

Inquit distribution, 15th to 20th centuries *continued*

	Initial	Medial	Final	Ø-stage
4. Henry Fielding, *Tom Jones*, 1749	23	69	7	1
5. Jane Austen, *Mansfield Park*, 1814	13	27	6	54
6. George Eliot, *The Mill on the Floss*, 1860	15	43	22	20
7. Charles Dickens, *Great Expectations*, 1860	31	37	16	15
8. Thomas Hardy, *Tess of the d'Urbervilles*, 1891	3	31	19	47
9. Joseph Conrad, *Lord Jim*, 1900	7	43	38	12
10. D. H. Lawrence, *Sons and Lovers*, 1913	1	29	46	24
11. Aldous Huxley, *Point Counter Point*, 1928	2	47	27	24
12. William Faulkner, *The Sound and the Fury*, 1929	3	69	25	3
	0	58	33	9
	5	64	27	4
13. Ralph Ellison, *Invisible Man*, 1947	4	41	25	30
14. Keith Waterhouse, *Billy Liar*, 1959	34	11	27	28
15. Muriel Spark, *Not to Disturb*, 1971	2	47	37	14
16. Paul Scott, *A Division of the Spoils*, 1975	22	6	8	64

The statistics are based on a sampling of 100 speeches in each text, except for *Oroonoko*, which does not have that many speeches. The tendency away from the initial inquit, despite the fluctuations, is clear. The three samples of *The Sound and the Fury* (each sample represents about 5% of the bulk of the text) suggest the consistency with which the distribution between inquit positions may be maintained.

A history of the inquit formula in English narrative reveals other sea-changes of interest to the critic. In Caxton or Lyly, for instance, the inquit in initial position is almost invariably embedded in a long sentence which conveys other information as well:

And whan vyenne herde speke of these tydynges / & sawe the grete honour & prys that she had goten and al was comen by this noble knyght / she said to ysabeau hyr damoysel / My suster sayd I not to you wel but late / that I was byloved . . .

William Caxton, *Paris and Vienne*

Amidst therefore these his extremities between hope and fear, he uttered these or the like speeches. [The speech which follows is 11 paragraphs long.]

John Lyly, *Euphues*

The initial inquit in the modern novel, on the other hand, tends to be something like an unobtrusive *I said* or, more rarely, a pungent *growled* or *snapped*. Moreover, nowadays the inquit tends to stand alone without elaboration; and it is shorter, like the speeches it accompanies, than during the eighteenth century.

This pattern reflects the narrator's withdrawal from the stance of interfering commentator and also a much stronger consciousness of people speaking not so much *about* a subject as *to* one another, a consciousness largely absent from renaissance narrative.[4] But the inquit is also subject to fashions. From the time of Fielding and Smollett on, eighteenth century novelists used speech for the purpose of highlighting dramatic climaxes, as reflected in the preference for "he cried" and "she exclaimed"; nineteenth century novelists show a preference for highly differentiated final inquits like *retorted Jerry* (Dickens) or *she breathed* and *I after an instant risked* (Henry James).[5] In modern popular literature the differentiated inquits are used to steer the sympathy of the reader (*he sneered, she bravely countered*), who needs to be constantly posted as to how he is to view what the characters say and do. The opposite tendency is followed by authors who insist on *showing* rather than *telling*,[6] and therefore prefer the zero-stage of the inquit.

5. *The question of author-specific habits*. Henry James brought the art of the inquit to a high polish, and his inventive use of the form even attracted comment from his critics. Some authors are acrobats of the inquit, and pride themselves on the variety of ways they manage to avoid the conventional and humdrum forms. Less obvious are the inquit-habits of Conrad and Lawrence, although distinctive in different ways, and the special arts of the zero-stage in later writers, for instance Ivy Compton-Burnett.

6. *Questions of authorship*. If authors show special and persistent characteristics in their use of the inquit, it may be that authorship problems, which abound in English narrative until the middle of the eighteenth century, can be attacked with inquit-characteristics as one of the parameters. In Robert Greene's romances, for instance, the inquit tends to the medial position. Recently Greene's authorship of *A Groatsworth of Wit* has been called in question,[7] yet the preference for the medial-inquit gives one pause, since the similarity to the treatment of inquits in Greene's euphuistic romances is remarkable. Here is a passage from *A Groatsworth*: ten speeches in a row, all but one of them with a medial inquit:

Lets then end talk, quoth Lamilia, and you (signior Lucanio) and I will go to the Chesse. To Chesse, said he, what meane you by that: It is a game, said she, that the first daunger is but a checke, the worst, the giving of a mate. Well, said Roberto, that game yee have beene at already then, for you checkt him first with your beauty, & gave your selfe for mate to him by your bounty. Thats wel taken brother, said Lucanio, so have we past our game at Chesse. Wil ye play at Tables then, said she: I cannot, quoth hee, for I can goe no further with my game, if I be once taken. Will ye play then at cards. I said he, so it bee at one and thirtie. That fooles game, said shee: Wele all to hazard, said Roberto, and brother you shall make one for an houre or two . . .

Greenes, Groatsworth of witte, bought
with a million of Repentance . . . London, 1592, D3r

The pattern is regular and in strong contrast to the prefixed inquits of Greene's great model, Lyly's *Euphues*. So the statistical treatment of inquits may provide a useful tool for ascertaining the authorship of doubtful works and readjusting traditional views of literary history.

Inquit Norms

Our questions alone may suggest that the inquit is subject to systematic study, and is not merely a matter of authorial caprice and unreflected habit. Certain unwritten laws seem to govern the length, form and position of inquits in narrative prose, and as we gain a sense of the governing norms and conventions, we can move from there to analysing departures from those norms. So we must begin by determining the norms.

Length of speech. A very short speech can take an initial or a final inquit, and no difference of meaning or style seems to result:

> A) He said, "Time to go."
> B) "Time to go," he said.
> *C) "Time," he said, "to go."

The last of these three versions is unlikely nowadays, since the speech is too short to allow a division. (The * indicates an unidiomatic locution.)

The longer the speech, however, the more awkward does the final position of the inquit become. The paragraph-length speeches in Lyly's *Euphues* are almost inevitably prefixed by an inquit: Lyly could hardly have Eubulus give Euphues a piece of his mind in a 250-word speech, followed by "he said". The constraint on inquits in final position seems to grow where a speech consists of more than one sentence or where a single sentence is more than 20 to 30 words long. A speech long enough to require indentation if quoted in a scholarly article requires an inquit in initial or medial position.

Thus we find that authors who give their characters long speeches, including Smollett, Dr Johnson, Peacock, Thackeray and Huxley, use the inquit in initial position to introduce such speeches. Authors that give preference to short speeches, which is the prevailing tendency in the twentieth century, strongly prefer the medial and final positions.

The inquit weighted with static modes. Both speech and report, the two dynamic modes, can have embedded in them passages in the two static modes, description and comment. Where report in the form of an inquit is weighted heavily with embedded description, it naturally grows longer and tends to the initial position, as in the following example from a story by James Joyce:

> She stopped, as if she were communing with the past, and then said shrewdly: "Mind you, I noticed . . ."

Description of the speaker is apparently felt to be more appropriate in the initial inquit, but a stronger admixture of comment fits better in an inquit that is in final position:

> "Will you tell me candidly – for I know nothing of her, and it is rather important that I should learn – what sort of person is Lady Caroline?'
> This frank question, put directly, and guarded by the battery of those innocent, girlish eyes, was a very hard question to be answered . . .
> D. M. Mulock, *John Halifax, Gentleman*

A long inquit in final position is hard to compose. "Long inquit" in this context refers to the fact that the inquit is enriched by description of the speaker or his situation, by report or by the narrator's comment. Take, for instance,

> He said, one hand on each knee, the carved briar hanging on one side, the voice hoarse and sounding a little exasperated by the opposition he was encountering, "would you mind . . ."

All the detail devoted to showing us how the speaker looks, his frame of mind and the quality of his voice, would be wasted on us if it came after instead of before the speech. The longer the inquit, in fact, the more likely that it *precede* rather than *follow* the speech. The modern tendency toward the shorter inquit or its elimination wherever possible therefore goes hand in hand with its migration from initial to final position.

Thus these rules go hand in hand. If
1. long speeches require an initial inquit and
2. long inquits come in initial position, it follows that
3. combinations of long speeches and long inquits almost invariably take the sequence inquit-speech. The opposite sequence is thinkable, but it would be hard to write, and a survey of narratives of different periods unearths no clear and unambiguous examples. There does seem to be, then, a *system* within which the position of inquits is determined.

The inquit and register shift. Some writers exploit the possibility of shifting from a colloquial inquit to a formal speech and back again, like P. G. Wodehouse, who has Bertie Wooster quote the pedantic and formal pronouncements of his butler, Jeeves. More normal, however, is a shifting up from speech to inquit:

> "I canna believe as yer really want me," he said, looking down at her with dark, glowing eyes.
> D. H. Lawrence, *The First Lady Chatterley*

The words of Mellors are in "intimate" register,[8] the inquit is neutral or consultative. Inevitably, authors that like to quote dialect speakers, like Emily Bronte and Dickens, are given to shifting down from the inquit, as are modern writers, like Lawrence or Steinbeck, who quote working-class speakers *in extenso*.

Where an author is given to "elegant variation", an instability in the register of the inquits themselves can result. *Replied* is rather formal, *answered* and *said* are neutral, stylistically unmarked forms.

Word Order in Inquits

To the modern reader's ear, the inquit in medial position as it appears in the eighteenth and nineteenth centuries has a somewhat formal or stilted look because it generally appeared in inverted form: *said he* instead of *he said*. (This is still the rule in modern German.) In Chaucer *he sayde* occurs as well as *sayde he*, but only *quod he*, never *he quod*. Chaucer found the inverted form, which he was certainly in no way shy of using, especially where metre or rhyme required, more appropriate to the one inquit than to the other. Where *quoth* is used later (as late as in Sterne's *Tristram Shandy*, in verse well into the 19th century), the inversion is also mandatory. "So the oiler quoth" in Crane's "The Open Boat" is an odd exception.

In the modern novel the habit of syntactic inversion applied to the medial inquit becomes optional, and is thus a matter of rhetoric (where an optional inversion is called an *anastrophe*). Such anastrophes tend to be retained in the medial, sometimes also in the final inquit[9] where the speaker is named:

medial: "Yes," said Miss Meydinger. "That would be a grand way."
H. G. Wells, *Love and Mr Lewisham*

final: "I'm not afraid of Eugenio," said Daisy with a toss of her head.
Henry James, *Daisy Miller*

Until late in the nineteenth century, this rule was also generally valid where a pronoun was substituted for the speaker's name:

"No," said she, "you must not lay aside your watch of Flora."
Maria Edgeworth, *Emile de Coulanges*

The development of modern narrative, however, pushed the verb to the rear:

"I know," he said. "Tell me the name of your dentist."

This rule holds even if the inquit is modified:

"Why are you in such a hurry, Tessa?" she said gently.
Joyce Carol Oates, *A Girl at the Edge of the Ocean*

But if a medial or final inquit with the speaker's name is modified, the anastrophe frequently occurs:

medial: "We'll find out," Angelo said calmly. "First let's see what happens next."

Harold Robbins, *The Betsy*

final: "Thank you, no," said Tessa politely.

Joyce Carol Oates, *A Girl at the Edge of the Ocean*

The rather spare, hard-boiled style of Robbins is naturally more likely to do without inquits in anastrophic form. The anastrophe, still standard in the Brontes and in Dickens, now suggests a touch of the flowery, the rhetorical, the self-conscious style. Yet in some authors the anastrophe still appears indiscriminately with the pronoun-verb sequence:

(pronoun + verb):   "How fine you look," he said, examining her from head to foot. "Really, quite the young lady!"

(verb + proper noun):   "Look here," said Otto, "this is the third day I've been watching you . . ."

both passages on one page of
Vladimir Nabokov, *Laughter in the Dark*

As Jespersen pointed out,[10] the anastrophe is less likely with verbs other than *to say*, so that a writer who used "said he" would nevertheless use "he whispered" and "he suggested". This may be because the focus in the simple "said he" is on *he*, and if we want to shift the focus to the verb, using a more specific, as it were "marked" form like *whispered*, it is only natural to place it in the second position, where the stress and focus seem naturally to belong. But this is a questionable kind of explanation, since it would obtain in our times only: in the eighteenth century, the inverted word order was virtually obligatory in the medial inquit, whether with "said", "replied", "returned" or "continued".

The matter becomes complicated when the inquit has four parts: a subject (the speaker's name or a pronoun), a verb of the *genera dicendi*, an indirect object, and a modifier:

(SVIMod)   My aunt said to him energetically:

James Joyce, "Araby"

A full list of the possible combinations could start with those which are most common:

(SVModI)   Bill said quietly to Jane
(ModSVI)   Quietly Bill said to Jane

Of the 24 thinkable combinations, some twelve are grossly ungrammatical, like:

(VModS)*   To Jane said quietly Bill

The remainder, which usually involve the topicalization of the modifier or the addressee, are available to the author aiming at certain emphases or rhetorical effects.

Of special interest here are those inquits which are in complementary distribution with one another, in that, for instance, the one is suitable only to the initial, the other only to the medial and final position. Thus the topicalization of the modifier, as in

Quietly Bill said to Jane

is suitable to an initial position only, whereas the topicalization of the verb, as in

a) Said Bill quietly to Jane
            or
b) Said Bill to Jane quietly

occurs most naturally when an inquit takes the medial position. The topicalization of the indirect object, on the other hand, is possible in the initial position, impossible in the medial and final:

a) initial: To Jane Bill quietly said, "let's go home before she starts her song and dance."
b) medial: *"Let's go home," to Jane Bill quietly said, "before she starts her song and dance."
c) final: *"Let's go home before she starts her song and dance," to Jane Bill quietly said.

Where the indirect object precedes the verb, inversion of verb and pronoun is awkward, if not impossible:

a)   To Jane Bill said
b) *To Jane said Bill

This is apparently because of a rule saying that if the indirect object is topicalized, a further topicalization (which is what the inversion of subject and verb amounts to) is not permissible.

Examples of three-part and four-part inquits, on which these hypotheses could be tested, one might add, are not as easily found in contemporary fiction as in that of the first quarter of the century, apparently because the description of the speaker or of his manner of speaking has been separated out of the inquit and now often stands by itself, becoming a substitute for the older style of inquit: a crypto-inquit, as it were:

She was clever and perceptive and compelled and cruel. "Look at me . . ."
William Golding, Free Fall

Frequently the crypto-inquit takes the form of a stage direction, followed immediately by direct speech:

> Diana pushed the scarf back revealing her brow and a strained-back strip of gleaming hair. "Miles is so upset about yesterday." "Damn Miles, if I may say so."
Iris Murdoch, Bruno's Dream

By comparison, the older three-part or four-part inquit seems a little primitive, overly explicit and obvious.

The conventions governing word order are, as we see, various and complex, and they have changed from epoch to epoch. Table 2 summarizes the more important ones, and suggests that some of them particularly require diachronic treatment:

Parameters governing word order in the inquit, medial position

Inversion using –	necessary	likely	unlikely	almost impossible
1. – quoth	+			
2. – cried	+ ca. 1670	+ ca. 1770	+ ca. 1870	+ ca. 1970
3. – said		possible		
4. – polysyl-labled verb			+	
5. – adverb or adverbial adjunct			+ 1870	+ 1970
6. – name instead of pronoun		+ ca. 1770	+ ca. 1970	
7. – indirect object preceding subject				+

The table also suggests certain incompatibilities; for instance:

– *quoth* makes syntactic inversion mandatory,
– rule 7 makes it virtually impossible.

It follows that the two cannot be, and, as far as we can ascertain, never could be mixed with one another:

  *To Jane quoth Bill

and even when "cried he" was the rule, as in Oliver Goldsmith, no indirect object would have been included in the inquit.

Among the shortcomings of the table is that it groups phenomena which are in fact diverse. The subject of the verb need not be a pronoun or a name – it may also be an epithet, like "the woman in white", which introduces other combinational constraints. Then too, adverbs are not the same as adverbial adjuncts: we can write

  He quietly said

but probably not

  *He in a soft voice said

since "in a soft voice" requires a position before or after the pronoun and verb. Finally, the table cannot reveal what happens when a number of parameters are simultaneously operative. Parameters 4 to 7, for instance, all apply to such an inquit as

  *To Jane whispered Bill hastily

where the rules push and pull in opposite directions, and it is hard to say whether the combination is only awkward or quite impossible. Since, as we have seen, a four-part inquit allows of 24 combinations, at least in theory, and we have 7 parameters to consider, the number of possibilities inviting inquiry goes into the hundreds, and it seems discreet not to pursue the matter here.

The Tense of the Inquit Verb

Direct speech in narrative comes in any tense whatever, but the present tense predominates. The inquit verb normally stands in the past tense and thus in contrast to the verbs in the speech it identifies. But the inquit may also be put in the present, though rarely in the present continuous. Interesting are those passages where the contrast of tenses is played with for rhetorical effect or where the difference is a matter of style register. In colloquial narrative even a mixture is permissible, as in "so I said to him, says I . . ." or for special stylistic effect. In *Moll Flanders*, for instance, the memoir-writing narrator sometimes prefers the past-tense-inquit for herself, the present-tense-inquit for her interlocutor at the time:

One morning he pulls off his diamond ring, and writes upon the glass of the sash in my chamber this line:

> You I love, and you alone.

I read it, and asked him to lend me the ring, with which I wrote under it, thus:

> And so in love says every one.

He takes his ring again, and writes another line thus:

> Virtue alone is an estate.

I borrowed it again, and I wrote . . .

But this is a usage in which Defoe is not consistent. Where he vacillates between inquits in the past and inquits in the present tense, however, there is a certain regularity in the shifts which invites closer examination, especially since the same phenomenon occurs in Fielding's dialogues. In some passages the inquit in present tense has a colloquial quality, whereas the inquit in past tense is formal. The difference, in other words, is a matter of style register.

An example of a systematic tense shift of a different kind is offered by Faulkner's *The Sound and the Fury*. Here chapters 1, 2 and 4 are told in the past; chapter 3, which is told by Jason Compson, uses *says* rather than *said* throughout, a technique which is clearly of a piece with the author's wish to shape a different narrative technique for each of the four perspectives from which the four chapters are told. What the effective function of this peculiar tense shift is, however, one can hardly determine.

It is a peculiarity of narrative verse that the inquit is often in the present tense:

> The Queen, so gracious, mild and good,
> Cries, "Is he gone! 'tis time he should."
> > Swift, "Verses on the Death of Dr Swift"

Not infrequently it occurs if the poem uses the historical present:

> Then up steps young Napoleon and takes his mother by the hand,
> Saying: "Mother dear, have patience until I'm able to take command."
> > "The Bonny Bunch of Roses O"

This pattern is presumably a relic of what was in the 16th and 17th century a standard inquit pattern in prose:

> His servant, though altogether past grace, yet for fashion-sake began to advise his master more wisely, saying:
> "For mine own part it maketh no matter . . ."
> > George Pettie, "Sinorix and Camma"

– the beautie of the Countesse representing it self before his eyes, made him

86

to alter his minde again, and to reject that which be before allowed, saying thus: "I feele in minde the cause of mine offence . . ."

William Painter, "The Countesse of Salesburie"

In modern prose, by contrast, the participle is little used for inquit purposes, except when the speech is supposedly made recurrently or habitually or to indicate audition by proxy. Exceptions are novels told wholly in the present tense, like Joyce Cary's *Mister Johnson*, or which are in past tense, but with the inquits in the present, like Mark Twain's *Huckleberry Finn*.

The Scale of Immediacy

The modern inquit, as we have seen, tends to be shorter than its predecessors, and tends to be separated from other narrative material, or even to disappear. Where it is imbedded or yoked to other phrases and clauses in a longer sentence, it tends to accrue to itself
– more report than description, and
– more description than comment.
This is surely due to a generally accepted convention according to which the four narrative modes are ranked on a kind of scale of immediacy. According to this scale a reader has more of the "sense of life" and fewer reminders that fiction is mediated by art if authorial comment is kept to a minimum. We might say that the illusionist function of literature is best served by a preference for

	1. speech
and less by	2. report, below which range
	3. description and
	4. comment.

The most obvious kind of mediation occurs in a fifth mode,

5. metanarrative,

which is no fictional mode at all, but the author's direct address to the reader, as in Fielding and Thackeray. Insofar as metanarrative can be considered a fifth mode, the three modes immediately preceding it may be considered "buffer-modes", since they inevitably intervene between *speech* and *metanarrative*: the transitional probabilities of the one being followed by the other seem to be practically nil, although one can construct an example:

In the fall of 1846 I started to make notes on my visits to Stratton Manor and on the supernatural events occurring there, and the resulting journals are the basis for the following story. "Zounds!" Lord Stratton had said to me one day, "you were a poor sort of writer if you failed to make up a masterpiece of the strange apparitions which have been plaguing this house!"

The jump over all the buffer-modes at a single bound is a little abrupt, but not inconceivable.

In the first half of the twentieth century, metanarrative was frowned upon altogether, until the self-conscious fictions of the 1960's, such as those of Nabokov and Barth, brought it into vogue again. But it is the other end of the scale that comes to be preferred: speech and, in some authors, as little else as possible. This view of what narrative should be, in fact, was shared by the founders of the English novel in the eighteenth century. Even in older fictions in which we find metanarrative, as in Defoe, there is on occasion a visible preference for the top end of the scale of immediacy by eliminating the inquit altogether and composing passages of unadulterated speech. One method is to slip into dramatic form, that is, to switch the mode of presentation in mid-career:

> "What do you want?" says John.
> "Why, what do you intend to do?" says the constable.
> "To do?" says John. "What would you have us do?"
> *Constable.* Why don't you be gone? What do you stand there for?
> *John.* Why do you stop us on the king's highway . . .
>
> Daniel Defoe, *A Journal of the Plague Year*

Another method is to convey dialogue in such a way that the speaker no longer needs to be named. The reader can be spared confusion, for instance, in that the speaker names his partner in the conversation occasionally:

> "Nay, Elinor, this reproach from you – you who have confidence in no one!"
>
> Jane Austen, *Sense and Sensibility*

This makes clear to us that it must be Marianne and not Elinor that is talking. When more than two persons participate in the conversation, of course, the method no longer works. An out-and-out foe of the inquit formula, like Ivy Compton-Burnett, gives the reader genuine puzzles in those family scenes where a number of persons take part in a conversation interrupted only now and then by an inquit.

The zero-stage. Aside from the three positions of the inquit, then, there is a zero-stage which, by the nature of non-existent entities, eludes investigation. As we have just seen, however, we can classify the techniques which allow the narrator to do without inquits:

1. Change of addressee.
2. Use of pronouns.
3. The speakers may have different dialects, style registers, viewpoints, subject matter.
4. Crypto-inquits tell the reader who is about to speak or has just spoken.

These techniques, however, are largely present in early narratives as well, and do not constitute a monopoly of the twentieth century story-teller. Defoe, for instance, uses many more inquits than we should expect to find in a contemporary writer. He could, however, perfectly well have left many of them away. Let us consider, for instance, a few lines of *Moll Flanders* and imagine that the inquits, here printed in square brackets, had been removed:

"Well," says the mother, "Then there's one son lost;" and she said it in a very mournful tone, as one greatly concerned at it. 'I hope not, madam," [says Robin:] "no man is lost when a good wife has found him." "Why, but child," [says the old lady,] "she is a beggar." "Why, then, madam, she has the more need of charity," [says Robin;] "I'll take her off the hands of the parish, and she and I'll bed together." "It's bad jesting with such things," [says the mother.] "I don't jest, madam," [says Robin;] "we'll come and beg your pardon, madam, and your blessing, madam and my father's". "This is all out of the way, son," [says the mother.] "If you are in earnest you are undone." "I am afraid not," [says he,] "for I am really afraid she . . ."

Once we know that a conversation is going on between Robin and his mother, an inquit paired with every subsequent speech is rather a luxury than a necessity. The reader is kept posted on who says what by means of signals in the speeches themselves as well as by the convention of closing and opening quotation marks. These signals were not, then, invented by modern writers who took it into their heads to eliminate inquits as much as possible. If the preference for the zero-stage is a mark of "progress" in narrative technique, it is only insofar as a growing awareness of the *redundancy* of inquits made it seem easy enough to do without them, and perhaps to explore and expand a wide variety of crypto-inquits, a variety which we cannot, indeed, find in the earlier periods. In that sense the growing preference for the zero-stage is part and parcel of the striving for a narrative economy in those areas (including, for instance, expositions, transitional summaries, and explanations of authorial purpose) where elaboration and profusion fail to add to what Ford Madox Ford, in gallicized English, called the *progression d'effet*. The modern writer saw, apparently, that many an inquit is ballast which one can do without, and which takes up the room one would prefer to make available for more important effects.

The Inquit and Stylistic Norms

The "laws" or norms of narrative which a close look at inquits, their structures and their connections to narrative contexts reveal, are to some extent, we must conclude, a matter of fashion. The norms change with time, and authors occasionally break the old norms and develop new ones. Thus we find very few laws relating to the inquit which are held to absolutely. Indeed, many a new awareness of a norm allows – may indeed positively invite – a "foregrounding" or deviation from that norm for rhetorical purposes. For the modern writer, in fact, the inquit norms are sufficiently manifold to invite deliberate and manifold contravention:

Said, Any good at cards? Said, No.
Said, Fine, Cavanaugh, take a hand of poker.
William Saroyan, "Ever Fall in Love with a Midget?"

The norm is that short inquits are put in final position. Saroyan does the opposite. The norm says that the zero-stage is appropriate where the name of the person addressed, Cavanaugh, is given. And the norm calls for a pronoun with "said" as well as quotation marks before and after directly quoted speech. Here, too, Saroyan breaks the convention. In short, Saroyan shows his awareness of the established norms and gets his special effects by deviating from them.

We have postulated that the forms and uses of inquits are subject to various regulations. Some of these have turned out to be absolute rules (probably one cannot write "he quoth softly that he loved her"); others are norms and conventions which can be played with in narrative for rhetorical and stylistic purposes. We have found, in other words, at least three stages of obligation:

1. *rules* (which are binding),
2. *norms* (rules which can be easily broken or altered or adjusted by time), and
3. *conventions* (norms, the original purpose and function of which is no longer clear to us).

Our investigation therefore gives a partial answer to the question which Searle has claimed to be crucial to his concept of speech acts, namely: "Are conventions realizations of rules?"[11] The conventions governing inquits, as we have seen, are in part norms of which some are binding rules: insofar as Searle is not merely tautologous (his question can be reduced to "Are conventions unformulated realizations of formulatable rules?") our answer to his question must be *yes*: the inquit conventions are not "mere conventions" the function of which is obscure, but a set of interrelated norms subject at least in part to authorial manipulation and, therefore, to critical analysis.

CHAPTER VI

Short Story Beginnings

Students of the short story like to speak of *closed* versus *open* beginnings and endings, but it is not easy to say exactly what these terms mean. Indeed, the concept of a closed beginning is a self-contradictory term, and the closed ending seems something of a tautology, rather like a black crow. Yet two easily remembered categories for the whole world of fiction ought to help make the business of explication simple and straightforward. Therefore the terms are worth investigating.

As to beginnings: stories start with more or less exposition. *More* means that the story does not begin immediately with an action, but that the reader is supplied with a background of both time and place, that the hero is introduced and characterized, and that antecedent events are summarized. This is the work of preparation called *procatasceue* in classical rhetoric and once considered the inevitable beginning of any discourse: its exposition. The story without exposition, by contrast, insofar as this is possible at all, starts without preparation or *medias in res*. These two extremes mark a wide continuum within which most stories will be found to reside. The narrative techniques which make the story seem to be positioned somewhere on this continuum are, as I hope to show, varied and manifold.

All this applies both to short stories and to novels, by and large. For several reasons, however, the opening of a short story is more important than that of a novel. Insofar as we can measure it in sentences and paragraphs at all, the opening may be shorter in a short story; but of course it occupies a greater percentage of the text. Then too, the short story tends to require a more tightly knit structure, so that the initial sounding of theme and tone is likely to reverberate through the middle and end in a way which is neither called for nor possible in a novel. In addition, novels often include blocks of exposition not at the beginning but later on in the course of the development: new scenes are described, new characters are introduced, more information about prior events is fed to the reader. Normally this occurs only in a limited way in the short story. Finally, the short story writer, with less space at his disposal, often tries to make his exposition as inconspicuous and brief as he can, whereas the author of a novel can afford to include a longer series of expositional elements before moving on to the heart of the matter; moreover, the reader of a novel will be prepared to spend longer on the preliminaries.

What I have said thus far presupposes what I believe frequently to be the case – that an opening or exposition is an identifiable portion of a fictional text and is usually over at a particular point. The theory of narrative modes can help us to find such points, when they exist, and help us define the kinds of opening.

As to short story endings: the traditional story shows how the conflicts are resolved, the characters achieve their aims or accept failure, the plot strands are drawn together and knotted up. The open ending, by contrast, stops in mid-air. The conflicts are *not* resolved. The story is supposed by the reader to run on beyond its fictional limits. The characters continue their lives – lives from which certain episodes are presented in the story.

Of course every story has a conclusion simply because it ends (*conclusion* from the Latin *conclusus*, to shut up); in practice, however, there exists a wide variety of openings and endings. The theory of narrative modes can help us define these varieties.

Since only a representative sample of texts will allow valid generalizations, some forty anthologies and collections of stories, including most of the major writers in this genre (see the bibliography) were drawn upon, yielding a corpus of six hundred British, American and Canadian short stories. These include 137 first published before 1900 and 463 published in this century. To allow comparison to the novel, three hundred of these were examined, half of them of this century, the other half of earlier date. The same works were examined both for the study of beginnings in this and for the study of endings in the following chapters. A table of the most relevant statistics can be found in the appendices.

Openings with Comment

Many tales open with a rather lengthy expository passage, telling the reader what the story is to be about. A story which starts with several sentences of this kind is clearly not of our time:

> Let nature be never so liberal to us in the complete forming of our bodies after the most exact copies of proportion, and let us be never so well accomplished in all our outward qualities so that we may imagine ourselves to be complete, yet if grace be not implanted on our hearts whereby to guide us in our actions, we are like a fair vessel at sea which is sufficiently furnished with all her sails and tackling, but yet wants the only thing to guide and steer her by, her rudder, without which it is very difficult to guide her to any safe harbour. The truth hereof we may every day experiment in ourselves, and . . .
> Francis Kirkman, "The Counterfeit Lady Unveiled"

Some readers may wish to define the short story in a way which excludes narratives of the kind Kirkman and his contemporaries wrote. But during the eighteenth and nineteenth centuries, when the story was more closely related to the essay than it is now, such openings were still popular, and were used by Scott, Poe and Hawthorne. The expository tone declares the preliminary remarks to be a kind of extraterritorial adjunct to the story proper. The effect is often increased by the narrator's references to the fact of his storytelling, a species of comment we have called *metanarrative*:

> The following narrative is given from the pen, so far as memory permits, in the same character in which it was presented to the author's ear; nor has he claim to further praise . . .
>
> Sir Walter Scott, "The Tapestried Chamber"

Among the six hundred stories which were surveyed for the purposes of this study, only five per cent (32 in all) begin with comment, and the figure is four per cent for the post-1900 sample. And here the essayistic method of comment is usually leavened with descriptive elements:

> We no longer groan and heap ashes upon our heads when the flames of Tophet are mentioned. For, even the preachers have begun to tell us that God is radium, or ether or some scientific compound, and that the worst we wicked ones may expect is a chemical reaction. This is a pleasing hypothesis; but there lingers yet some of the old, goodly terror of orthodoxy.
>
> O. Henry, "An Unfinished Story"

A similarly essayistic exposition, with a latent quantum of metanarrative, is also used in one story of Fitzgerald's:

> Begin with an individual, and before you know it you find that you have created a type; begin with a type, and you find that you have created – nothing. That is because we are all queer fish, queerer behind our faces and voices than we want anyone to know or than we know ourselves. When I hear a man proclaiming himself . . .
>
> F. Scott Fitzgerald, "The Rich Boy"

The second paragraph goes on in the same style: "There are no types, no plurals", and the third as well: "Let me tell you about the very rich." The story consists of eight numbered sections, of which the first is wholly devoted to a discursive treatment of the story's theme. Of course no law says that exposition is forbidden to the modern short story. Yet writers seem to feel the force of such a taboo, and these examples from O. Henry and Fitzgerald constitute lone outposts. No doubt a story which opens with a few words of unalloyed comment is conceivable nowadays, but it is certainly not in fashion.

Openings with Description

The heyday of lengthy expository description was the nineteenth century. Short stories, like novels, often began with a setting of the scene so extensive that it would not do to quote more than a very much truncated example here:

Among the few features of agricultural England which retain an appearance but little modified by the lapse of centuries, may be reckoned the high,
grassy and furzy downs, coombs, or ewe-leases, as they are indifferently
called, that fill a large area of certain counties in the south and south-west.
If any mark of human occupation is met with hereon, it usually takes the
form of the solitary cottage of some shepherd.

Fifty years ago such a lonely cottage stood on such a down, and may
possibly be standing there now . . .

Thomas Hardy, "The Three Strangers"

As the *essay* is the purer form of the beginning with comment, the *sketch* is the
purer form and (for the nineteenth century short story) progenitor of such a
beginning as Hardy's. In our age we expect that the description at the
beginning of a story will turn out to be its chief setting, which it may be on
occasion in nineteenth century stories too, such as Hawthorne's "The
Maypole of Merry Mount" or Hardy's "The Withered Arm". But in many a
landscape description which open stories by Irving or Hawthorne, the scene is
apparently depicted for its own sake – here Zavarzadeh's term "phenomenalistic" is indeed appropriate – the description, then, has little direct relevance
to the plot of the story which follows. This judgement applies to many a
passage in Kipling: in one of his stories, for instance, the opening words are
direct speech, yet in the fifth paragraph the action is interrupted by the
following description:

"Is it officially declared yet?" . . .
Martyn picked up the *Pioneer* from the table, read through the telegrams
once more, and put up his feet on the chair-rests. It was a hot, dark,
breathless evening, heavy with the smell of . . .

Rudyard Kipling, "William the Conqueror"

The "dark, breathless evening" turns out to be no more than a small period in
the time-scheme of the story as it enfolds; the description does not serve the
reporting of fictive events, but is designed to convey the feel of a tropical
evening. The speech with which the story opens turns out to be a modal
façade (see Chapter I), behind which the reader finds a proper description for
the purpose of establishing atmosphere.

Description may also function as a figure of testimony (see Chapter II)
especially when it focusses on topographical or historical facts which the
reader thinks to be accurate. Story expositions with description therefore
tend to be "etic" or contextual, whereas middles and endings tend to be
"emic" or cotextual,[1] that is, to contain references interior to the fiction rather
than verifiable in the outer, nonfictional world.

During the course of the twentieth century, short story expositions have
become neater and shorter, but they have not been done away with
altogether: the opening with description reigns unabated. Of the stories
surveyed here, 228 (38%) begin with description, no different a percentage
than that which obtained before 1900. So the movement is not away from
description, but toward a use of it in special ways:

1. Description is less likely to occur as a block of several paragraphs at the beginning. At word and phrase level, description is present in any story whatever; at sentence and paragraph level, however, its heyday seems to be past. Whereas a block of description was a standard opening in the nineteenth century, there is a tendency in the twentieth century to tuck the block away later in the story, as in the Kipling quoted above or as in Lawrence's "The Horse Dealer's Daughter".

2. Description is now devoted less to landscapes than to city-scapes and interiors:

> It was the dead hour of a November afternoon. Under the ceiling of level mud-coloured cloud, the latest office buildings of the city stood out alarmingly like new tombstones, among the mass of older buildings. And along the streets the few cars and the few people appeared and disappeared slowly as if they were not following the roadway or the pavement but some inner, personal route. Along the road to the main station, at intervals of two hundred yards or so, unemployed men and one or two beggars were dribbling slowly past the desert of public buildings to the next patch of shop fronts.
>
> V. S. Pritchett, "The Fly in the Ointment"

3. In the contemporary short story the relevance of the description to what follows is less obvious than it was in Poe or Hawthorne. The Pritchett story just quoted from, for instance, takes the form of a conversation in a factory between a father and his son: the theme of business in difficulty is the common denominator of the block description which opens the story and of the central scene, which takes place neither in the street nor in an office building. Indeed, one can still find stories of the "poetic" kind which seem to include description for its own sake:

> From the oval-shaped flower-bed there rose perhaps a hundred stalks spreading into heart-shaped or tongue-shaped leaves half-way up and unfurling at the tip red or blue or yellow petals marked with spots of colour raised upon the surface; and from the red, blue or yellow gloom of the throat emerged a straight bar, rough with gold dust and slightly clubbed at the end. The petals were voluminous enough to be stirred by the summer breeze, and when they moved, the red, blue and yellow lights passed one over the other, staining an inch of the brown earth beneath with a spot of the moist intricate colour. The light fell either upon the smooth, grey back of a pebble, or . . .
>
> Virginia Woolf, "Kew Gardens"

Here the description has become an art form in itself. This is not to say that the description is unfunctional, but that it is of dubious relevance to the plot, or to an understanding of the motives behind the behaviour described. The same may be said of the following opening of a Joyce story:

The grey warm evening of August had descended upon the city and mild warm air, a memory of summer, circulated in the streets. The streets, shuttered for the repose of Sunday, swarmed with a gaily coloured crowd. Like illumined pearls the lamps shone from the summits of their tall poles upon the living texture below which, changing shape and hue unceasingly, sent up into the warm grey evening air an unchanging, unceasing murmur.

James Joyce, "Two Gallants"

Here we have a city-scape again, yet a rather romantic one and not what we should normally associate with the proclaimed style of "scrupulous mean-ness" or with the sparse and dreary atmosphere of Joyce's *Dubliners*. And it is of arguable relevance to the action that follows.

In "Araby", too, the atmosphere at the climax of the story, in the bazaar, is not that which is deftly sketched in by the opening paragraph:

North Richmond Street, being blind, was a quiet street except at the hour when the Christian Brothers' School set the boys free. An uninhabited house of two storeys stood at the blind end, detached from its neighbours in a square ground. The other houses of the street, conscious of decent lives within them, gazed at one another with brown imperturbable faces.

James Joyce, "Araby"

In other words, the setting offers a way into the story insofar as it creates the relevant atmosphere, but it is no longer a setting *within which* the story proper will take place.

4. Description of place and time still occurs in the modern story, but at least as often the description is devoted to the characters:

Michael Lowes hummed as he shaved, amused by the face he saw – the pallid, asymmetrical face, with the right eye so much higher than the left, and its eyebrow so peculiarly arched, like a "v" turned upside down . . .

Conrad Aiken, "Impulse"

Where the character is alone, or where the events are seen through his eyes, as in Aiken's story, the mirror-look is a stand-by for exposition. A mere window-pane will also serve:

Vincent Bishop, standing at his hotel room window saw in momentary reflection from the windowpane a nervous young man with dark eyes and undisciplined black hair.

Brian Moore, "Uncle T"

Such a brief self-portrait can also serve as an effective conclusion to a story:

He tried to recapture the feelings of the morning, but when he looked at himself in the mirror all he saw was the staring face of a fat frightened old man.

Hugh Garner, "The Yellow Sweater"

The mirror-trick is also used by Huxley, not in the first sentence but nevertheless as part of the exposition:

> Mr Hutton came to a pause in front of a small oblong mirror. Stopping a little to get a full view of his face, he passed a white, well-manicured finger over his moustache. It was as curly, as freshly auburn as it had been twenty years ago. His hair still retained . . .
>
> Aldous Huxley, "The Gioconda Smile"

Huxley often devotes another block of description to each of the other important characters as they appear on the scene. An alternative technique is to describe or at least identify the important characters all at once at the outset:

> There were two white men in charge of the trading station. Kayerts, the chief, was short and fat; Carlier, the assistant, was tall, with a large head and a very broad trunk perched upon a long pair of thin legs. The third man on the staff was a Sierra Leone nigger, who maintained that his name was Henry Price.
>
> Joseph Conrad, "An Outpost of Progress"

> Mrs Halloran had a nephew in the priesthood but that didn't stop her from drinking like a fish. Her husband, big Flatfoot Halloran, of the thick neck and braised-beef face, had been a patrolman on the Montreal waterfront, but gin and cahoots with the Black Hook Gang had got him off the cops some years before.
>
> Leo Kennedy, "A Priest in the Family"

Huxley's method makes the exposition less obviously expositional, whereas the other method allows for a cleaner, uninterrupted sequence of events once the story is started. One of the few differences in the use of narrative modes between the novel and the short story is that the novel often includes a detailed physical description of the *dramatis personae*. Such descriptions are not impossible in short stories, but they are exceptions and not usual to the form.

5. The obviousness of description in the modern story is reduced, then,
– by reducing the size of the block of exposition,
– by distributing the exposition over the first few pages, and, above all,
– by mixing description with the other narrative modes, primarily report. Such mixing works well with description:

> Grey puffs of sand arose and moved across the hillside; the rain peppered the road with spots of mud. Pfeffer sprinted up the derelict footway and arrived at the cottage out of breath.
>
> Irving Layton, "Vacation in La Voiselle"

A single sentence of description like this hardly strikes us as an exposition any more. In many stories the very first sentence mixes description and report:

Through level lines of streaming snow, a huge figure loomed large and portentous.

Alan Sullivan, "The Essence of a Man"

Through the bloody September twilight, aftermath of sixty-two rainless days, it had gone like a fire in dry grass – the rumour, the story, whatever it was. Something about Miss Minnie Cooper and a Negro.

William Faulkner, "Dry September"

Day had broken cold and gray, exceedingly cold and gray, when the man turned aside from the main Yukon trail and climbed the high earthbank, where a dim and little-traveled trail led eastward through the fat spruce timberland.

Jack London, "To Build a Fire"

Our awareness of exposition, on the other hand, is heightened by the use of the past perfect tense ("had gone like a fire", "had broken cold"), a phenomenon we must return to in connection with report. It is probably the wish to reduce this expositional quality and to give the scene a greater sense of immediacy that causes some writers to use the present tense where the past would be more normal:

A stout man with a pink face wears dingy white flannel trousers, a blue coat with a pink handkerchief showing, and a straw hat much too small for him, perched at the back of his head. He plays the guitar. A little chap in white canvas shoes, his face hidden under a felt hat like a broken wing, breathes into a flute; and a tall thin fellow, with bursting overripe button boots, draws ribbons – long, twisted, streaming ribbons – of tune out of a fiddle. They stand, unsmiling, but not serious, in the broad sunlight . . .

Katherine Mansfield, "Bank Holiday"

Here a preponderance of description (a sequence of three descriptions of persons) is broken by report ("plays the guitar", "breathes into a flute"). A similar beginning is this one:

Braggioni sits heaped upon the edge of a straight-backed chair much too small for him, and sings to Laura in a furry, mournful voice. Laura has begun to find reasons for avoiding her own house until the latest possible moment, for Braggioni is there almost every night. No matter how late she is, he will be sitting there . . .

Katherine Anne Porter, "Flowering Judas"

Here too description is immediately followed by report, the characters are introduced together and in the present tense: except for the indication of habitual action ("he will be sitting there"), the opening is practically devoid of expositional elements.

Thus far we have assumed that the static modes, comment and description, are suitable to exposition, whereas the dynamic modes, report and speech, are the modes of the *medias in res* openings. But we see, without having yet examined the use of the dynamic modes in short story beginnings, that the difference applies in tendency only, not absolutely. For description in particular can be made to seem less expositional by means of various devices. On the other hand, it will be made to seem even more expositional when a strong admixture of metanarrative is added:

> Along the sea of Solway, romantic on the Scottish side, with its woodland, its bays, its cliffs, and headlands, – and interesting on the English side, with its many beautiful towns with their shadows on the water, rich pastures, safe harbours, and numerous ships, – there still linger many traditional stories of a maritime nature, most of them connected with superstitions singularly wild and unusual. To the curious these tales afford a rich fund of entertainment, from the many diversities of the same story; some dry and barren, and stripped of all the embellishments of poetry; others dressed out . . .
>
> Allan Cunningham, "The Haunted Ships"

The story is introduced by a description and then by a disquisition on the source and varieties of such stories as well. Such a doubling up of the two static modes, description and comment, gives the reader a very distinct sense of being led only gradually into the story. Then too, both static modes give an even stronger impression of expositionality when the present tense is used: the result is an even more strongly non-narrative frame, or half frame, for the story being introduced. Thus we have in the Cunningham opening a very proper "beginning" – a distinct and fair-sized antechamber to the larger chamber of fiction which follows.

The expositional quality of description is also increased by connecting it
– with the report of anterior events, and
– with references to habitual actions on the part of some of the characters.
But since both of these two techniques are varieties of report, it is best to deal with them in the next section.

Openings with Report

Detailed analysis of the modern short story has shown that report and speech have become the dominant modes of the short story in this century, with speech the great favourite.[2] But only report vies with description in the opening sentences of modern short stories, occurring four times as much as does speech (40% for report as opposed to 11% for speech). For the period before 1900 the figures are 31% for report and 8% for speech. In other words, the two dynamic modes are more strongly favoured now. The turn seems to come just before the First World War, in the period of James Joyce's *Dubliners*:

> Old Jack raked the cinders together with a piece of cardboard and spread

them judiciously over the whitening dome of coals. When the dome was thinly covered his face lapsed into darkness but, as he set himself to fan the fire again, his crouching shadow ascended the opposite wall and his face slowly re-emerged into the light. It was an old man's face, very bony and hairy.

James Joyce, "Ivy Day in the Committee Room"

Even this beginning is not unadulterated report: the modifiers *old*, *judiciously* and *whitening* in the first sentence are more or less descriptive, and in the next two sentences, as well as in the following ones not quoted here, description increasingly predominates. A similar movement to other modes is evident in the other Joyce story which opens with report:

> The bell rang furiously and, when Miss Parker went to the tube, a furious voice called out in a piercing North of Ireland accent:
> "Send Farrington here!"
> Miss Parker returned to her machine, saying to a man who was writing at a desk:
> "Mr Alleyne wants you upstairs.'

James Joyce, "Counterparts"

Despite the descriptive modifiers, *furiously*, *furious* and *piercing*, the opening is certainly *medias in res*, with its alternation of report and speech. It is as clear an example of the opening with scenic report as is to be found in the anthologies and collections studied here. If the opening with scenic report is a markedly modern one, Joyce's openings, although written before the First World War, are still more modern than much of what followed later.

The other examples are from Hawthorne's *Twice-Told Tales*, written about seventy years earlier:

> The sexton stood in the porch of Milford meetinghouse, pulling lustily at the bell rope. The old people of the village came stooping along the street. Children with bright faces tripped . . .

Nathaniel Hawthorne, "The Minister's Black Veil"

> One day, in the sick chamber of Father Ephraim, who had been forty years the presiding elder over the Shaker settlement at Goshen, there was an assemblage of several of the chief men of the sect.

Nathaniel Hawthorne, "The Shaker Bridal"

> Young Goodman Brown came forth at sunset into the street at Salem village; but put his head back, after crossing the threshold, to exchange a parting kiss with his young wife. And Faith, as the wife was aptly named, thrust her own pretty head into the street, letting the wind play with the pink ribbons of her cap while she called to Goodman Brown.
> "Dearest heart," whispered she, softly and rather sadly, when her lips

were close to his ear, "prithee put off your journey until sunrise and sleep in your own bed tonight."

Nathaniel Hawthorne, "Young Goodman Brown"

Hawthorne and Joyce, then, get as close to a beginning with report as any, and they are rather overrepresented in our six hundred stories, since all fifteen of the stories in Joyce's *Dubliners* are included, and twenty-six stories by Hawthorne. In the other 559 stories it is surprisingly difficult to find a dozen clear examples. More common is that some form of scenic or panoramic report is mixed with other elements in the first sentence. Report seems to behave like some of those chemicals which have to be kept tightly stoppered in jars: let out, they immediately combine with other materials.

The scenic report of an action is not by its nature expositional, but becomes so in various ways: for instance, by the inclusion of references to events which had occurred earlier on:

> For no very intelligible reason, Mr Lucas *had* hurried ahead of his party.
> E. M. Forster, "The Road to Colonus"
> [italics mine]

> The fighting *had* been hard and continuous, that was attested by all the senses.
> Ambrose Bierce, "The Coup de Grace"
> [italics mine]

Here, as in most cases, *anteriority* is suggested by the use of the past perfect tense. Anteriority may also be indicated by prepositions like *after* or *before*:

> *After* they had eaten, Big Tom pushed the cracked and dirty supper things to the back of the table . . .
> Hugh Garner, "One, Two, Three Little Indians"
> [italics mine]

> Late in the afternoon *after* Mrs Boldescu's funeral, her four children returned to the shop.
> Mavis Gallant, "The Legacy"
> [italics mine]

The continuation of anteriority is usually signalled by further use of the past perfect:

> It was not until *after* he arrived home from taking his mother to the railway station that he began to realize how tired he *had become*. "Now, don't work too hard while I'm away, Len," *had been* her last words on kissing him, and before he left the train. While he was riding slowly homeward his thoughts *had been* busy hopping from one detail to another . . .
> Raymond Knister, "Mist-Green Oats"
> [italics mine]

Eight years *before* he *had seen* his friend off at the North Wall and wished him godspeed. Gallaher *had* got on. You could tell that at once by his travelled air, his well-cut tweed suit, and fearless accent. Few fellows had talents like his and fewer still could remain unspoiled by such success. Gallaher's heart was in the right place and he *had* deserved to win. It was something to have a friend like that.

Little Chandler's thoughts ever since lunch-time *had been* of his meeting with Gallaher, of Gallaher's invitation and of the great city London where Gallaher lived. He was called Little Chandler because, though he was but slightly under the average stature, he gave one the idea of being a little man. His hands were white and small, his frame was fragile, his voice was quiet and his manners were refined. He took the greatest care of his fair silken hair and moustache and used perfume discreetly on his handkerchief. The half-moons of his nails were perfect and when he smiled you caught a glimpse of a row of childish white teeth.

As he sat at his desk in the King's Inns he thought what changes those eight years *had brought*.

James Joyce, "A Little Cloud"
[italics mine]

Here too, the expositional quality is increased both by descriptive passages and by the amount of comment imbedded in the narrated monologue of Little Chandler; it is counteracted by elements suggesting a particular place and time where something was done or seen (*since lunch-time, at his desk*). Signals of anteriority naturally decrease as the story progresses, but wherever they recur, the sense of exposition returns — what in German is called *nachgeholte Exposition*. In early story-telling, for instance in Defoe, such forms of exposition are sometimes introduced by "I neglected to mention that . . ." or "the reader should know that . . .", a tactic that would be considered primitive, or at least a symptom of bad narrative planning, in a contemporary short story, except where it serves to characterize an inept narrator. Even the more discreet "it will be remembered" calls attention to the narrator-reader relationship and is therefore no longer favoured:

> There was commotion in Roaring Camp. It could not have been a fight, for in 1850 that was not novel enough to have called together the entire settlement. The ditches and claims were not only deserted, but "Tuttle's grocery" *had contributed* its gamblers, who, *it will be remembered*, calmly continued their game the day that French Pete and Kanaka Joe shot each other to death over the bar in the front room.
>
>
>
> Bret Harte, "The Luck of Roaring Camp"
> [italics mine]
>
>

Writers as distant in literary history from one another as Hawthorne and Hemingway like to imbed whatever passages of anteriority they think appropriate to the exposition in at least a fragment of straight report or description, where time, place and action are each briefly suggested. This sequence has been and still is enormously popular. Our earliest examples are once more from *Twice-Told Tales*:

> At nightfall once, in the olden time, on the rugged side of one of the Crystal Hills, a party of adventurers were refreshing themselves after a toilsome and fruitless quest for the Great Carbuncle. They *had come* thither, not as friends nor partners in the enterprise, . . .
> Nathaniel Hawthorne, "The Great Carbuncle"
> [italics mine]

> Passing a summer, several years since, at Edgartown, on the island of Martha's Vineyard, I became acquainted with a certain carver of tomb-stones, who *had traveled and voyaged* thither from the interior of Massachusetts in search of professional employment. The speculation *had* turned out so successful that my friend . . .
> Nathaniel Hawthorne, 'Chippings with a Chisel"
> [italics mine]

Joyce uses the same technique: arousing interest in a situation and then sketching in the events that had led to this situation:

> Two gentlemen who were in the lavatory at the time tried to lift him up: but he was quite helpless. He lay curled up at the foot of the stairs down which he *had fallen*. They succeeded in turning him over. His hat *had rolled* a few yards away and his clothes were smeared with the filth and ooze of the floor on which he *had lain*, face downwards. His eyes were closed and he breathed with a grunting noise. A thin stream of blood trickled from the corner of his mouth.
> James Joyce, "Grace"
> [italics mine]

> There was no hope for him this time: it was the third stroke. Night after night I *had passed* the house (it was vacation time) and *studied* the lighted square of window: and night after night I *had found* it lighted in the same way, faintly and evenly. If he was dead, I thought, I would see the reflection of candles on the darkened blind for I knew that two candles must be set at the head of a corpse.
> James Joyce, "The Sisters"
> [italics mine]

In each example the thrust of the beginning is increased by the use of the pronouns "him" and "he", which lack referents, and at the same time that thrust is impeded by the apparent wish to supply information about earlier events:

> We got up at four in the morning, that first day in the east. On the evening before we *had climbed* off a freight train at the edge of town, and with the

true instinct of Kentucky boys *had found* our way across town and to the race track and the stables at once.

> Sherwood Anderson, "I Want to Know Why"
> [italics mine]

Usually the first sentence contains a time indicator, to help define the previous events, as in our examples:

At nightfall once (Hawthorne)
several years since (Hawthorne)
at the time (Joyce)
this time (Joyce)
four in the morning (Anderson)

The depiction of anterior events is often an unnecessary exercise — it is frequently exchangeable or expendable, or, in structural terms, "indexical" rather than functional.[3] Consider the beginning of "The Battler":

> Nick stood up. He was all right. He looked up the track at the lights of the caboose going out of sight around the curve. There was water on both sides of the track, then tamarack swamp.
> He felt of his knee. The pants were torn and the skin was barked. His hands were scraped and there were sand and cinders driven up under his nails. He went over to the edge of the track down the little slope to the water and washed his hands. He washed them carefully in the cold water, getting the dirt out from the nails. He squatted down and bathed his knee.
> That lousy crut of a brakeman. He would get him some day. He would know him again. That was a fine way to act.
> "Come here, kid," he said. "I got something for you."
> He *had fallen* for it. What a lousy kid thing to have done.
> They would never suck him in that way again.
>
> Ernest Hemingway, "The Battler"
> [italics mine]

Although one could argue that the remembered scene with the brakeman is germane to some of the themes which the story goes on to develop, like gratuitous violence and the humiliation of the physically weak, it is also exchangeable, if not expendable. As so often with a literary convention, it is easier to identify the convention of the anterior event in expositions than to explain why it is there. Perhaps, having proved itself useful in many contexts, it takes on a life of its own. It comes to seem appropriate because it is traditional rather than functional.

Some modern narratives show a deliberate attempt to avoid anteriority and yet to include material which would once have looked like this (hypothetical) opening:

One evening Mrs Liebig *had been taken* by her grandson to see a play.

But it seems to be more elegant to slip such material into a conversation, even if this conversation is thus made rather unlikely. This is how the story opens in fact:

> All the way home in the taxi and in the lift up to her flat on the seventh floor Mrs Liebig kept on talking. Sometimes she spoke of the play, making comments to Maurice in the form of questions to which she did not await the answer. The lights of Regent Street and Oxford Street flashed momentarily through the taxi window, caught in the saxe-blue spangles of the ornament that crowned her almost saxe-blue neatly waved hair, reflected in the mirror of her powder compact which seemed always to occupy her attention in taxis. "Was the father of the girl a fraud then?" she asked, and, "Why didn't the mother make him work?" "I suppose," she said, "that the old man had used him to get rid of his mistress." Then, "What a play," she exclaimed, "for a boy of your age to take his grandmother to!"
>
> Angus Wilson, "After the Show"

Only at this point is the relationship of the two characters returning from the theatre revealed. Whether a more obvious anteriority with the past perfect tense or a phrase like "after the play" would have been less effective is a problem of taste and style – and of literary fashion.

The phenomenon we have called *anteriority* often appears with the related one of depicting habitual actions, which might be seen as a kind of anteriority as well:

> When the literary gentleman, whose flat old Ma Parker cleaned every Tuesday, opened the door to her that morning, he asked after her grandson.
>
> Katherine Mansfield, "Life of Ma Parker"

In this story the anterior view follows much later; in fact, it constitutes the central material of the story. More usual is the presentation in parallel of both anterior and habitual action:

> In the morning the Corams *used to leave* the Pension, which was like a white box with a terracotta lid among its vines on the hill above the town, *and walk* through the dust and lavish shade to the beach. They were a couple in their forties.
>
> He *had never been* out of England before, but she *had spent* half her youth in foreign countries. She *used to wear* shabby saffron beach-pyjamas with a navy-blue top which the sun had faded.
>
> V. S. Pritchett, "Handsome is as Handsome Does"
>
> [italics mine]

In each of the following passages habitual action is expressed by the use of *ever* or *never*:

> Yesterday afternoon the six-o'clock bus ran over Miss Bobbit. I'm not

sure what there is to be said about it; after all, she was only ten years old, still I know no one of us in this town will forget her. For one thing, nothing she *ever* did was ordinary, not from the first time that we saw her, and that was a year ago.

Truman Capote, "Children on Their Birthdays"
[italics mine]

It was Joe Dillon who introduced the Wild West to us. He had a little library made up of old numbers of *The Union Jack, Pluck* and *The Halfpenny Marvel*. Every evening after school we met in his back garden and arranged Indian battles. He and his fat young brother Leo, the idler, held the loft of the stable while we tried to carry it by storm; or we fought a pitched battle on the grass. But, however well we fought, we *never* won siege or battle and all our bouts ended with Joe Dillon's war dance of victory. His parents went to eight-o'clock mass every morning in Gardiner Street and the peaceful odour of Mrs Dillon was prevalent in the hall of the house.

James Joyce, "An Encounter"
[italics mine]

The new recruit had been with the gang since the beginning of the summer holidays, and there were possibilities about his brooding silence that all recognized. He *never* wasted a word even to tell his name until that was required of him by the rules . . .

The gang met every morning in . . .

Graham Greene, "The Destructors"
[italics mine]

A wide variety of means can suggest habitual action, so that it has become a stock technique of exposition in the short story: it is to be found in the expositions of about two thirds of all stories and one in five novels (see Appendix B for an exact tabulation), and is thus more ubiquitous than one might suppose, much more so than are the "generalizing iterations" which Genette has discovered in Proust,[4] and which are not a phenomenon of expositionality. As long as the phenomenon of *habituality* persists, we retain the sense of an exposition, even though the predominant narrative mode may still be report:

My husband is in Atlantic City, where they are trying out "Dear Dora", the musical version of "David Copperfield". My husband wrote the score. He *used to* take me along for these out-of-town openings, but not any more.

He, of course, has to spend almost all his time in the theater and that leaves me alone in the hotel, and pretty soon people find out whose wife I am and introduce themselves, and the next thing you know they are inviting us for a week or a weekend at Dobbs Ferry or Oyster Bay. Then it is up to me to think of some legitimate-sounding reason why we can't come.

In *lots of cases* they say, "Well, if you can't make it the twenty-second, how about the twenty-ninth?" and so on till you simply have to accept. And Ben gets mad and stays mad for days.

. . . Ben never turned down their invitations and often . . .

Ring Lardner, "Liberty Hall"

[italics mine]

This passage, although mostly in the mode of report, has a flavour of exposition about it because no particular scene and action has yet begun – that is, it has the quality of *anteriority* without any of its special markers – and because the actions and reactions described are habitual or repetitive.

The Lardner passage, although it is in part an example of scenic report, also contains elements of what Percy Lubbock calls *panoramic narrative:*[5] both time and space are seen, as it were, through a telescope. Panoramic report is by its nature more expositional than is scenic report. The actions depicted in anterior report, it should be added here, need not be panoramic but often are, as some of our earlier examples show:

> . . . what changes those years had brought (Joyce)
> . . . had come thither . . . (Hawthorne)
> . . . had traveled and voyaged . . . (Hawthorne)
> . . . had found our way across town (Anderson)
> . . . had spent half her youth in foreign countries (Pritchett)
> . . . had been with the gang since the beginning of the summer holidays (Greene)

The kinds of report, then, which tend to be expositional – the anterior view, the habitual action and the panoramic scene – are birds of a feather which have some tendency to flock together, although each can also occur separately or in combination with any of the other two. In our own day the opening with panoramic report is practically taboo. For a clear example we can, however, look to Defoe:

A gentleman of a very good estate married a lady of also a good fortune, and had one son by her, and one daughter, and no more, and after a few years his lady died. He soon married a second venter; and his second wife, though of an inferior quality and fortune to the former, took upon her to discourage and discountenance his children by his first lady, and made the family very uncomfortable, both to the children and to their father also.

The first thing of consequence which this conduct of the mother-in-law produced in the family, was that the son, who began to be a man, asked the father's leave to go abroad to travel. The mother-in-law, though willing enough to be rid of the young man, yet because it would require something considerable to support his expenses abroad, violently opposed it, and brought his father also to refuse him after he had freely given him his consent.

Daniel Defoe, "In Defence of his Right"

The events of about twenty years are contained in a single paragraph of two sentences. The second paragraph covers perhaps months or weeks, later on we move to scenic report ("one evening after the") and speech. The exposition, if we may call it that, covers too extensive a ground to suit modern taste.

Not only do two paragraphs contain the makings of a novel – too much information is given here at once. Another striking example of this phenomenon is contained in the same anthology, the Everyman *English Short Stories*:

> During the tyme that the famous Citie of Constantinople remained in the handes of the Christians, emongst many other noble menne, that kepte their abidyng in that florishing citie, there was on whose name was Apolonius, a worthie duke, who beyng but a verie yong man, and euen then newe come to his possessions whiche were verie greate, leuied a mightie bande of menne, at his owne proper charges, with whom he serued against the Turke, duryng the space of one whole yere, in whiche tyme although it were very shorte, this yong duke so behaued hym selfe, as well by prowesse and valiaunce shewed with his owne handes, as otherwise, by his wisedome and liberalitie, vsed towardes his souldiors, that all the worlde was filled with the fame of this noble duke. When he had thus spent one yeares seruice, he caused his trompet to sounde a retraite, and gatheryng his companie together, and imbarkyng theim selues he sette saile, holdyng his course towardes Constantinople: but beeyng vppon the sea, by the extremitie of a tempest whiche sodainly fell, his fleete was deseuered some one way, and some an other, but he hym selfe recouered the Ile of Cypres, where he was worthily receiued by Pontus duke and gouernour of the same ile, with whom he lodged, while his shippes were newe repairyng.
>
> Barnaby Rich, "Apolonius and Silla"

To our ears this does not sound like the beginning of a short story because of the panoramic view and because of the overly efficient way of providing the reader immediately with answers to what journalists call the five w's: *when, where, who, what, why.* Even in compressed form, as in Hawthorne, this consideration of the five w's makes an unmodern impression:

> At nightfall once, [when], in the olden time, on the rugged side of one of the Crystal Hills [where], a party of adventurers [who] were refreshing themselves [what] . . .
>
> Nathaniel Hawthorne, "The Great Carbuncle"

Hawthorne often achieves this effect; it seems likely that he used it to bring the reader into the story very quickly, even if in an obviously expositional way:

> Rambling on foot in the spring of my life and the summer of the year, I came one afternoon to a point which gave me the choice of three directions.
>
> Nathaniel Hawthorne, "The Seven Vagabonds"

A story can be opened, as we see, with scenic as well as with panoramic report. Put in other terms: character, place, time and action are essential dimensions of a story, but nowadays they may not be introduced all at once. That is rather the mark of a nineteenth century story:

> As Mr John Oakhurst, gambler, stepped into the main street of Poker Flat on the morning of the twenty-third of November 1850, he was conscious of a change in its moral atmosphere since the preceding night. Two or three men, conversing earnestly together, ceased as he approached, and exchanged significant glances. There was a Sabbath lull in the air, which, in a settlement unused to Sabbath influences, looked ominous.
>
> Francis Bret Harte, "The Outcasts of Poker Flat"

We cannot complain of too much exposition here: the opening with scenic report is direct, the infusion of description is more than merely decorative, there is a form of speech in the very next paragraph. Yet four of the five w's are too neatly and too completely presented for modern tastes. Ambrose Bierce is capable of the same kind of beginning:

> Jerome Searing, a private soldier of General Sherman's army, then confronting the enemy at and about Kenesaw Mountain, Georgia, turned his back upon a small group of officers, with whom he had been talking in low tones, stepped across a light line of earthworks, and disappeared in a forest.
>
> Ambrose Bierce, "One of the Missing"

The necessary background information is deftly delivered, the story seems to be off to a flying start. Yet such a beginning would not be written by a serious practitioner of the modern short story. The closest we come to it is in the following:

> I met him first in a hurricane; and though we had gone through the hurricane on the same schooner, it was not until the schooner had gone to pieces under us that I first laid eyes on him. Without doubt I had seen him with the rest of the Kanaka crew on board, but I had not consciously been aware of his existence, for the *Petite Jeanne* was rather overcrowded. In addition to her eight or ten Kanaka seamen, her white captain, mate, and supercargo, and her six cabin passengers, . . .
>
> Jack London, "The Heathen"

Here there is not as much compression or as great a wealth of data as in the panoramic report with which Barnaby Rich or Daniel Defoe open the stories quoted from above, but still enough that the whole passage is, though report, a clear example of exposition.

Report, we must conclude, is suitable for beginning a story *medias in res*, but it also allows as fully expositional an opening as do the static modes, comment and description.

The Opening with Speech

The two dynamic modes report and speech have become the favourites of modern storytellers, but in particular speech. Many a modern short story contains no comment or description at sentence-level at all, but only in imbedded form. Speech, on the other hand, is a universal ingredient of narrative and is in some stories the dominant mode, at least in terms of the sheer number of lines within quotation marks. Yet few stories open with speech: of the six hundred stories surveyed here, only 68 (11%). And those 68 include a number of arguable examples, since inquit-sentences were included in the group, that is, openings like that of Willa Cather's "Neighbor Rosicky", which opens with a reporting phrase:

> When Doctor Burleigh told neighbor Rosicky he had a bad heart, Rosicky protested.
> "So? No, I guess my heart was always pretty good. I got a little asthma, maybe. Just a awful short breath when I was pitchin' hay last summer, dat's all."
>> Willa Cather, "Neighbor Rosicky"

Stories which open with speech do not necessarily, of course, continue in the same fashion. We have noted the trick of the "modal façade": often the first few words are in quotation marks, after which no dialogue follows for a paragraph or even for a page or two:

> "Halloa! Below there!"
> When he heard a voice thus calling to him, he was standing at the door of his box, with a flag in his hand, furled round its short pole.
>> Charles Dickens, "The Signalman"

The opening words, as here, often constitute a kind of puzzle; the resolution is left to material in the other modes:

> "Well, Mabel, and what are you going to do with yourself?" asked Joe, with foolish flippancy. He felt quite safe himself.
>> D. H. Lawrence, "The Horse Dealer's Daughter"

The paragraph which follows is primarily anterior report. The exposition which explains the problem formulated by Joe in his question follows some seven pages later. Thus the import of the opening words is, on first reading, quite obscure. The words in the speech are no more than a kind of bait to the reader. Such tactics on the part of the author are not uncommon:

> "Tell you what we'll do; we'll shake for it."
> "That suits me," said the second man, turning, as he spoke . . .
>> Jack London, "The Faith of Men"

For about a page after this, no further dialogue follows. The opening with speech, we find, is more often than not a façade, to be followed later by the necessary exposition:

> "Miss Spence will be down directly, sir."
> "Thank you," said Mr Hutton, without turning round.
> Aldous Huxley, "The Gioconda Smile"

> "They say he's worth a million," Lucia said. He sat there in the little hot damp Mexican square, a dog at his feet, with an air of immense and forlorn patience.
> Graham Greene, "Across the Bridge"

In each story a good deal of description and anterior report follow the relatively lively opening with speech. This is true for the Dickens and Lawrence stories just quoted from as well as these by London, Huxley and Greene. We have already quoted the description of the "hot, dark, breathless evening" during which the following words are spoken:

> "Is it officially declared yet?"
> "They've gone as far as to admit extreme local scarcity, and they've started relief-works in one or two districts, the paper says."
> Rudyard Kipling, "William the Conqueror"

The later exposition fills in the background: who is speaking, to whom, in what situation.

Modes Imbedded in Speech

It should be pointed out that speech is a mode defined by its form, whereas comment, description and report are defined in terms of the subjects of discourse. These subjects are also those with which any speech is likely to concern itself. In other words, every speech in some manner comments, or describes or reports. *Indirect speech* opening a story can, for instance, contain the theme of the story:

> My father said sometimes a man comes to change his way of thinking.
> Douglas Spettigue, "The Haying"

A general theme is formulated, which turns out to be the moral of the story. But it would be hard to find a second example of this kind: comment imbedded in speech is as rare now as the opening with comment alone. More common is the opening with description: for instance, a central character is introduced and described by another. Thus we have a standard opening with description packed up, as it were, in the mode of speech, as in Greene's "Across the Bridge", just quoted: "They say he's worth a million", or more extensively:

III

"But this painter!" cried Walter Ludlow, with animation. "He not only excels in his peculiar art, but possesses vast acquirements in all other learning and science . . ."

Nathaniel Hawthorne, "The Prophetic Pictures"

The characterization continues at some length.

Just as common, however, is that an opening with speech contains report:

"She's coming, Caffin." Two grinning faces appeared outside the mosquito house. The wire mesh gave them the look of early press photographs, grey and blurred.

Caffin, a pale, fat young man, lying on the bed in a singlet, glared savagely at them.

Joyce Cary, "Government Baby"

Speech, then, usually contains one of the other modes, but it also poses special problems of definition when we try to sort out exactly which modes they are:

"My aunt will be down presently, Mr Nuttel," said a very self-possessed young lady of fifteen; "in the meantime you must try and put up with me."

Framton Nuttel endeavoured to say the correct something . . .

Saki, "The Open Window"

The "self-possessed young lady" is not reporting anything, but foretelling an action. Statements about future actions, negations, questions and passives can be interpreted as transformations of declarative sentences:

"You will not find [negation + future] your father greatly changed [description]," remarked Lady Moping [reporting phrase = report], as the car turned into the gates of the County Asylum [description, since we do not impute independence or volition to the car].

"Will he be wearing a uniform?" [future + interrogative] asked Angela.

"No, dear, of course not. He is receiving the very best attention." [passive]

It was Angela's first visit [description] and it was being made at her own suggestion. [report: anterior]

Ten years had passed since the showery day . . . [report: anterior]

Evelyn Waugh, "Mr Loveday's Little Outing"

The passage presents most of the problems one meets in the subcategorization of speech.

Non-referential Modes in Speech

We have assumed thus far that all narrative belongs to one of our four modes, and this is for most purposes of explication true. But speech in particular has functions other than reporting, describing and commenting, so that we may find, especially if we segment our texts at the word and phrase-level, fragments which do not fit, like Dickens' "Halloa! Below there!" This is of course speech, but our further subdivisions of speech do not work, since *hello* is neither report, description nor comment. It is an expression used to establish contact with another person which Malinowski called the "phatic" use of language: "a type of speech in which ties of union are created by a mere exchange of words."[6] Jakobson suggests that the various functions of language, including the "phatic", can be attached to the six points of his communication model:[7]

```
                        context
                        message
Addresser ---------------------------------------------------------------Addressee
                        contact
                        code
```

Each point involves a different function:

```
                        Referential
                        Poetic
Emotive ------------------------------------------------------------- Conative
                        Phatic
                        Metalingual
```

Since narrative, especially in written form, is almost exclusively referential, the modes report, description and comment are in fact three subfunctions of the referential use of language. In speech, however, other functions operate as well, as in the Dickens opening, or in

"Well, Mabel, and what are you going to do with yourself?"

in which the "well" is phatic, the "Mabel" both phatic and conative, and so forth. Such non-referential modes are also to be found in first-person narratives:

You know, this is the first time Tom and I have been with real friends since we were married.

Ring Lardner, "Who Dealt?"

For the most wild, yet homely narrative which I am about to pen, I neither expect nor solicit belief.

Edgar Allan Poe, "The Black Cat"

In the latter example, the author refers to himself, to his narrative (Jakobson is aware that the term "poetic" may be stretched a little to include all references to the message) and by implication to the reader or listener as well.

The Lardner-opening contains some elements of report, but the Poe-opening is exclusively non-referential, if we stay within Jakobson's system – of course both the narrator and the reader may be seen in another sense as part of the context as well as part of the fiction; and insofar as this is the case, "I neither expect nor solicit belief" may also be classed as description of character.

Our survey of short-story openings has, in fact, revealed very few examples of the non-referential functions, and these, it should be added, are sometimes very hard to classify exactly. The *poetic* function, for instance, is rarely as obvious as in Scott:

> The following narrative is given from the pen, so far as memory permits . . .
>
> "The Tapestried Chamber"

And it may be no more than implicit in a single pronoun, as here:

> It all began one June evening in the main hall of the provincial museum.
> Roger Lemelin, "The Stations of the Cross"

To see the "it" as an example of the "poetic" function is both questionable in itself and no very substantial addition to an interpretation of the story. On the whole, then, the non-referential functions, although they do crop up in narrative, especially as a subcategory of speech and in first-person narration, hardly reduce the importance of the four chief modes.

Both the four modes and the non-referential categories of Jakobson together do not offer sufficient subcategories for absolutely every conceivable utterance in narrative. Consider, for instance:

> Certainly such places exist. One could find them on a map for sure.

This statement neither reports nor describes; it is not referential in the usual sense, for there is some doubt, even within the terms of the fiction, that the places referred to exist. Nor is the statement emotive, conative, poetic, phatic or metalingual. In the terms of the speech act theory associated with the name of John R. Searle,[8] it insists, attests and predicts. If we accept Ohmann's classification of performative verbs,[9] both sentences are "attesters", even though they refer merely to something which exists, perhaps, only in the imagination of the speaker.

If we wish to categorize all forms of speech and its submodes, then, we probably need not only the modes and the language functions of Jakobson's model but speech act theory as well. But subcategorization by speech acts is not very productive of critical insight, at least not in the present state of the art. The modes of report and description consist, in Ohmann's terms, almost exclusively of attesters and verdictives, with the latter occurring more frequently in description than in report. Comment, understandably enough, tends to the use of "responsibility establishers", namely "ascribers" and "implicators", with some "future directors" as well – mostly "wishes", "influencers", "exhortations" and "conditionals". Only in the mode of speech do we find the whole gamut of the eighteen categories suggested by Ohmann.[10] We can conclude that the three non-speech modes are themselves fundamental categories of communication, as Searle calls the speech acts, whereas the mode of speech itself is an encompassing category containing multitudes. Only speech, then, contains such a variety of kinds of expression that a microscopic examination may demand a supplementary set of categories which neither the chief narrative modes, their submodes nor the non-referential functions have to offer.

Important to the reader of narrative expositions, indeed, are not the subcategories of speech but how the story-opening with speech functions in reference to what follows. For we have seen that speech is generally no substitute for explication, by which it is almost inevitably followed. Speech gives us an opening *medias in res*, which on closer inspection turns out to be a gentle fraud, for stories almost always require exposition, for obvious reasons: we are plunged from reality into fiction, into a strange environment. It is like the first day at a new job. Before anything very effective can be accomplished, persons, places and things must be either introduced or discovered. There is nothing wrong with exposition *per se*, and in some stories the exposition is more artful and effective than are the speeches of the characters. If the opening with speech is thought to belong to the higher forms of narrative art, this is only because it gives the illusion of an immediate plunge into the story, not because exposition, which tends to be less interesting than action or dialogue, can be done away with altogether.

The opening with speech is natural to what has been called *analytic* rather than *synthetic* narrative:[11] it poses a riddle or a puzzle and teases us to read on and discover the solution. There is always something unnatural about it, a kind of putting the cart before the horse, because natural, unstilted dialogue tends to be rooted in a situation which the reader cannot at the outset know. Therefore the standard opening with description is more natural, and we can understand why it is by far the most popular technique. The opening with speech, by contrast, involves rather a reversal of the sequence of presentation that would lead most quickly to the orientation of the reader.

Essential to the technique of speech-openings, then, is the signal to the reader that he is being thrown into a context to which he lacks the key, at least at the outset. This signal may be reinforced by other techniques, like the opening with *yes*:

"Yes," said the dealer, "our windfalls are of various kinds. Some customers are ignorant, and then I touch a dividend on my superior knowledge . . ."

Robert Louis Stevenson, "Markheim"

Here we are never told what statement the *yes* refers to. That is not always so:

"Yes," said Miss Le Petyt, gazing into the deep fireplace and letting her hands and her knitting lie for the moment idle in her lap. "Oh, yes, I have seen a ghost. In fact I have lived in a house with one for quite a long time."

"How you *could —!*" began one of my host's daughters; and "*You,* Aunt Emily?" cried the other at the same moment.

Sir A. T. Quiller-Couch, "A Pair of Hands"

Here is another example from a story that seems to begin with speech, although we might also consider it a straight first-person story, like Lardner's "Who Dealt" or Thurber's "You Could Look It Up", except that it continues in inverted commas throughout:

> "Yes, indeed, my grandfather wass once in jail," said old Mrs McTavish, of the county of Glengarry, in Ontario, Canada; "but that wass for debt, and he wass a ferry honest man whateffer, and he would not broke his promise – no, not for all the money in Canada – If you will listen to me, I will tell chust exactly the true story about the debt, to show you what an honest man my grandfather wass.
>
> E. W. Thomson, "The Privilege of the Limits"

The opening *yes* is a mere trick, then, insofar as we never find out to whom it was addressed. It is like the *and*, which connects something we can never know to that which is presented.

> And after all, the weather was ideal.
>
> Katherine Mansfield, "The Garden Party"

Different in kind are the other devices of the analytic opening, like the use of the deictic *here* or *then*, the definite article attached to an object which we are then introduced to, and the personal pronouns, the reference of which must eventually be clarified:

> Eight years before *he* had seen his friend off . . .
>
> James Joyce, "A Little Cloud"

> I had known *her* for some considerable time before I came to know *him*.
> Anthony Hope, "The Prince Consort"

> I met *him* first in a hurricane . . .
>
> Jack London, "The Heathen"
[all italics mine]

But as we see, these are mechanisms of the *medias in res* opening which apply to description and report as well as to speech, and which are clear signals to the reader that he is to find his way into the fiction without benefit, at least for the time being, of an exposition.

Conclusion and Summary

The short story, in contrast to the novel, generally contains only a few characters and events, so that the exposition can be made comparatively efficient; but even stories which seem to begin *medias in res* normally have an exposition, though this may not be evident in the first sentence.

Exposition generally consists of description and certain kinds of report: panoramic, anterior and habitual. The theory of narrative modes helps us to classify the kinds of openings which writers have in fact used and to examine more closely which kinds have been favoured. *Expositionality* is an effect to be seen in connection with the modes, but is also increased and decreased by a number of other techniques and devices. The chief of these can be displayed in the following table:

The Dynamics of Expositionality

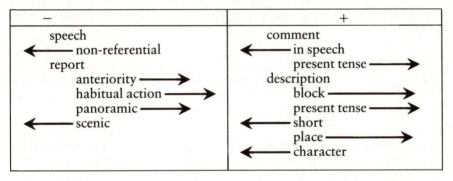

−	+
speech	comment
← non-referential	← in speech
report	present tense →
anteriority →	description
habitual action →	block →
panoramic →	present tense →
← scenic	← short
	place →
	← character

CHAPTER VII

How Stories End I: the Static Modes

Endings are interesting. Writers obviously devote special care to their composition and readers (not only professional critics) probably give them particular attention. We expect endings, much more than beginnings, to show what the story was about, what special effect was to be achieved. The classical short story theory, that of Edgar Allen Poe, focuses on this effect:[1]

> ... having conceived, with deliberate care, a certain unique or single *effect* to be wrought out, he then invents such incidents – he then combines such events as may best aid him in establishing this preconceived effect.

We do not know whether most writers consciously do what Poe demands. Yet in many stories the end seems somehow prior to that which goes before, like the final "God-given line" around which poets are sometimes said to write their poems. Thus the ending may dictate the steps needed to prepare for it: consider the revelation of "the black cat" in Poe's story of that name, or the suicide of Seymour Glass in the last sentence of Salinger's "A Perfect Day for Bananafish". In these stories, as in any "twist-in-the-tail" narrative, the conclusion is of paramount importance and deserving of closer examination.

We have sorted story openings into a few distinct categories, but this formalistic approach does not work so well with endings. By the time the reader arrives at the end of a story he has probably amassed a fund of information about character, event and theme. This information, unavailable at the beginning, is available in the reader's mind as he finishes reading the story and is thus at the disposal of the writer shaping the story's close. The reader's lack of prior knowledge at the opening forces the narrator to shape it with primarily formal elements, then, and writers have found countless ways of ringing the changes on these elements. Endings are even more various and harder to classify. They are also apparently harder to write well.

Yet on closer inspection we will find that a limited set of techniques is used in story endings again and again. These techniques are to some extent governed by and discoverable through a consideration of the narrative modes employed.

Open and Closed Endings

The most common division made is that between open and closed endings. In the closed ending the action does not simply stop. A variety of signals is used to announce that the story is drawing to a close. Often some earlier element in the work is repeated, though rarely in quite so obvious a manner as in the following example from the seventeenth century:

> With this last prize he thinks it high time to fly no longer at rovers, but to take up and settle, and accordingly carries himself, his impudence, and plaister-box, to Banbury and there sets up a professed chirurgeon, as the beginning of our history set forth.
>
> Elkanah Settle, "The Complete Memoirs of the
Life of that Notorious Impostor Will. Morrell"

This is an extreme example of linking the end to the beginning. But a similar effect is achieved where a summary of the story is given, or a panoramic after a succession of scenic views. Also popular to the present day is a final symbolic event, or a "natural" ending of the sort often used to close a play or a poem.[2] This event may be a departure, the closing of a door or window, or the death of a character (the latter in 43 of the 600 stories surveyed).

In an open ending, on the other hand, action and dialogue continue to the very end; conflicts, if any, are left unresolved or insoluble, or the "slice of life" is left uncovered and without any particular container: hanging, as it were, in mid air. The action is suspended rather than concluded.

What "suspended" often means is that the time scheme of the story is not enclosed in a frame making use of one of the static modes. Description and comment, as we have seen, are the two static of the four modes: they convey little or no sense of time passing. Their use allows an essentially non-narrative epilogue with a strongly pictorial or essayistic bias. The open endings, by contrast, tend to make use of speech and report: the clock of the plot ticks until the very last moment, possibilities suggested in the course of the story are left unexplored or at least unresolved. The ideal of a tapering off of narrative toward the end of a story therefore involves a sequence of modes moving from speech and report to the space-centered description and the final comment, the abstractions of which are often without reference to space or to time. Often the end stands in the present tense in contrast to the past in which most narration, including description, tends to be formulated. An even stronger sense of conclusion results from the author's camera seeming to withdraw from dialogue and action, focussing instead on the characters themselves, on the setting, finally on the narrator and the process of narration itself:

> The grass had long been green on the graves of Shepherd Fennel and his frugal wife; the guests who made up the christening party have mainly followed their entertainers to the tomb; the baby in whose honour they all had met is a matron in the sere and yellow leaf. But the arrival of the three strangers at the shepherd's that night, and the details connected therewith,

is a story as well known as ever in the country about Higher Crowstairs.
Thomas Hardy, "The Three Strangers"

Typical of such a conventional ending are the rhetorical flourishes, including the Shakespeare quotation, "sere and yellow leaf", the final sentence introduced by a conjunction, the withdrawal from scenic to panoramic report, the capsule summary of the chief action ("arrival of the three strangers") and the present tense of the final utterance.

The closed ending, in other words, is brought about by a combination of various kinds of content and technique. That is why the world of stories is not easily divisible into those with open and those with closed endings. We will find, it is true, especially in the traditional and more conventional stories of the nineteenth and earlier twentieth centuries, clear cases of closed endings. But, especially in the modern short story, we will find mostly endings which are *more or less* closed. Rarely does a story show absolutely none of the strategies explored below with which a work of fiction can be given a final flourish or recognizable finish. "Writers rarely resist the urge to conclude more forcefully."[3] When we speak of the open ending, therefore, this cannot be taken in an absolute sense: we probably mean a story which is less obviously closed than it might have been.

In the twentieth century the open ending has become more or less the standard strategy, whereas the stories of Poe, Hawthorne and Melville usually have closed endings, although perhaps not quite as closed, if one can measure degrees of closedness, as did the stories of their predecessors. For the most closed kind of ending is that which eschews the chief narrative modes altogether and slips into metanarrative. My sampling of 600 stories contains 22 examples (under 4%), and most of these were published before 1900, indeed, a number of them before 1800, that is, before the short story as a recognizable genre is usually said to have existed. Sometimes the metanarrative close is marked expressly as a postscript to the story:

> Postscript
> Let the reader take notice we hear there is a rumour of a false copy which is likely to come forth. Let him beware of it, lest it abuse the memory of the dead.
> Anonymous, "The Triumph of Truth"

A similar address to the reader is that of Richard Head:

> Postscript
> Reader, let me assure thee that this is no fiction, but a true relation of Mr Jackson's life and conversation, penned by his own hand and delivered into mine to be made public for his countrymen's good, . . .
> Richard Head, "Jackson's Recantation"

The signals of *metanarrative* are few and clear: the narrator refers to himself, or to the reader, or to his story, or any two or three of these in combination. As in the two "postscripts" just quoted, the ending may be a distinct section of the story:

> It is unnecessary to add more – the imagination of the reader can supply the rest; and, we may only add, that Grizel Cochrane, whose heroism and noble affection we have here hurriedly and imperfectly sketched, was, tradition says, the grandmother of the late Sir John Stuart of Allanbank, and great-great-grandmother of Mr Coutts, the celebrated banker.
>
> J. M. Wilson, "Grizel Cochrane, A Tale of Tweedmouth Muir"

> So ends my story, friend. The cattle-drover left us that night and we saw no more of him. Only before going he gave the piebald and the silver trappings to Sotelo. Six months after his visit, Sotelo also received a letter from him to say that his marriage with Elaria had taken place; and the letter was accompanied with a present of seven cream-coloured horses with black manes and hoofs.
>
> W. H. Hudson, "The Story of a Piebald Horse"

Or the ending may contribute some finishing touches to the plot and a gentle transition from report to metanarrative close:

> But being forced to lie a good while before he could purchase his liberty, as being charged with actions to a great value, then it was that Mrs Cellier, having heard of Don Tomazo's fame and believing him brisk for her turn, gave him her first visits which produced those transactions between them that have lately made so great a noise in the world. For an account whereof, the reader is referred to the *Narratives* themselves.
>
> Anonymous, "Don Tomazo, or the Juvenile Rambles of Thomas Dangerfield"

All these examples have in common the shift to the present tense:

> Let the reader take notice
> let me assure thee
> it is unnecessary
> So ends my story
> the reader is referred

Such a shift of tense is a frequent signal of many conclusions: especially in metanarrative endings, a little less so in the endings with comment and description, and often perceptible even in endings using the dynamic modes (see Chapter VIII). It is typical of what Labov (analysing a collection of oral narratives registered by tape recorder) calls the "coda" to anecdotes and stories.[4] So it is a frequent phenomenon, not one restricted to metanarrative, but almost inevitable and more obvious there than in other types of ending.

Metanarrative endings are no longer in fashion. There are only a few clear examples in stories of the last fifty years to be found. One is by Sherwood Anderson, first published in 1933:

I shall not try to emphasize the point. I am only explaining why I was dissatisfied then and have been ever since. I speak of that only that you may understand why I have been impelled to try to tell the simple story over again.

> Sherwood Anderson, "Death in the Woods"

This example, like one from Updike to be noted below, is from a first person story. Since the metanarrative ending in a third-person story is now practically unknown, we may conclude that a full definition of modern short story technique might well stipulate that metanarrative endings in third-person stories (83% of those surveyed here) are now taboo.

Some of the stories from which the above quotations are drawn have also been quoted in the discussion of how stories begin. It should not be surprising that the story with a strongly closed ending is likely to have a strongly expositional opening as well. There is a modal consonance, as it were, which diminishes a little in the modern period, although we shall find it there too. Here is how the two stories quoted above because of their postscripts begin:

"As the memory of good men . . ."

> Anonymous, "The Triumph of Truth"

"How vain are the thoughts . . ."

> Richard Head, "Jackson's Recantation"

Like the postscripts, these statements are in the present tense, and they display the chief marks of extreme expositionality: authorial comment in the present tense, unmitigated by an admixture from the other modes. Some of the early stories I have quoted because of their metanarrative endings, like "Don Tomazo" or "The Counterfeit Lady Unveiled", begin with an address to the reader. This tendency toward modal consonance suggests the complementary hypothesis: that stories with wholly unexpositional beginnings will tend to have open endings, and that a large middle range of stories will display a mixture of techniques which seem to follow less obvious laws of narrative.

Endings with Comment

Like metanarrative, comment too has come to be dispensed with in endings. In the nineteenth century it was sometimes combined with metanarrative:

"Moi?" returned the Frenchman, standing back from his easel, and looking at me and at the figure, quite politely, though with an evident reservation: "Je dis, mon cher, que c'est une spécialité dont je me fiche pas mal. Je tiens que quand on ne comprend pas une chose, c'est qu'elle ne signifie rien."

My reader thinks possibly that the French student was right.

> Dante Gabriel Rossetti, "Hand and Soul"

But even in its time this technique is an exception, and at least the comment itself is imputed to the character rather than to the narrator, who only steps in to assert his agreement.

In the twentieth century the metanarrative/comment conclusion is a great rarity:

> . . . the momentous moral of this story being, An expected gift is not worth giving.
>
> John Updike, "Wife-Wooing"

This is as "pure" (see Chapter III for this term) a comment as one is likely to find in a contemporary story. But even here we find several of the techniques with which modern fiction in general seeks to make comment palatable, including the use of irony (here the new twist to an old cliche).

Another method of making comment appear less intrusive is to integrate it with other modes and thus make it appear less of a monolithic block:

> "No, I want you, I want you", was all he answered, blindly, with that terrible intonation which frightened her almost more than her horror lest he should not want her.
>
> D. H. Lawrence, "The Horse Dealer's Daughter"

This passage, like those to follow, should illustrate the thesis that endings with comment, almost as strongly as those with metanarrative, are of the closed kind, and that at the same time a number of elements may be operative with which the effect of closure is weakened. In the example above the comment is not imposed as a syntactically self-contained block, and it applies not to the whole but only to the latter section of Lawrence's story. Then too, the final sentences depict not a settled love relationship but one which is just beginning. In other words, an ending which is because of the element of comment a closed one in tendency also has in it, both in terms of form and of content, narrative techniques of the open rather than of the closed ending.

In both the Updike and the Lawrence examples, then, we find techniques used in twentieth century fiction to make endings with comment palatable. Brevity and the integration in other modes are two of these techniques. Authors also distance themselves from the final comment in other ways: by the use of irony (as in Updike), and by imputing the comment to an inside view: that is, to the speech, the thought (as in the Lawrence example above) or the narrated monologue of a character.

Simply to impute the comment to the narrator of a first-person story, on the other hand, has little effect:

> Thus saying, he limped off, leaving me in admiration at his intrepidity and content; nor could I avoid acknowledging, that an habitual acquaintance with misery serves better than philosophy to teach us to despise it.
>
> Oliver Goldsmith, "The Disabled Soldier"

Although the narrator rather than the author conveys the comment, the heavily closed effect is not thereby mitigated: there are too many abstractions in too large a block of the one mode, formulated in too serious and rhetorical a fashion. The same must be said of the conclusion of our nineteenth century example, also a first-person tale:

> Sometimes from out the folded paper the pale clerk takes a ring – the finger it was meant for, perhaps, moulders in the grave; a bank-note sent in swiftest charity – he whom it would relieve, nor eats nor hungers any more; pardon for those who died despairing; hope for those who died unhoping; good tidings for those who died stifled by unrelieved calamities. On errands of life, these letters speed to death.
> Ah, Bartleby! Ah, humanity!
>
> Herman Melville, "Bartleby"

The author, in other words, cannot hide behind his narrator to make that mode less obvious or more dynamic which, by its nature, is not so. He *can* make his comment less intrusive by giving it an ironic twist, making it very brief, and putting it into the mouth or mind of a character, or by a combination of these techniques.

Irony

The endings just quoted are certainly meant to be taken by the reader at face value, even if it is not the author himself who addresses him. This is so even if the narrator himself casts some doubt on the validity of his own generalisations, as Hawthorne does almost habitually:

> Does it not argue a superintending Providence, that, while viewless and unexpected events thrust themselves continually athwart our path, there should still be regularity enough in mortal life to render foresight even partially available?
>
> Nathaniel Hawthorne, "David Swan"

> I had likewise gained perplexity; for there was a strange doubt in my mind, whether the dark shadowing of this life, the sorrows and regrets have not as much real comfort in them – leaving religious influences out of the question – as what we term life's joys.
>
> Nathaniel Hawthorne, "Chippings with a Chisel"

A certain diffidence is suggested by the question mark in the first example and the "strange doubt" with which the second one is introduced, but the message is considered to be generally true, as the use of the present tense indicates.

After the middle of the nineteenth century, however, endings containing an ironic twist appear:

> It is an honest town once more, and the man will have to rise early that catches it napping again.
>
> Mark Twain, "The Man that Corrupted Hadleyburg"

In the twentieth century, perhaps, we will be made uneasy by any conclusion with authorial comment, even if it contains a measure of irony:

Romance at short notice was her speciality.
Saki, "The Open Window"

This comment strikes a more modern note than do those of Hawthorne, both because of its ironic touch and its brevity. Nevertheless it may disturb the reader who thinks that any comment whatsoever, ironic or not, is an authorial intrusion and therefore unwanted. In the Saki story, one might add, it is also unnecessary. The action of the story had made quite clear enough that the "speciality" of the girl was "romance at short notice". We do not require the summary statement to get the message. Indeed, this story – like any passable story – has charms which a curt summary will fail to do justice. Even an ironic concluding comment, then, will blunt rather than sharpen the point that has been made – at least for a reader who has grown up with Hemingway, Faulkner and Salinger.

Comment from inside views

The problem is not only that we have come to expect a story to speak for itself, which is to say, to speak primarily in the dynamic modes. If there must be a comment, it should at least stem from a character rather than from a narrator – it must present an "inside" view:

Perhaps they promised that there would always be women in the world who would spend their brightest, freshest, rarest hours to nurse and protect that superiority he cherished in his heart.
F. Scott Fitzgerald, "The Rich Boy"

Even then, it is a moot point whether the inside view will save this conclusion from the strictures of a critical reader. The rhetoric of the narrator is obvious in these final sentences, and that may make the comment seem intrusive, even if it were not to seem so otherwise.

Fitzgerald's sketch of Anson Hunter is one of the rare examples of a modern short story which begins with both metanarrative and comment: "Begin with an individual, and before you know it you find that you have created a type . . ." We have, then, a consonance of the static modes between beginning and end. And the "type" promised us at the outset is not inadequately caught in the abstractions of the concluding summary. Something of this defense will also apply to the following:

The common soldier of the American volunteer army had returned. His war with the South was over, and his fight with nature and against the injustice of his fellow-men, was begun again.
Hamlin Garland, "The Return of the Private"

This summary, with some minor changes, might just as well apply to later stories with the same theme, such as Hemingway's "Soldier's Home"—except that Hemingway avoids final comment, apparently in the belief that the other modes must carry the "message", if any, of the tale.

There is another difference between the examples of conclusions with comment of, on the one hand, Goldsmith, Melville and Hawthorne, and, on the other, Saki, Fitzgerald and Garland. The older authors make judgements of universal application, the later ones judge only the particular person or situation. This limitation can make even authorial comment less obtrusive, especially if its authorial nature is doubtful or at least not very obvious:

> And it was to this shore, through that chaos, by those currents, that their little boat had been brought out of the past finally to safety and a home. But ah, the storms they had come through!
>
> Malcolm Lowry, "The Bravest Boat"

The exact source of the final exclamation is unclear. And the comment would strike us more forcefully as comment if the exclamation read, "But ah, all lovers need time to adjust to one another's ways!"

Even a comment of more general application can be dared if it seems to be primarily applied to the fictional character or situation:

> Jake wrote out a cheque, but unhappily. Being the old kind of Jew, a Diaspora Jew, he was bound to feel guilty either way.
>
> Mordecai Richler, "This Year at the Arabian Nights Hotel"

Typical of this kind of comment is that, in contrast to the sweeping generalizations with which Hawthorne often ends his stories, the past rather than the present tense is used: thus the effect is less that of the "coda" in which a bridge from the narrated past to the narrative present is accomplished.

Finally, there is the concluding comment imputed to a character in a story who is thus endowed with a choric function:

> "And will you, dare you, wed this lady on such terms?" demanded Colonel Dagworth, turning sternly to Sir Richard Warden. "No," he replied, "I'll none of her; take her—she is yours. I will bestow her upon you with my own hand at the marriage altar; and all I ask in return is, for you to bear me witness among your brother cavaliers, that you found one generous foe among the conquerors of Colchester."
>
> Agnes Strickland, "The Love Quarrel"

> ". . . this cup, fashioned no doubt by elfin skill, but rendered harmless by the purification with fire, the sons and daughters of Sandie Macharg and his wife drink out of to this very day. Bless all bold men, say I, and obedient wives!"
>
> Allan Cunningham, "The Haunted Ships"

Then the woman folded her fat, pudgy hands; her head sank low on her breast; and she sobbed, "God's will be done!"

Frederick Philip Grove, "Snow"

In these examples the "closing" effect is recognizable even to the reader ignorant of the story other than the ending. A less closed effect is achieved where the final comment occurs in narrated monologue rather than direct speech and where that comment is brief:

But at that he had to hide his face. He put his face into her bosom and his arms enfolded her.
Spoilt their evening! Spoilt their being alone together! They would never be alone together again.

Katherine Mansfield, "The Stranger"

Lady Ormskirk had had a son at last. By George, how pleased the old dowager must be! He would write her a note of congratulation by the next mail. Abas would make a very good house-boy. That fool Cooper!

W. Somerset Maugham, "The Outstation"

We should note that these endings are blended into the final section especially well; that is, unlike some of the earlier examples, they are not conclusions that could be easily pried loose from the main fabric. It helps that they are transported not by an author's or a narrator's voice but by a consciousness clearly within the fictional world. Then too, they are short and thus unobtrusive, like our final and more famous example:

He waited for some minutes listening. He could hear nothing: the night was perfectly silent. He listened again: perfectly silent. He felt that he was alone.

James Joyce, "A Painful Case"

Endings with Description

Like comment, description is a static mode suitable to the closed ending. As we found in examining the kinds of description in story beginnings, however, it can be used in different ways, some of which seemed highly expositional, others less so. A similar set of variations, we find, determines to what extent the ending of a story with description is felt to be closed:

Closed	*Not so closed*
1. block description	1. short description
2. of place	2. of person
3. pure	3. mixed with dynamic modes
4. unfunctional	4. functional

A longer block description of place, then, unmixed with report or speech and of minimal relevance to the action of the story is most clearly a combination which results in a closed ending:

A cloud, small, serene, floated across the moon. In that moment of darkness the sea sounded deep, troubled. Then the cloud sailed away, and the sound of the sea was a vague murmur, as though it waked out of a dark dream. All was still.

Katherine Mansfield, "At the Bay"

The rhetorical flourishes, the repeated alliteration and the emphasis on a panorama growing increasingly still reinforce our sense of conclusion. These elements together create a sense of a non-narrative frame in distinct contrast to the content of the preceding narrative. The very fact that a landscape is being described suggests the presence of a frame, since stories are by and large about people rather than places:

There was this house, and the other wooden houses that had never been painted, with their steep patched roofs and their narrow slanting porches, the wood-smoke coming out of their chimneys and dim children's faces pressed against their windows. Behind them there was the strip of earth, ploughed in some places, run to grass in others, full of stones, and behind this the pine trees, not very tall. In front were the yards, the dead gardens, the grey highway running out from town. The snow came, falling slowly, evenly between the highway and the houses and the pine trees, falling in big flakes at first and then in smaller and smaller and thicker flakes that did not melt on the hard furrows, the rock of the earth.

Alice Munro, "The Time of Death"

A shorter description than this, even if mixed with some report and speech, has an equally closed effect if the rhetorical heightening is there and the subject is death:

"Anyhow, this she told me, that my blue woman, as fair as flax, had died and was buried in the neighbouring churchyard (the nearest to, though miles distant from, Trevarras). She repeatedly assured me, as if I might otherwise doubt so sophisticated a fact, that I should find her grave there, her 'stone'.

"So indeed I did – far away from the elect, and in a shaderidden north-west corner of the sleepy, cropless acre: a slab, scarcely rounded, of granite, with but a name bitten out of the dark rough surface, 'Femina Creature'."

Walter De La Mare, "The Creatures"

And when he had lived long, and was borne to his grave a hoary corpse, followed by Faith, an aged woman, and children and grandchildren, a goodly procession, besides neighbours not a few, they carved no hopeful verse upon his tombstone, for his dying hour was gloom.

Nathaniel Hawthorne, "Young Goodman Brown"

The short story of the twentieth century rarely displays the pure block of description at the end which results in such distinctly closed endings as these. But even a sentence or two reestablishing an atmosphere and without direct reference to the story's characters or events and apparently not preparing the ground for further action suggests a distinct close:

> There was no movement, no sound, not even an insect. The dark world seemed to lie stricken beneath the cold moon and the lidless stars.
> William Faulkner, "Dry September"

This is so even if the conflicts of the story are not all resolved and the plot threads are not all reunited. The block panoramic description of landscape, especially if it is related only loosely to what has happened in the story, furnishes a recognizable frame. Such a frame often has a heightened rhetorical finish and, especially in stories of the 19th and early 20th century, a reference to the chief character's death:

> Nothing could be more undeathlike than this place; nothing could be more right for a man who had helped to do the work of great cities and had always longed for the open country and had got it at last. Rosicky's life seemed to him complete and beautiful.
> Willa Cather, "Neighbor Rosicky"

Less closed an effect is gained where the description of place is quite short or is mixed with a small amount of report:

> Looking back from the mounting grade before the track curved into the hills he could see the firelight in the clearing.
> Ernest Hemingway, "The Battler"

> Ma Parker stood, looking up and down. The icy wind blew out her apron into a balloon. And now it began to rain.
> Katherine Mansfield, "Life of Ma Parker"

Description of Persons

Concluding descriptions of persons rather than places play a small role in endings. The block description of character, perhaps understandably enough, is reserved exclusively for beginnings, at least as far as the 600 stories examined here furnish evidence. Closing descriptions of character are inevitably short:

> Little Chandler felt his cheeks suffused with shame and he stood back out of the lamplight. He listened while the paroxysm of the child's sobbing grew less and less; and the tears of remorse started to his eyes.
> James Joyce, "A Little Cloud"

He rushed beyond the barrier and called to her to follow. He was shouted at to go on but he still called to her. She set her white face to him, passive, like a helpless animal. Her eyes gave him no sign of love or farewell or recognition.

James Joyce, "Eveline"

Gazing up into the darkness I saw myself as a creature driven and derided by vanity; and my eyes burned with anguish and anger.

James Joyce, "Araby"

In each of these examples from Joyce's *Dubliners*, the closed effect is increased by rhetorical heightening and by the admixture of abstractions ("tears of remorse", "no sign of love or farewell", "a creature driven and derided by vanity"), which remind us of the earlier conclusions with comment. Although there is little sense of a frame here, each ending contains a climax of self-recognition essential to the rounding off of the story.

Description of Persons Mixed with other Modes

More common is the ending in which a short description of a person is mixed with one of the other modes. By and large these endings are, of course, less closed than are those so far discussed, unless the theme of death is central:

Oddly secure in the dark, the dark of the cinema, the dark of her personal fear, she felt protected. She thought: Il prie pour moi. She saw, as plainly as if it had been laid in her arms, her child, her personal angel, white and swaddled, baptized, innocent, ready for death.

Mavis Gallant, "Bernadette"

He stood and fumbled in his pockets (for a knife) while he faced Kayerts, who was hanging by a leather strap from the cross. He had evidently climbed the grave, which was high and narrow, and after tying the end of the strap to the arm, had swung himself off. His toes were only a couple of inches above the ground; his arms hung stiffly down; he seemed to be standing rigidly at attention, but with one purple cheek playfully posed on the shoulder. And, irreverently, he was putting out a swollen tongue at his Managing Director.

Joseph Conrad, "An Outpost of Progress"

Also with a tendency to the closed end of the scale are final short descriptions of a person where they are yoked to a comment of an obvious kind:

Above the bed there was a big text in a deep-black frame: –

Lost! One Golden Hour
Set with Sixty Diamond Minutes.
No Reward Is Offered
For It Is Gone For Ever!

"Yer grandma painted that," said grandpa. And he ruffled his white tuft
and looked at Fenella so merrily she almost thought he winked at her.
Katherine Mansfield, "The Voyage"

How closed such a short description is in actual effect, however, must
depend not only on its formal qualities, such as length, use with other modes,
rhetorical heightening, and so forth, but also on its degree of integration with
the whole text. In Conrad's "An Outpost of Progress", the end of which is
quoted above, the concluding description of the suicide is both a climax and
conclusion to what has gone before. In Katherine Mansfield's "The Voyage",
however, both the comment contained in the framed text and the description
of the grandfather constitute new information, by and large unconnected
with the sketch of which the story consists; it pulls no threads together, it
summarizes nothing, and therefore is very much "open". In her story, "The
Singing Lesson", by contrast, the concluding description of the music teacher,
who has just heard from her fiancée that he is not leaving her after all,
summarizes her state of mind, which has been the central subject of the story
all along.

And this time Miss Meadows' voice sounded over all the other voices – full,
deep, glowing with expression.
Katherine Mansfield, "The Singing Lesson"

It is hard to say in absolute terms whether any story ending is "open" or
"closed", but this one is certainly more "closed" than that of "The Voyage".
For it shows us the final stage of a development which has been traced for us,
step by step. It suggests no further step yet to come which would be relevant to
the singing lesson which the story has described.

As in story beginnings, the description in endings is more often than not
mixed with report. Both the final action and the description tend to be iconic
in the modern short story, to point to a larger significance beyond themselves
and to summarize something of central importance in the story:

They gazed, squinting in the sun, at the flying red thing, and he turned away
and saw in the shadow of her cheek and on her lips and chin the dark rich
red of the pulp and juice of the crushed raspberries.
Hugh Hood, "Flying a Red Kite"

Here the father, who had despaired of seeing the sense of his own existence,
finds a meaning in life, or at least regains self-confidence, by witnessing his
little daughter's pleasure at flying a kite and finding some wild raspberries.
The sight of her juice-stained face is the answer to the central question which
the story had put: what makes life worth living? The epiphany is shared by the
father with the reader. For the reader who grasps the significance of the
description, the story is "closed". So it is in the following examples:

Now truly she was furious. She had been on the defensive before but now

131

she attacked. Tried to get off her father's lap and fly at me while tears of defeat blinded her eyes.

William Carlos Williams, "The Use of Force"

The "tears of defeat" signalize the psychological as well as physical victory of the doctor, who has succeeded in prying open the child's mouth and diagnosing her diphtheria. The abstraction, "defeat", is a word-level, minimal comment on the state of the child, which makes the description into a closed ending.

The boy and the girl said nothing. Darling laughed embarrassedly, looked hard at them sitting there, close to each other, shrugged, turned and went toward his hotel, the sweat breaking out on his face and running down into his collar.

Irwin Shaw, "The Eight-Yard Run"

Here the hero has relived the moment of his triumph on a football field, fifteen years earlier. Then too, he had been aware of the spectators and of the sweat running down his back, and the repetition of these two images from the opening of the story completes the frame. A similar effect is gained by the following text, which might at first glance seem to constitute an "open" ending:

To Quebec – 20 miles
To Quebec – 18 miles

The signs were pointed in the same direction.
"Crazy. Everything is crazy," Pfeffer muttered. He turned down the road, and soon he was covered by the white dust his feet raised.

Irving Layton, "Vacation in La Voiselle"

As in the previous example, there is a phenomenon of recurrence operative here; the seemingly irrelevant detail of white dust is linked to the opening of the story:

Grey puffs of sand arose and moved across the hillside; the rain peppered the road with spots of mud. Pfeffer sprinted up the derelict footway . . .

The story is framed by the focus on Pfeffer coming and then going, and on the state of the ground he has to traverse. The inconclusiveness of the story's action, the lack of effective contact between the hero and the other characters, point to an "open" end; but the use of description, though brief and mixed with report, works in the opposite direction. One can hardly say which effect predominates.

We have considered the effects of length (block vs. short), object (place vs. person) and modal purity (pure vs. mixed) as primary dimensions which allow us to arrive at some rough measure of the effect of description. Other dimensions which either reinforce or cut across these effects have suggested themselves; these must be looked at more systematically in connection with the dynamic modes, report and speech.

Description of Things

Descriptions of things are rare in openings especially, but also infrequent in closings, though certainly they would not strike one as unusual:

> The dagger lay next to the hearth, the tip of the thin blade still smeared with wet blood.

A possible opening for a murder story, one would think, but made up here for lack of a published example. Story *endings*, by contrast, do occasionally focus on a thing:

> "Though it's no good buying newspapers . . . Nothing ever happens. Curse this war; God damn this war! . . . All the same, I don't see why we should have a snail on our wall." Ah, the mark on the wall! It was a snail.
> Virginia Woolf, "The Mark on the Wall"

The mark on the wall is thus explained. The thing is named, in other words, to furnish a solution to the question posed by the story's title. Here is another example:

> It was later, when they had left her a while to be alone with him, that she knelt and touched his hand. Her eyes dimmed, still it was such a strong and patient hand; then, transfixed, they suddenly grew wide and clear. On the palm, white even against its frozen whiteness, was a little smear of paint.
> Sinclair Ross, "The Painted Door"

The smear of paint, seen through the eyes of the heroine (a clear case of substitutionary perception), tell both her and the reader simultaneously that her husband witnessed her act of adultery. That is why he had gone out into the Canadian winter to allow himself to freeze to death, brushing his hand on the door she had freshly painted. Here is yet another example:

> Corley halted at the first lamp and stared grimly before him. Then with a grave gesture he extended a hand towards the light and, smiling, opened it slowly to the gaze of his disciple. A small gold coin shone in the palm.
> James Joyce, "Two Gallants"

Again, the object signalizes the central (and sordid) action. In each example the object can hardly be said to be described; rather it is named, in the Ross and Joyce texts provided with a descriptive adjective. Block descriptions of things seem to be unsuitable for story endings: another "empty set" which further search might be able to fill, and which certainly could be filled if some story writer thought it worth the trouble. Interesting for our purposes here is the fact that description, whether of places, persons or things, tends to effect a closed rather than an open ending, unless some other overriding factor or set of factors establishes an exception to the rule.

The factors we have found operative thus far may be summarized as follows:

Closed	Less closed
Metanarrative	
block (long)	fused (short)
Comment	
authorial/narratorial	choric
block (long)	fused (short)
Description	
block (long)	fused (short)
of place	of person
pure, or mixed with *comment*	mixed with dynamic modes
unfunctional (distinct	functional
"frame" effect)	
rhetorically heightened	same style register as bulk
	of story
subject: death	—
iconic	—

CHAPTER VIII

How Stories End II: the Dynamic Modes

The static modes, comment and description, as we have seen, furnish clear examples of closed endings. The effect may be supported by elements of content and narrative technique, such as the subject of the hero's death or a rhetorically heightened language. Yet this effect is by no means inevitable; a number of other narrative elements may intervene and undercut, rather than support, the effect of the narrative mode.

The dynamic modes, report and speech, by contrast, are conducive to an open effect. They tend to produce open endings where they appear in their pure forms or mixed with one another. This is not the effect, however, when they occur mixed with the static modes or metanarrative. They also attract a large number of other narrative elements (more than do the static modes) which may support or undercut such effects as they naturally possess.

In their simplest form, stories which end with report or speech have open endings insofar as the final sentences fail to round out some earlier element of narrative: instead, the action or the final bit of dialogue seems to exist for its own sake or to point to some future event. So the ending can be seen in parallel to the *in medias res* beginning: we can leave the action *in medias res* as we have entered it:

> But today she passed the baker's by, climbed the stairs, went into the little dark room – her room like a cupboard – and sat down on the red eiderdown. She sat there for a long time. The box that the fur came out of was on the bed. She unclasped the necklet quickly; quickly, without looking, laid it inside. But when she put the lid on she thought she heard something crying.
>
> Katherine Mansfield, "Miss Brill'

If we do not closely examine the relevance of this action to what has gone before, we may term this an *in medias res* conclusion, and label it as *open*. To the phenomenon of anteriority in story beginnings, where a connection to what has gone before is suggested, we can add the parallel phenomenon of *posteriority* at the end: the suggestion of a future action:

> He wanted his life to go smoothly. It had just gotten going that way. Well,

that was all over now, anyhow. He would go over to the schoolyard and watch Helen play indoor baseball.

Ernest Hemingway, "Soldier's Home"

Here too, the ending seems to be open. An open ending, however, cannot like the metanarrative "postscripts" of old, be investigated in isolation. On a second look we find that even these apparently open endings are like the birthmark in Hawthorne's story of that name, with their roots reaching even to the very heart of the story. In Mansfield's "Miss Brill" the crying Miss Brill hears echoes of her own desolation: her loneliness, her rejection by the girls who had made fun of her in her old fur necklet. And in Hemingway's "Soldier's Home" the future action to which the last sentence points is symptomatic of the state of the ex-soldier; it is thus an indirect comment on the central theme. So it is only in a superficial sense that these stories seem on first reading to have open endings.

The nature of these two endings is symptomatic. For what is available for our exploration is not a wide variety of open endings with report, but a variety of factors with which the openness of endings with report is modified or altogether cancelled out. Some of these factors have to do with content, others with technique and presentation, for instance, modal choice, style and tone. One or more of these factors almost inevitably plays a role. Although endings with comment and description, then, are usually closed in a more obvious way, endings with report may be termed *less* closed, but rarely out-and-out open.

The content which makes for a more closed ending, even with report, is primarily of two kinds. The first is that which tells of the hero's disappearance or death.

The Ending with Death

Of some 184 stories which end with report and are surveyed here, about one quarter refer to the main character's death. Before the nineteenth century, insofar as one may speak of short stories in that period at all, it was natural enough to end the tale this way: a story was often little else than a "bald scenario for a novel", as Edith Wharton put it – a curtailed novel or brief fictional biography with the usual pious close:

And in the end, this worthy man ended his life in London with great honour.

Thomas Deloney, "Sir Thomas Eyer"

The moral sentiment allowed of more extension where the main character had been duly punished for his or her iniquity:

Thus have I brought this unlucky woman from her birth to her burial . . . if we give ourselves over to ill company or our own wicked inclinations, we are infallibly led to the practice of those crimes which, although they may be pleasing at the present, yet they have a sting behind, and we shall be sensible thereof when we shall be hurried to an untimely end, as you have seen in the vicious life and untimely death of this our Counterfeit Lady.

Francis Kirkman, "The Counterfeit Lady Unveiled"

Or the death of the main characters could be suggested in the "they lived happily ever after" style:

They had several children, but none survived them; and Melissa, upon the death of her husband, which happened about seven years ago, retired wholly from town to her estate in the country, where she lived beloved, and died in peace.

John Hawkesworth, "The Story of Melissa"

. . . concluded with her the marriage daie, which was presently accomplished with great ioye and contentation to all parties: and thus Siluio hauyng attained a noble wife, and Silla his sister her desired houseband, they passed the residue of their daies with suche delight, as those that haue accomplished the perfection of their felicities.

Barnaby Rich, "Apolonius and Silla"

In the nineteenth century, death is often named indirectly, with a poetic circumlocution, in which the title of the tale is sounded once more:

Some months after, dragged to the gibbet at the tail of a mule, the black met his voiceless end. The body was burned to ashes; but for many days, the head, that hive of subtlety, fixed on a pole in the Plaza, met, unabashed, the gaze of the whites; and across the Plaza looked toward St Bartholomew's church, in whose vaults slept then, as now, the recovered bones of Aranda; and across the Rimac bridge looked toward the monastery, on Mount Agonia without; where, three months after being dismissed by the court, Benito Cereno, borne on the bier, did, indeed, follow his leader.

Herman Melville, "Benito Cereno"

"Tell the boys I've got The Luck with me now"; and the strong man, clinging to the frail babe as a drowning man is said to cling to a straw, drifted away into the shadowy river that flows forever to the unknown sea.

Bret Harte, "The Luck of Roaring Camp"

The pathos here is not quite of a piece with the story itself. But it is apparently thought appropriate to both a report of death and to the end of a story. Here is another example:

And so passed Otoo, who saved me and made me a man, and who saved me in the end. We met in the maw of a hurricane and parted in the maw of a shark, with seventeen intervening years of comradeship, the like of which I dare to assert has never befallen two men, the one brown and the other white. If Jehovah be from His high place watching every sparrow fall, not least in His kingdom shall be Otoo, the one heathen of Borabora.

Jack London, "The Heathen"

Not so many modern stories end in death, whereas the stories of Poe, Hawthorne and Melville often do. Where the ending with death is not appropriate to the modern plot, however, it can be presented in the guise of a dream, which we may consider a special form of a virtual mode:

And Geraldine lay awake, dreaming that death had closed the last door in the old house.

Anne Hébert, "The House on the Esplanade"

I dreamt that just before dawn I crept out of the house and went through the yard. And all the letters Noreen had ever made out of grain there while she was feeding the chickens had all sprouted up into green letters of grass and wheat. Someone touched me on the shoulder and said sadly, *I haven't got a spoon*, but I ran away without answering across the fields into the bush. There was a round pond there surrounded by a grove of young chokecherry trees. I pushed through these and came to the edge of the pond. There lay the Bully looking almost pitiful, his arms and legs bound with green ropes made out of nettles. He was drowned dead, half in the water and half out of it, but face up. And in the dim light of the dawn I knelt down and kissed him gently on the forehead.

James Reaney, "The Bully"

Whereas the nineteenth century story tends to wrap the character's death up in a mixture of comment and description, many a modern story concludes with a brief report of the physical event:

The second crash sounded from below. Pepé swung forward and toppled from the rock. His body struck and rolled over and over, starting a little avalanche. And when at last he stopped against a bush, the avalanche slid slowly down and covered up his head.

John Steinbeck, "Flight"

You could see what was going to happen; and we called out, our voices like lightning in the rain, but Miss Bobbit, running toward those moons of roses, did not seem to hear. That is when the six o'clock bus ran over her.

Truman Capote, "Children on their Birthdays"

Each of these stories finishes in the mode of report, so that the endings are abrupt; they are nevertheless closed. A century earlier the effect would probably have been less prosaic and more closed: the final sentences would probably have been dressed with authorial comment and with a heightened style.

138

The death of a character can also yield a less closed effect by rendering it as an event posterior to the limits of the story:

He emptied the ashtray containing his nail parings and cigarette butts into the toilet, and swept the floor with a shirt, so that there would be no trace of his life, of his body, when that lewd and searching shape of death came there to find him in the evening.

John Cheever, "Torch Song"

The character is to die, as it were, after the story itself is over, which suggests an open ending. And the mundane details which dominate the first part of the sentence are unsuitable to a grand finale. But the sense of openness is decreased not only by the fact of death but also by the rhetorical flourish ("lewd and searching shape of death") with which it is conveyed as well as by the cadence of the final words: the pattern "to find him/ in the evening" = x x́ x/ x x x́ x is a *cursus trispondiacus*, a clause-ending such as we find in Cicero's verse. This cadence is rather that of a traditional than of a contemporary story ending:

. . . to teach us to despise it.

Oliver Goldsmith, "The Disabled Soldier"

. . . were crumbled into fragments.

Nathaniel Hawthorne, "Ethan Brand"

In this sense Cheever's concluding clause uses a traditional cadence of conclusion. Thus the various factors which suggest open versus closed in his final sentence tug in contrary directions; so the ending cannot be classified as open simply because it takes the narrative mode of report, nor closed simply because the character is to die.

The report of a death is the most obvious and frequent of ways to end a story. Also available is the wedding, which is a staple of the novel. But less than one percent of short stories end with it, even if one includes such doubtful cases as Lawrence's "The Horse Dealer's Daughter": but it does seem rather likely that the doctor will ask Mabel to marry him. Apparently the short story does not offer enough scope for the to and fro of a courtship, unless the story is allowed to run on to an unusual length, like Hardy's "The Distracted Preacher". Instead, the short story makes do with minor closing actions: shutting a door, going to sleep, ending a telephone conversation, getting up from a chair or simply departing.[1] Departures are often made more conclusive by the he-did-not-look-back *topos*; a handful of examples will help make clear how strongly this *topos* has become entrenched:

He did not look back.

William Faulkner, "Barn Burning"

. . . nor was he ever seen again.

Duncan Campbell Scott, "The Tragedy of the Seigniory"

. . . they did not see her again.

Yves Thériault, "Anguish of God"

The man walked straight ahead and didn't look back.

Don Bailey, "A Few Notes for Orpheus"

He begins to walk. Away from the town and out into the open country. Scorns to look back.

David Helwig, "In Exile"

A variant is the she-did-not-answer *topos*. These topoi are also used in the modern novel, but much less frequently. The repeated use of a closing *topos* (not only in the mode of report) can gradually turn what was at first an apparently *open* ending into a recognizable cliché and thus into a conventional signal that the story is over. Thus the he-did-not-look-back *topos* might have struck a reader of fifty years ago as open. To the reader of today it will perhaps seem an unambiguous example of a *closed* ending. As I have attempted to show elsewhere, the *topos* has ancient roots, but it is particularly vital in our time in the Canadian short story.[2]

Endings which Repeat Beginnings

A second technique is often used to give a story what Frank Kermode has called "sense of an ending":[3] something from the story's beginning is repeated, most often the title of the story. In the nineteenth century this is sometimes less a matter of content than of rhetoric, and occasionally makes a somewhat "arty" impression:

While I gazed, this fissure rapidly widened – there came a fierce breath of the whirlwind – the entire orb of the satellite burst at once upon my sight – my brain reeled as I saw the mighty walls rushing asunder – there was a long tumultuous shouting sound like the voice of a thousand waters – and the deep and dank tarn at my feet closed sullenly and silently over the fragments of the "House of Usher".

Edgar Allen Poe, "The Fall of the House of Usher"

Here, at least, the final words fit the sense, whereas in Hawthorne the effect is sometimes highly artificial:

"And I," observed Peter Goldthwaite, with reviving spirits, "have a plan for laying out the cash to great advantage."

"Why, as to that," muttered John Brown to himself, "we must apply to the next court for a guardian to take care of the solid cash; and if Peter insist upon speculating, he may do it, to his heart's content, with old Peter Goldthwaite's Treasure."

Nathaniel Hawthorne, "Peter Goldthwaite's Treasure"

Hold out your vessel, my dear! There it is, full to the brim; so now run home, peeping at your sweet image in the pitcher as you go, and forget not, in a glass of my own liquor, to drink – "Success to the Town Pump!"
Nathaniel Hawthorne, "A Rill from the Town Pump"

". . . I begin to grow weary of a town life, sir. Will you show me the way to the ferry?" "No, my good friend Robin, – not tonight, at least," said the gentleman.
"Some few days hence, if you wish it, I will speed you on your journey. Or, if you prefer to remain with us, perhaps, as you are a shrewd youth, you may rise in the world without the help of your kinsman, Major Molineux."
Nathaniel Hawthorne, "My Kinsman, Major Molineux"

In all three examples the title of the story is mentioned by a character, who is presumably not responsible for the title. It seems less of an artifice, perhaps, to have a title repeated in authorial report:

"Damn it all!" he thought; "this is childish. This is as bad as Alicia!" And he set to work to paint in his celebrated manner – spindleberries.
John Galsworthy, "Spindleberries"

Originally she'd intended just to look at him across the room while she let Mr Huws-Evans talk to her, but after what had happened she left Mr Huws-Evans to unpack his crisps and put them in bowls while the brother (it was funny to think that he was Mr Huws-Evans too, in a way) took her across the room, sat her on the sofa and started talking about interesting things.
Kingsley Amis, "Interesting Things"

The fact that the repetition of the title is a conventional technique makes it more out of place in the Amis than the Galsworthy story, since the Amis story does not, by and large, stick to time-worn narrative clichés. If the Amis story ended with a clause like "and started talking to her about his work" we would have a more clearly open ending. The repetition of the title, however, strongly reduces the "openness" which report, left *in medias res* and with an element of posteriority ("started talking"), would otherwise possess.
Short story writers have found various ways of reducing the apparent artificiality of the title repetition. One is to alter the title a little, shaping it to the context of the final sentence:

And that, I conclude, is but another evidence of the complete and final triumph of the egg – at least as far as my family is concerned.
Sherwood Anderson, "The Egg"

She has to cry, Mrs Thompson thought. She has to have it out. She rocked slowly, tapping her foot, trying to remember how she'd felt about things when she was twenty, wondering if her heart had ever been broken, too.
Mavis Gallant, "My Heart is Broken"

141

Again, the total effect must be seen in the light of the other factors brought into play: Anderson's ending smacks strongly of comment ("evidence of the complete and final triumph"), which makes his ending more closed, whereas Gallant's ending is more open, in part because the final words are thoughts of a character in a third-person story (in our system, that is, a submode of speech), in part because of the participle "wondering", in part because the title is presented in altered form – in third rather than first person.

A different effect is gained where the title is used as a motif which a first-person narrator sounds:

> Darn him, what did he want to do like that for? I keep thinking about it and it spoils looking at horses and smelling things and hearing niggers laugh and everything. Sometimes I'm so mad about it I want to fight someone. It gives me the fantods. What did he do it for? I want to know why.
>
> Sherwood Anderson, "I Want to Know Why"

> So I can't tell you the exact margin we win the pennant by. Maybe it was two and a half games, or maybe it was three and a half. But it'll all be there in the newspapers and record books of thirty, thirty-one years ago and, like I was sayin', you could look it up.
>
> James Thurber, "You Could Look it Up"

It seems, by comparison, less artful to tuck the title away in the final sentence like this, even if the formality of the conclusion is then increased by a brief summary statement:

> Thus the friends, who had met with such glee, parted in a very different mood; Lord Woodville to command the Tapestried Chamber to be unmantled, and the door built up; and General Browne to seek in some less beautiful country, and with some less dignified friend, forgetfulness of the painful night which he had passed in Woodville Castle.
>
> Sir Walter Scott, "The Tapestried Chamber"

How much less conventional is the technique of Henry James about a hundred years later, who makes the title work for him in the conclusion of "The Beast in the Jungle", where the conclusion is both climax and resolution of the puzzle which the title posed:

> He saw the Jungle of his life and saw the lurking Beast; then, while he looked, perceived it, as by a stir of the air, rise, huge and hideous, for the leap that was to settle him. His eyes darkened – it was close; and, instinctively turning, in his hallucination, to avoid it, he flung himself, on his face, on the tomb.
>
> Henry James, "The Beast in the Jungle"

The beast, of course, is not "really" there, but appears only in the imagination of the fictional figure: it is a "virtual" form of the perception-by-proxy submode which has come to be widely used in the modern short story.

Artful in a different way is the ending of Joyce's "The Dead": it also capitalizes on images of death; but it is more closed because its rhetoric contrasts with the "scrupulous meanness" of the language earlier on, and because it conveys, in contrast to the Henry James example, where we may be tempted to imagine John Marcher's next move after getting up from May Bartram's tomb, no sense of a posterior action:

> It was falling, too, upon every part of the lonely churchyard on the hill where Michael Furey lay buried. It lay thickly drifted on the crooked crosses and headstones, on the spears of the little gate, on the barren thorns. His soul swooned slowly as he heard the snow falling faintly through the universe and faintly falling, like the descent of their last end, upon all the living and the dead.
>
> James Joyce, "The Dead"

"The Beast in the Jungle" ends in a more conventional way however, insofar as its final sentence looks back to what was developing in the story and also to what must come after: John Marcher's life after the loss of the woman who could have given his life a meaning. Many stories end in this Janus-headed fashion, looking simultaneously backward and forward. The repetition of the title is only the most obvious way to effect the backward look. This can also be done by a renewed reference to the theme which the story develops:

> Later, the dog whined loudly. And still later it crept close to the man and caught the scent of death. This made the animal bristle and back away. A little longer it delayed, howling under the stars that leaped and danced and shone brightly in the cold sky. Then it turned and trotted up the trail in the direction of the camp it knew, where were the other food-providers and fire-providers.
>
> Jack London, "To Build a Fire"

Here we have the conclusion with the chief (or only) character's death to round out the action, and an oblique reference in "fire-providers" to the central action indicated in the title. Both the reference to death and the title-echo belong to the "closed" variety of narrative; but here they are balanced by the *in medias res* departure from the scene. And, at least from the point of view of the dog, who is the witness and source of information, the final action, "trotted . . . in the direction of the camp", looks forward beyond the confines of the story.

The Janus-headed ending combines the final look back which is essential to the closed ending and which both metanarrative and comment inevitably convey, with the suggestion that life goes forward which is essential to the open one, and which usually demands some form of report, albeit mixed with other modes:

She slammed the door and, as the taxi moved off, leaned toward the window and waved. He stood there uncertainly, waving back, radiant with relief. Then, as she disappeared around the curve of the drive, he ran quickly up the steps to find his friends, and safety.

Elizabeth Taylor, "A Red-Letter Day"

In this story the child reenters his boarding school at the end of his mother's visit; the day was mostly an agony of uncertainty and instability which he is glad to exchange for the "safety" of the surroundings to which he has grown accustomed. Thus "to find his friends" looks forward, but the word "safety" indicates what his mother was unable to provide that day and thus summarizes and closes. The abstraction represents a fragment of comment, for it labels the psychological state which the visiting day, the red-letter day of the title, jeopardized. The Janus-face consists, then, half of report, half of comment. The same structure, but reversed, is contained in the following example, in which the report looks backward, the comment forward to the narrator's continuing preoccupation with the terrible accident recounted in the story:

A short time ago I was driving past the main gate of the Malloy-Harrison plant, and I noticed McKillup tending the gates. One uniform sleeve was empty, and the other ended above one of those steel mechanical hands. The sight of him brought it all back to me, but I'd as soon forget it if I could.

Hugh Garner, "E Equals Mc Squared"

Here the open effect of report is enforced by the posteriority of the very last words, "if I could". On the other hand, there is the look backward in time, separated from the main action and giving us a brief glimpse of the crippled McKillup (the "Mc" who has been brutally "squared" in an industrial accident) – a closing effect, almost a postscript. This closing effect is reinforced by the return from the past tense of the report to the present conditional of the final clause, "if I could" – a common signal of conclusion. The passage, then, includes a number of pushes and pulls, the forces of which are hard to weigh up against one another.

The Janus-effect, then, is gained by a combination of
– some form of repetition or capping or resumé,
– often with a shift of verb tense, but balanced by
– a reference to the future, the phenomenon here called *posteriority*.

The first set of effects may be subsumed under the heading *epanalepsis*, the rhetorical figure reducible to the formula

x . . . x

That is: an element which begins a clause, sentence, paragraph, or larger unit of discourse is repeated at the end. The obvious example is a repetition of the title of the work. Less obvious is other verbal repetition, especially in the longer narrative. E. M. Forster is said to have wanted to begin *A Passage to*

India with the word "except" and to end it with the word "extraordinary".[4] (He ended it differently, in fact.) Few novel readers would have caught the epanalepsis if Forster had in fact kept to his intention.

Even more likely to escape notice at first reading is the repetition of themes, emotions and images which were sounded at the beginning of the work:

> But spite of my treatment, and spite of my dissuasive talk of him to my neighbours, the lightning-rod man still dwells in the land, still travels in storm time and drives a brave trade with the fears of man.
> Herman Melville, "The Lightning-Rod Man"

Here not only the title of the story is sounded again, but also the thunderstorm described in detail at the opening. Then too, "trade with the fears of man" has been shown, though not labelled with these words. Again, there are several kinds of epanalepsis here, which, together with the shift to the present tense and the suggestion of posteriority, yield the typical Janus-effect.

Epanalepsis, then, may be verbal, but also scenic, psychological, modal, and so forth. Thus it may suggest a kind of frame (assuming that the reader notices the repetition) and contribute to the effect of a closed ending. Often it is a matter of interpretation. If the reader thinks of the *lily* as a death-symbol, then the structure of Joyce's "The Dead" is epanaleptic:

> Lily, the caretaker's daughter . . .
> . . . upon all the living and the dead.

If the reader sees both the preface to "The Counterfeit Lady" and its "postscript" as metanarrative, this story too is of the epanaleptic type. Naturally the one kind of epanalepsis weighs more heavily than the other. As some of the examples quoted have shown, the frame-effect may be mitigated by techniques working in the opposite direction, or reinforced by techniques also conducive to a "closed" effect.

Often an ending in the mode of report and, to a lesser extent, of speech, will echo elements tucked away in the interior of the story:

> Robin waited a little, then, with the very shadow of a sigh, walked to the window. He looked out for a moment at the gathering dusk, then got a chair, climbed on to it and carefully took down the water-colour from the wall.
> Hugh Walpole, "Bachelors"

The reader needs to remember that Robin liked this particular water-colour and his brother did not. But since the brother was to marry and move out of the house, Robin meant to leave the picture on the wall. Once his brother's engagement is called off, however, Robin is delighted to return to his old subservient ways, to adjust his own taste to that of his more dynamic brother. Taking down the picture is therefore a symbolic act which seals Robin's glad acceptance of his brother's return.

A similar example of epanalepsis is the following:

> No, it was too difficult. "I'll – I'll go with them, and write to William later. Some other time. Later. Not now. But I shall *certainly* write," thought Isabel hurriedly.
> And, laughing in the new way, she ran down the stairs.
> Katherine Mansfield, "Marriage à la Mode"

The phrase "in the new way" is not only an oblique reference to the title; it also echoes a phrase near the opening:

> "*Dear* William! I'm sure you did!" She laughed in the new way.

So the last sentence of the story constitutes a final condemnation of Isabel: she has acted despicably in her attempt to keep up with her modish friends, and will go on "in the new way."

Strictly speaking, these are not examples of epanalepsis: the water-colour is not mentioned at the beginning of Walpole's story, and "the new way" is only gradually unfolded in Mansfield's. In the terminology of rhetoric, what we have here is a case of *diacope*, repetition after an interval: . . . x . . . x . . . or *polyptoton*, repetition with a difference: . . . x . . . x' . . . But such repetitions as we have noted can also be seen as occurring at the beginning and end of a narrative movement or segment; so the term *epanalepsis* will serve for a broad palette of similar phenomena.

Epanalepsis, in its narrower sense of a more or less exact verbal repetition, does not seem to occur in endings with comment, although conceivably it could (if, for instance, the story's title contained an abstract *message* repeated at the end). It occurs only rarely with description, but often with endings where report and speech predominate. This is a paradoxical finding, since those narrative modes most suitable to a potentially open ending also best lend themselves to a technique the function of which is to frame – that is, to achieve a closed effect. But the paradox is valid. Each narrative mode, we find, brings with it a set of predispositions only. These are reinforced or negated by other functions which may support or run counter to the effect of the mode. Endings in which all the functions tend in only one direction are the exception rather than the rule.

Techniques which Mitigate the Open Effect of Report

The closing reference to the death of a character, the final reference to the story's title and the other less obviously epaleptic endings are mostly manipulations of content, although some of the examples cited might just as well be thought of as narrative techniques. There remain a set of phenomena which are to be categorized as *technical* in the stricter sense: modal, panoramic/scenic, and stylistic.

The mixture of report with comment, as we have seen, is a phenomenon which helps close what would otherwise be a quite open ending:

. . . to find his friends and safety.

Elizabeth Taylor, "A Red-Letter Day"

. . . drives a brave trade with the fears of man.

Herman Melville, "The Lightning-Rod Man"

Such an admixture of the narrator's comment is a species of authorial interference, of telling as opposed to showing. The interference is patently a matter of mode rather than point of view: it is a species of telling, whether the comment is thought to occur in the discourse of an author, narrator, reflector, first-person narrator, fictional figure or whatever. Thus such an admixture of comment at the end of a story is perhaps an unmodern technique. One can say in its defence that it constitutes a highly attenuated version of the blatantly moralizing comment which we find in medieval and renaissance narrative and in the more immediate predecessors of Irving, Poe and Hawthorne.

In the use of *panoramic* as opposed to *scenic* report, the famous distinction of Percy Lubbock's, there is also a clear historical development. Panoramic report contributes to a closed effect, scenic to an open one, if we leave the other factors discussed above or yet to be examined out of account. The ultimate in panoramic endings is that employing the *tableau*, a quasi-simultaneous presentation of the main characters in a single view:

> The train of withered mourners, the hoary bridegroom in his shroud, the pale features of the aged bride, and the death bell tolling through the whole, till its deep voice overpowered the marriage words, all marked the funeral of earthly hopes. But as the ceremony proceeded, the organ, as if stirred by the sympathies of this impressive scene, poured forth an anthem, first mingling with the dismal knell, then rising to a loftier strain, till the soul looked down upon its woe. And when the awful rite was finished, and with cold hand in cold hand the married of eternity withdrew, the organ's peal of solemn triumph drowned the wedding knell.
>
> Nathaniel Hawthorne, "The Minister's Black Veil"

Adding to the closed effect are the references to marriage and to death, the admixture of comment, and the rhetorically heightened final sentence, with its regular iambic close. More mixed in its effects is the following tableau, which has a number of details and close-up views that smack of the scenic as well as of the panoramic:

> For one instant the party upon the stairs remained motionless, through extremity of terror and of awe. In the next, a dozen stout arms were toiling at the wall. It fell bodily. The corpse, already greatly decayed and clotted with gore, stood erect before the eyes of the spectators. Upon its head, with red extended mouth and solitary eye of fire, sat the hideous beast whose craft had seduced me into murder, and whose informing voice had consigned me to the hangman. I had walled the monster up within the tomb!
>
> Edgar Allen Poe, "The Black Cat"

147

Although this ending, like that of "The Minister's Black Veil", is a mixture of report and description without more than a touch of submerged comment ("seduced me into murder"), the effect is that of a closed ending. Except for the reference to the hangman, the details are facts and images which occurred earlier in the story, and which are adequately drawn together in a dramatic tableau.

Now it would be convenient if we could ascribe to the ending with panoramic report a closed effect, and to scenic report an open one. This rule might be valid too, other things being equal. But they rarely are. For the ending with scenic report almost inevitably contains an epanaleptic detail, or it shows a symbolic or iconic action: one which typifies the central values of the story. The endings quoted above from Hawthorne's "A Rill from the Town Pump", James' "The Beast in the Jungle" and Amis' "Interesting Things" may serve as examples. Some stories, like Porter's "Flowering Judas", seem to be deliberately constructed with such a concluding scene in view:

> . . . and from the Judas tree he stripped the warm bleeding flowers, and held them to her lips. She saw that his hand was fleshless, a cluster of small white petrified branches, and his eye sockets were without light, but she ate the flowers greedily . . .

We must conclude, therefore, that panoramic report is suited to a closed, scenic report to an open ending, but only potentially. For scenic report is habitually rendered less open by one or more of the other elements under discussion here.

Considerations of Style

To these elements belong a set of stylistic ones, some of which have been noted in passing. We need not try to settle here the vexed question, how style is to be defined. It is convenient to treat it under the three headings of *diction*, *syntax* and *rhetoric*.

The diction of short story endings frequently takes a sudden leap from that which came before – upward toward pathos or sublimity, or, less frequently, downward into the mundane or vulgar.

For the purposes of literary analysis we need a wider range of categories than the concept of *style register* usually yields, but the five categories suggested by Martin Joos in *The Five Clocks*[5] is nevertheless convenient:

1. frozen
2. formal
3. consultative
4. casual
5. intimate

Literature can make little use of registers 1 and 5. The nineteenth century story tends to use registers 2 and 3, modern narrative favours 3 and 4. Thus the nineteenth century story ending often shows a shift up to register 2:

> . . . the organ's peal of solemn triumph drowned the wedding knell.
> Nathaniel Hawthorne, "The Minister's Black Veil"

The twentieth century writer more often starts at register 4, and moves up from there. But the technique is essentially the same, and the range hardly less, for the highly formal close which Hawthorne can make use of is no longer appropriate:

> He emptied the ashtray containing his nail parings and cigarette butts into the toilet, and swept the floor with a shirt, so that there would be no trace of his life, of his body, when that lewd and searching shape of death came there to find him in the evening.
> John Cheever, "Torch Song"

Here we see the last-minute shift from a casual to a formal diction, which of course corresponds to the shift in the object of discourse – from "nail parings" to the "searching shape of death." Usually the move to a higher plane of diction is made more gradually, and often it goes hand in hand with the search for an abstract statement of truth which is essentially the final movement from the dynamic mode of report to the static ones of description and comment:

> Again, the terror the acknowledgement of wasted years and death. Valentin, responsive and confident, still nestled in his arms. His cheek touched the soft cheek and felt the brush of the delicate eyelashes. With inner desperation he pressed the child close – as though an emotion as protean as his love could dominate the pulse of time.
> Carson McCullers, "The Sojourner"

The infusion of comment into so many short story endings, in fact, may stem not so much from the author's wish to put the story into a clearer focus by means of an abstraction as from the need to elevate the diction at the end, thus giving a signal, as it were, that the work is over. This signal consists of a shift upward, as a rule, but a shift downward is also possible:

> I crushed it into the mud with my foot. In a way you could call it Hunky's epitaph. But even that didn't seem enough. Not by a goddam long shot!
> Hugh Garner, "Hunky"

The shift downward is naturally easier to accomplish if it involves a shift from poetic report to profane speech:

> Low along the prairie sky the dying sunshine lingered, faintly blushing the length of one lone, grey cloud there. The Ben said:
> "Let that there goddamn owl go."
> W. O. Mitchell, "The Owl and the Bens"

The effect is often heightened by letting the speech contain one of the other techniques of closure – an epanaleptic utterance, for instance, or a shift into comment.

An examination of how *syntax* is used to signalize a closing can be based on the four kinds of syntax available:

normal
inverted
elaborated
fragmentary

The assumption here, as in the discussion of diction, is that the stylistic phenomena which will interest us consist of deviations from the norm. Thus inverted syntax can appear especially at the end of a story to heighten the effect:

> ... a goodly procession, *besides neighbours not a few* [my italics], they carved no hopeful verse upon his tombstone, for his dying hour was gloom.
> Nathaniel Hawthorne, "Young Goodman Brown"

Or the syntax can be *elaborated* (we have quoted a number of examples (Hawthorne, Hardy, Lawrence, Fitzgerald) or *fragmented*:

> Ah Bartleby! Ah humanity! (Melville)
> But ah, the storms they had come through! (Lowry)
> That fool Cooper! (Maugham)
> The Corams against the world. (Pritchett)

In each case it is not so much the kind of syntactical deviation that counts, but the fact of the deviation from what came before.

As to *rhetoric*, the ways in which authors use it to celebrate the story's conclusion are as multitudinous as the rhetorical figures themselves. Only a few examples can be given here. In general favour are all forms of repetition (my italics):

> anaphora: *Spoilt* their evening! *Spoilt* their being alone together! They would never be alone together again.
> Katherine Mansfield, "The Stranger"

> epistrophe: And now, had it all come *to an end*? It had all come foolishly *to an end*.
> Conrad Aiken, "Impulse"

> symploce: *Now that thing is gone, that thing is gone*, I cannot cry. I cannot care. That thing will come back no more.
> F. Scott Fitzgerald, "Winter Dreams"

epizeuxis: *Spare me, spare* me your consolations, they are unavailing to a sorrow such as mine!

Mrs Gore, "Dorathea"

Next to these and other forms of repetition in frequency is a variety of plays with conjunctions. One convention, namely the final clause with *and*, is so natural that it is perhaps not to be counted a deviation at all, except that it often effects an elegiac, solemn close:

. . . and they sing ballads no more.

Thomas H. Raddall, "Blind MacNair"

. . . and was afraid to sleep again.

Katherine Anne Porter, "Flowering Judas"

. . . and they felt that they could then be interpreters.

Stephen Crane, "The Open Boat"

In each case, we should note, the effect of the statement is to comment on how the past connects with or is contrasted to the present: it is the effect of a final glide, not quite open, not quite closed: a variety of the Janus-faced conclusion.

Of the 600 stories surveyed here, 85 end with an and-clause, whereby these were counted only where they occurred after a full stop, a semi-colon or a dash. Another 34 stories end with but-clauses. Clearly this is one of the durable *topoi* of narrative endings. It is almost as popular in the novel: we find it in Defoe, Fielding, Walpole, Radcliffe, Austen, and Charlotte Bronte.

Where the final sentence begins with *and*, a variety of effects is gained, but they have in common the tone of after-thought — that is, of a conclusion which does not loudly proclaim itself as such. The effect is more *closed*, of course, where a character's death is involved:

And when he had lived long, and was borne to the grave . . .

Nathaniel Hawthorne, "Young Goodman Brown"

With the appropriate diction, the closing sentence with *and* can assume a biblical flavour:

And I was Penitent; for in my heart I had always despised him a little.

James Joyce, "An Encounter"

The use of a final sentence with *and* as a conclusion-signal is a favourite of Joyce's and also of Katherine Mansfield. The latter uses it twice in twist-in-the tail endings:

Blushing more crimson than ever, but looking at her severely he said, almost angrily: 'Excuse me, Mademoiselle, you dropped this.'

And he handed her an egg.

Katherine Mansfield, "Feuille D'Album"

He stopped, he turned. But when she saw his timid, puzzled look, she gave a little laugh.
"Come back, Mr Dove," said Anne. And Reginald came slowly across the lawn.

Katherine Mansfield, "Mr and Mrs Dove"

(Reginald's response to Anne indicates his step toward a liaison which had seemed doomed.) Again, these are Janus-faced endings. The excision of the *and* would in each case make for a more abrupt ending. Certainly each *and* suggests that the action is closely connected to what has come before, but this is not inevitably its function:

And now it began to rain.

Katherine Mansfield, "Life of Ma Parker"

Here the final sentence seems a mere afterthought, which might have been used to introduce a further action. The *and* reduces the effect of an otherwise open ending because it has the character of a much-used formula: in Labov and Waletzky's transcriptions of oral narratives, twelve out of fourteen transcriptions include as one of the final sentences a beginning with *and*.[6] Thus such an ending goes hand in hand with the other closing-techniques already discussed, as in the following:

And Geraldine lay awake, dreaming that death had closed the last door in the old house.

Anne Hébert, "The House on the Esplanade"

To be considered here is the use of the participle ("dreaming"), the alliteration ("dreaming . . . death . . . door"), the death-theme, the use of a virtual mode ("dreaming that"), and the non-scenic report which amounts, taken together with the preceding section not quoted here, to a tableau. In other words, the *and*-sentence is part and parcel of a set of conventions used in story closings.

Unlike the final clause with *and*, the final sentence with *and* is more patently a stylistic deviation which has come to be accepted as a narrative convention – which is not to say that it is used as such consciously. It is a convention of long standing: if one cuts the *and* away from "And they lived happily ever after" one retains a dry and unsatisfying conclusion which violates some kind of unspoken law, a law which is of course much older than the form of the short story itself.

If degrees of stylistic variation could be measured, the *and*-sentence would certainly be more deviant, though sanctioned by convention, than the *and*-clauses. The latter occur in every story, the *and*-sentence is often used only once, and then at the very end. An in-between status is probably held by the final *and*-sentence after a semicolon:

> . . . ; and the tears of remorse started to his eyes.
>
> > James Joyce, "A Little Cloud"

> . . . ; and my eyes burned with anguish and anger.
>
> > James Joyce, "Araby"

> . . . ; and his eyes filled up so much with tears . . .
>
> > James Joyce, "Clay"

The reference to *eyes* is a chance finding which results from our narrow focus on story endings and cannot be gone into here, except to note that we will find it once more just below in the quotation from Joyce's "Eveline". Relevant, however, is the finding that of the fourteen stories in Joyce's *Dubliners*, nine conclude with some special use of a conjunction.

Although the conclusion with *and* apparently goes back to a convention of oral narrative, it appears in the short story almost exclusively in the modes of report and description. The only example in the mode of speech in our sample of 600 stories is that of Sir A. T. Quiller-Couch's "A Pair of Hands", but even there the final sentence only happens to be the end of a story told by a fictive narrator, and is thus no clear example of a final *and*-sentence in dialogue.

Almost as frequent a narrative convention is to end the story with a lack of conjunctions normally to be expected (asyndeton) or a superfluity (polysyndeton):

> asyndeton: So shall he read elder truths, sad truths, fearful truths.
>
> > Thomas de Quincey, "Levana and our Ladies of Sorrow"

> She saw, as plainly as if it had been laid in her arms, her child, her personal angel, white and swaddled, baptized, innocent, ready for death.
>
> > Mavis Gallant, "Bernadette"

> And this time Miss Meadows' voice sounded over all the other voices – full, deep, glowing with expression.
>
> > Katherine Mansfield, "The Singing Lesson"

> Perhaps they promised that there would always be women in the world who would spend their brightest, freshest, rarest hours to nurse and protect that superiority he cherished in his heart.
>
> > F. Scott Fitzgerald, "The Rich Boy"

> polysyndeton: . . . *and* he turned away *and* saw in the shadow of her cheek *and* on her lips and chin the dark rich red of the pulp and juice of the crushed raspberries.
>
> > Hugh Hood, "Flying a Red Kite"

Her eyes gave him no sign of love *or* farewell *or* recognition.

James Joyce, "Eveline" [my italics]

Both asyndetic and polysyndetic structures seem to work best when three lexical units (words, phrases, clauses, sentences) are involved. This, too, is a stylistic convention that may occur anywhere in a prose text, but appears with very high frequency at the end of a story. The play with conjunctions in the conclusion has become a narrative convention and thus a signal to the reader that the author has consciously shaped the language of his final phrases. If we can place the manipulation of conjunctions in a hierarchy of effects, probably we would rate it as a relatively weak one among the techniques of signalling the story's end. For the conjunction can, especially with report, also suggest a continuing action or an afterthought, and thus render more open what would, on other counts, amount to a more closed ending. That depends on the context in each case.

The range of rhetorical figures used to close short stories is almost as wide as that found in poetry, even including forms of parallel and transverse alliteration such as would make an Elizabethan euphuist nod his head in approval. Of course the more common figures are also those most used, especially the ever-popular simile:

Her dark coat fell open, and her white throat – all her soft young body in the blue dress – was *like a flower* that is just emerging from its dark bud.

Katherine Mansfield, "The Young Girl"

There was nothing funny at all. Nothing anywhere. But I poked about for an answer.
"Why, this," I said, holding the bird by its beaded cord. "This, of course."
He looked at it a long time. "Yes," he said, seriously. "Yes, I suppose it is quaint," and he smiled.
It was *as though* a pearl was smiling.

P. K. Page, "The Green Bird"

And they caught the rhythym, and the faith, and the new words, Mammii Ama straightened her plump shoulders. *Like a royal palm* she stood, rooted in magnificence, spreading her arms *like fronds*, to shelter the generations.

Margaret Laurence, "A Gourdful of Glory"
[my italics]

In this last example we also see once more the polysyndetic structure of "And they caught . . . and . . . and", the final elevation of style register and the touch of comment in the diction ("magnificence") as well as the purport of the simile, "like a royal palm." Indeed, the piling up of such stylistic deviations toward the end of the story is not unusual:

(parallelism
(conclusion with
and)
(inverted syntax)

And pulseless and cold, with a Derringer
by his side and a bullet in his heart,
though still calm as in life, beneath
the snow lay he who was at once the
strongest and yet the weakest of the
outcasts of Poker Flat.

(parallel
structure:
isocolon)

(parallel structure:
homoioteleuton;
paradox)

— Francis Bret Harte, "The Outcasts of Poker Flat"

Familiar, too, is the conclusion with death, the general elevation of style register in the diction, the elaborated syntax, the panoramic view, the implicit report of events in the mode of description, and the epanaleptic use of the story's title. Such a heaping up of signals which are standard fare in story endings allows little doubt but that this is a closed rather than an open ending.

Finally, there is a kind of ending which has become conventional in the last century: almost one in every ten of the stories surveyed here has an ironic ending. These endings need not be looked at here in detail because most of them take the form of speech rather than report. The ironic endings in report include two that might also be considered as reported speech or thought, both of them from *Dubliners*:

"Come down, dear, Mr Doran wants to speak to you."
Then she remembered what she had been waiting for.
                                    James Joyce, "The Boarding House"

"What do you think of that, Crofton?" cried Mr Henchy. "Isn't that fine? What?"
Mr Crofton said that it was a very fine piece of writing.
                                    James Joyce, "Ivy Day in the Committee Room"

The other three cases are also borderline, since they include reports of a character's mental state or reported speech:

She didn't even recognize him again.
                                    Katherine Mansfield, "Her First Ball"

Small wonder that Ben was credited at the Lamb's Club with that month's most interesting bender.
                                    Ring Lardner, "Liberty Hall"

"Dead a week," said the officer curtly, moving on, mechanically pulling out his watch as if to verify his estimate of time. Six o'clock and forty minutes.
                                    Ambrose Bierce, "One of the Missing"

The final phrase is not, properly speaking, report either, but *substitutionary perception* — what the officer, having mistaken his brother's time of death, sees when he consults his watch.

Even these few examples allow us to draw four conclusions.

1. Irony occurs at the end of a story rather than at the beginning because it normally depends on the discrepancy between a statement and contextual information. The latter is established in the course of the story, and thus provides opportunities for irony not easily available earlier on – although there are stories which introduce irony on the first page, such as some by Ring Lardner and Stephen Leacock.

2. Irony is a special form of rhetorical heightening, which we have already identified as a story-closing signal. Thus it is another of the many techniques which, when used with otherwise open endings, reduces that openness.

3. Irony is easiest to achieve with the mode of speech. Once the story has established the values of the narrator, the character can contradict these values and thus create an irony which the alert reader will recognize. Such irony is most readily achieved by letting the psychology of a character appear in a mode different from that which reveals the ideology of the narrator.[7]

4. The conclusion with irony is a modern development: the quotation from Ambrose Bierce is one of the very few examples which the period before 1890 will yield.

The Open Ending with Report

Our working hypothesis has been that an ending with *report* is potentially of the *open* variety. In practice, however, this hypothesis is not to be substantiated. What we find instead is a variety of influences and techniques which work in the other direction; and where several of them occur, it would seem, they have a cumulative effect. Some of them apply to the static modes as well, but they are of special interest where they counteract the natural tendency of the dynamic modes. The chief ones were:

A. Content: 1. posteriority
             2. death and departure
             3. epanaleptic elements
             4. Janus-headed structures
B. Technique: 1. mix with static modes
             2. panoramic report, tableau
             3. style: diction, register, syntactic deviation, rhetorical effects and tropes, including and-clauses, polysyndeton, etc.
             4. irony

Yet the endings discussed in this section are different from those using *metanarrative* and comment; and we can assume on the part of the authors surveyed a leaning towards open rather than closed endings. Why then are so many elements introduced which tend to neutralize the presumably desired effect of an open ending?

One reason may be this: the short story has been thought of since the time of Poe as a form of narrative art in which all the parts have a function, all of them subservient to the central effect. Openings and closings have been observed to be especially functional, economic.[8] As soon as the critic thinks he sees how the end of the story functions, that is, how it may be related meaningfully to that which came before, he sees it as an arrow pointing back into the story; he integrates it into the total plan, and thus interprets it, rightly or wrongly, as a neatly tied bow on the bouquet. As Parker and Binder argue in a recent study of Melville and Mark Twain, "however uncomfortable a bolus it proves, almost any ending can be swallowed by a modern critic determined to prove the unity of a novel . . ."[9] This is perhaps more true of the reader of a short story, which is generally, rightly or wrongly, presumed to have a tighter structure than a novel requires. To grasp the ending of a story as totally open, the reader would have to see it as a blind alley or an excrescence, a useless extension outside the narrative economy; in other words, artistically inferior. No writer will want to write such an ending; at least, not deliberately. As in language generally, narrative aspires to a grammaticality which no author will wish casually to violate. So there are no really open endings in our anthology pieces: if there were, they would be *bad* pieces. And yet, the open ending seems to be a modern ideal.

One way out of this paradox is that the writer uses speech for the story ending. For the narrator can attribute ill-formed, narratologically ungrammatical utterances to his figures which he might not want to attribute to himself. He can pour into the mold of speech a variety of irrelevancies. Whether he will wish to do so is another matter, for of course the ventriloquist is fully responsible, though less obviously, for what his puppets say.

The ending which reports a seemingly insignificant or an irrelevant action poses a special problem for the critic. For if he labels such an ending as open, he so much as proclaims that for him the final sentences of the story are meaningless, or at least uninterpretable. Consider the following example:

> Ethel did not check his babbling. She was aghast at the narrowness of the escape, and for a long time kept silence. At last she said: "Such a marvellous deliverance does make one believe in Providence."
>
> Mr Lucas, who was still composing his letter to the landlord, did not reply.
>
> E. M. Forster, "The Road from Colonus"

It is indeed not easy to make out what effect Forster meant to achieve with this ending. Is it perhaps a story designed to point out the senility of old Mr Lucas; or is the utterance of his daughter so naively sentimental that her father sees fit to ignore it? This reading would suggest that the events on the road to Colonus were a merely natural disaster, a fact which Forster points up by ironically attributing to Ethel a silly and irrelevant judgment. We cannot be sure. So the critic who claims to have found a genuinely open ending is in effect confessing his inability to interpret it. If he is later given a plausible explanation for that ending, he will probably reclassify it as closed. In other words, the openness or closedness of an ending is only in part a property of the text. It is also in part a function of the reader's response.

Endings with Speech

Speech, as we have shown, can include all the other modes. It does not seem to include *metanarrative*, of course: why would a figure in a story refer to the story in which he appears? At most he might refer to a story if he has himself been telling it:

> "Faith, sir," replied the story-teller, "As to that matter, I don't believe one-half of it myself."
>
> Washington Irving, "The Legend of Sleepy Hollow"

And a modern story is certainly conceivable in which a character, as in Pirandello's play, would set out in search of a short story to contain him. But that would be merely an exception to prove the rule.

Speech that conveys comment is of two kinds: straight and ironic. In the first case the figure acts as a mouthpiece for the narrator. It is certainly significant that such a choric use of speech conveying comment is hardly a twentieth century phenomenon:

> "O, deep is the ploughing of grief! But oftentimes less would suffice for the agriculture of God. Upon a night of earthquake he builds a thousand years of pleasant habitations for man. Upon the sorrows of an infant he raises oftentimes from human intellects glorious vintages that could not else have been. Less than these fierce ploughshares would not have stirred the stubborn soil. The one is needed for earth, our planet, — for earth itself as the dwelling place of man; but the other is needed yet oftener for God's mightiest instrument, — yes" (and he looked solemnly at myself), "is needed for the mysterious children of the earth!"
>
> Thomas De Quincey, "Savannah-La-Mar"

> We drove a quarter of a mile or so in silence, and when we had gone thus far Lady Troughton made what appeared to me to be the only remark that could possibly be made. "Poor little goose!" said Lady Troughton.
>
> Anthony Hope, "The Prince Consort"

Even here there is a trace of irony as well. In our age, however, the ironic comment is a standard technique for closing the story:

> The girl gazed at him as if through a window at a new discovered sky, "Yes, yes, in Government charge — of course, I'll do anything." Suddenly she caught Bing's hand and kissed it. "God sent you to me."
>
> Joyce Cary, "Government Baby"

> "Who did it to you, Mr Schwartz?"

Maurie wept.
"Anti-Semeets," Edie said later.

Bernard Malamud, "The Jewbird"

Whereas "poor little goose!" is an intentionally ironic comment made by a fictional figure, "God sent you to me" and "Anti-Semeets" are seriously meant statements which happen to be at odds with what we have learned in the story. This technique, which demands a more subtle judgment of the reader, is the more common one in the modern short story. Oddly enough, almost none of the novels surveyed make use of the effect.

Where irony results from the narrator's treatment of his materials, the usual mode is comment, less obvious are ironic report and description. Where irony results from a discrepancy between the narrator's views and those of a character, the usual mode of the character is speech: the character says what the narrator indicates to be mistaken, exaggerated, or even ridiculous. Or the character is simply unreliable or naive. We come to realize this either because we can compare what the character thinks to what we know of the world or on the basis of discrepancies between the presumably reliable narrator and one or more of the characters. Some of the possible configurations of reliability are as follows:

		narrator	character	
both are reliable	1	+	+	consonant
one is reliable	2	+	−	dissonant
one is reliable	3	−	+	dissonant
both are unreliable	4	−	−	?

Consonances and dissonances arise not only on the basis of differing reliability but also morality, religious persuasion, political belief, sympathy and so forth. There can be cross-currents too. We may find Jane Austen's Emma unreliable but sympathetic, Mr Knightley reliable but unsympathetic. But let us stay with reliability/unreliability as the yardstick for a moment. Type 1 is standard fare in fiction and can be called *consonant narration*: both narrator and character are more or less trustworthy. Types 2 and 3 are more interesting. Type 2 is normal − we trust the narrator if there is no marked evidence that we should not. Type 3 is less usual, for it is difficult for a narrator to shape a reliable character and at the same time plant evidence in his own work to shed doubt on his own words. Yet the trick is in fact manageable even in first-person narration, where one might think it impossible: in Goldsmith's *The Vicar of Wakefield* the Vicar includes in his story traces of contradictory evidence, so that the reader comes to know more about the characters than does the narrator himself. Thus the Vicar reports a conversation which allows the reader to see that Mr Burchell is Squire Thornhill in disguise, a fact to which the narrator himself is blind. Another classical example is Ford Madox Ford's *The Good Soldier*. In each of these works we are made aware of dissonances because information contained in one of the submodes of speech is contradicted by information transported by another.

As to type 4, it might seem to constitute a quite empty set. For if both narrator and character are unreliable, the work would seem incapable of presenting a vantage point from which to judge their unreliability. But as early a novel as the first version of Gascoigne's *The Adventures Passed by Master F. J.* of 1573 includes a narrator who pretends to publish the adventures of a friend whose reliability the narrator himself calls into question. At the end of the story the narrator-editor throws aspersions on his own "thriftlesse historie". So we can trust neither the informant, who shows himself to be a casuistical hypocrite, nor the narrator pretending to tell the story. The multiple unreliability, one should add, does not add up to consonance as does multiple reliability, but rather to a multiple dissonance. Even the final words in the mode of metanarrative, the mode least open to query, casting aspersions on itself in mock modesty as it does, is obviously open to doubt.

If a final word is to cast doubts on how the preceding narrative is to be taken, it tends to appear in our day in the mode of speech rather than metanarrative or comment. Altogether almost a third of the 600 stories surveyed here end with speech, although only a tenth of them begin with it. Sometimes the closing speech presents the climax of the story, sometimes it formulates the message or calls that which preceded it in question. It tends to include some of the formal signals typical of story endings in the other modes. If often begins with the conjunctions *and* or *but*, as though the final words of the story were a mere afterthought, it tends to be very short and to take the form of a question.

The increasing popularity of the closing with speech is shown by the fact that only 2% of the novels before 1700 end in this mode, whereas it is 20% of our pre-1900 short stories and almost 40% of the post-1900 sample. To understand this phenomenon, we have to consider several other facts:

1. The incidence of speech has gone up in this century altogether: from 8% in the beginnings of stories published before 1900 to over 20% in the Anglo-American story after 1900 and in the body of the stories themselves,[10] as well as in the endings.
2. The rise of speech in endings has been gained at the expense of the static modes, which supplied just over half of all endings before 1900 and only a quarter in the modern period.

These changes may have a number of different causes. The beginning with metanarrative or comment was natural enough in renaissance story-telling, where deductive thought-processes were the rule. Apparently it seemed "natural" to begin with a general statement and then proceed to illustrate it. In many a story influence by the Italian conventions of story-telling (as in the voluminous collection of William Painter, *The Palace of Pleasure*), the story is often presented as a mere *exemplum*: the narrative illustration of a moral principle. The conclusion, then, took the form of a summarizing statement or a *dubbio*: throwing the question open to the supposed audience.[11] This is a narrative convention which the story has retained more tenaciously than has the novel. The obvious form of it was widespread and (we might now think) a little heavy-handed in the nineteenth century:

> Does it not argue a superintending Providence, that, while viewless and unexpected events thrust themselves continually athwart our path, there should still be regularity enough in mortal life to render foresight even partially available?
>
> Nathaniel Hawthorne, "David Swan"

The *dubbio* in our time is more likely to take another form: it is briefer, studded with fewer abstractions which belong to comment, and imputed to the speech of a fictional figure. But the story it ends may be just as much in the *dubbio*-line; and just as strongly reveal the question as a *closing* gambit:

> Eloise shook Mary Jane's arm. "I was a nice girl," she pleaded, "wasn't I?"
>
> J. D. Salinger, "Uncle Wiggily in Connecticut"

In the earlier English reception of the *dubbio*-form, of course, the narrator made his intention clear at the very opening, not only the ending, of his story. That made the use of speech unlikely, though not impossible, as the opening mode.

In the eighteenth and nineteenth centuries we find a further hindrance to the use of speech, especially to open a story. By and large the narrative was *synthetic* rather than *analytic*: it devolved from a set of premises in logical and chronological order, rather than from a puzzle to be solved. It is logical and "natural" that we have first a speaker, then his speech. The other way around – speech first, and later a revelation as to who had spoken – would seem a rhetorical *hysteron proteron*: an illogical, communicatively illformed sequence likely to confuse the reader, or at any rate to demand more of his attention and acuity. And the *ending* with speech was the exception rather than the rule for another set of reasons: for one thing, it was not thought necessary to conceal the presence of a narrator; for another, the vogue for open endings is a post-Victorian development, with some notable exceptions; and finally, the ending with speech prohibits a number of rhetorical flourishes which were standard technique. Frank Kermode suggests that there are "period rules for endings"[12] and perhaps he has in mind some of the *topoi* discussed above. Direct colloquial speech practically prohibits several of the *topoi* which the earlier "period rules" demanded:

– the quasi-obligatory raising of the style register,

– the epanaleptic close,
– the extended use of asyndetic or polysyndetic elements, and
– the closing tableau.

Any and all of these are theoretically possible with direct speech. But in practice they seem to demand the static modes or narratorial report.

On the other hand, the ending with speech goes hand in hand with another set of *topoi*, which seems to constitute a further set of "period rules". One of these *topoi* is the penchant for syntactic fragments (like "By when?" or "Tonight") in contrast to the usual well-formedness of story beginnings and of endings in the narrator's own voice. Another is the brevity of the final sentence. Over 15% of our stories end with a sentence of five words or less, and most of these endings are in the mode of speech or in first-person narration. The rate for the Canadian short story is 20%.[13] Only 3% of the beginnings of stories are as short. In fact, the story openings that are often quoted by critics are short, although not quite short enough to be included in our figure of 15%, since some of them contain more than five words:

I am a rather elderly man.

Herman Melville, "Bartleby"

None of them knew the color of the sky.

Stephen Crane, "The Open Boat"

And after all the weather was ideal.

Katherine Mansfield, "The Garden Party"

Soon now they would enter the Delta.

William Faulkner, "Delta Autumn"

These examples are drawn equally from the period before 1900 and after, as are the *very* short beginnings (five words or less). The short concluding sentence, by contrast, is found in only 3% of the pre-1900 stories. The brief and snappy conclusion, in other words, has become a convention of the modern story. It is almost never used in the novel before 1900, and only rarely in the novel of our day: some exceptions are Forster's *A Passage to India*, Cheever's *The Wapshot Chronicle* and Bellow's *Herzog*.

Like the ending with report, the final speech tends to include a negation: the words *ever* and *never* are favourites with some authors but simple *nos* and *nots* predominate. The query "Isn't it, darling?" at the end of Mansfield's "The Garden Pary" is thus an agglomeration of the modern closing *topoi*:

1. speech
2. five words or less
3. question
4. syntactic fragment
5. negation

What is missing is the inception with "and" or "but", the irony that direct speech at the close so often expresses, and the use of one of the virtual modes. The latter frequently occurs with an ironic twist in *virtual speech*:

And with that strange power of imagination that was peculiarly his own, he could already hear her whispering over his grave, "Oh, how splendid of you . . . how noble!"

Arthur Schnitzler, "The Death of a Bachelor"

Or in *virtual thought*:

. . . ; but they were both in such a state, for different reasons, that neither of them thought it strange.

Mavis Gallant, "Acceptance of Their Ways"

The increasing use of the virtual forms of speech has taken place by a gradual usurpation of thought and substitutionary perception as well. Probably they tend to occur at the ends of stories because these modes yield poetic effects, attracting to themselves metaphorical language, psychological speculation and the spinning out of fanciful dream visions. When these visions take on an extended life of their own, we can hardly call them submodes of speech any more. There occurs a kind of break-through beyond speech, thought and substitutionary perception to a realm of the character's own making, which includes substitutionary report, perhaps even a whole world of substitutionary narration:

In her mind's eye she is always advancing, she is walking between lanes of trees on a June day. She is small and slight in her dreams, as she is in life. She advances toward herself, as if half of her were a mirror. In the vision she carries Ruth, her prettiest baby, newly born, or a glass goblet, or a bunch of roses.

Mavis Gallant, "Malcolm and Bea"

Occasionally in modern narrative, in other words, the quantity of virtual modes used results in a new quality of narration, which theorists of socalled "postmodernist" narrative have given such terms as "surfiction"[14] and "fabulation".[15] The fictional figure generates a second-stage fiction of his own, and this is on occasion so extended that such a term as *reported thought* no longer seems applicable. Compared to the novel, however, the short story of the 1970's has only a little to offer in the postmodernist way. It is too early to say whether the new fashion will be replaced by another one before the short story is greatly influenced, or if the short story will eventually follow the most recent developments of the novel. If it does, our model of the submodes of speech may require extension. At the moment, even where patches of "fabulation" occur to grace the ending of a story, the submodes I have suggested seem adequately to encompass most of the phenomena to be registered. Such outbreaks of substitutionary narration as occur at the ends of stories may be subsumed under the umbrella of "poetic" effects with which story endings are signalled. That these may give us the sense of the higher style registers associated with the closed ending of a story is nothing especially new.

I have noted that almost a third of the stories I have analyzed end with speech. Together with the endings in report about 62% (374 out of 600) of the stories therefore end with one of the dynamic modes. The figure would be higher did not about a quarter of the stories chosen carry a publication date before 1900. Whether the dominance of the dynamic modes constitutes progress in narrative technique is another question. Enough stories of the 1970's contain so much comment and even straight passages of metanarrative that we must question the continuing popularity of report and speech. Perhaps a turn has already taken place. It is not the purpose of this survey to venture a definite judgement, but only to offer a seismograph to register such quakes and eruptions of story-telling practice as have taken place in recent generations.

Conclusion: Novel and Short Story

The narrative modes are fundamental categories of narration. It is a cliché of Anglo-American criticism that categorization is a waste of time – worse, that its pursuit deadens the critic to a sense of the uniqueness of a work of art. But categories can be glasses through which not only the general law but also the particular phenomenon can be discovered. For the critical process, like most attempts at definitions, works by going alternately in two directions: first classification, then differentiation. That, at least, has been our method here: first to reduce, to simplify, to see the phenomenon as the example of a category; second, to look at different manifestations of that category, paying homage to the particular.

The object of gross groupings, then, is to allow a subtle differentiation which would not otherwise have been possible. This means viewing criticism as an empirical science, which seeks to discover laws generally applicable, and then as an art, confronted by a flux of individual manifestations of that law. The results are those of close textual analysis generally: the attempt to simplify reveals unsuspected complexities. If one may speak of a grammar of narrative competence, that grammar, like the grammar which linguists explore, is found to contain a number of rules hitherto uncodified, but also to hint at a further set of rules which our analysis cannot, or cannot yet, hope to codify. So the attempt to simplify also results in a new sense of the complexity of texts. Then too, laws make criminals. The very statement of a law, such as "stories begin with descriptions of landscapes and people, but not of things", is an open invitation to the writer looking for new ways to break with traditional practice. A statement of the categories of narrative grammar is a form of generative grammar, pointing to "empty sets" waiting to be filled. Most will be fillable by novelists and by short story writers. But perhaps not all of them.

The debate is now a century and a half old whether a short story is the same as a novel, only shorter, or inherently a different genre with its own rules, a thesis stated most forcefully by Brander Mathews in 1883 and in a number of published variants in 1885, 1888 and 1901.[1] It is contained in Poe's theory of the short story, but his definitions are also of doubtful validity. Even his dictum, that the nature of the short story derives from the fact that it can be read at a single sitting, is questionable. An avid reader confronted by a novel that appeals to him may well read it to the end practically without interruption. The so-called "explosive principle",[2] the idea that the story will depict a turn of fate,[3] the rule that it be devoted to a single predominating incident[4] are all correct, and provable with suitable examples. But each principle can be rendered null and void by citing counter examples. The simpler definitions encompass certain tendencies only, but not binding laws.[5] Even the compilers of the *Short Story Index*[6] pay lip service to the conventional definition, which has it that every short story worthy of the name is a carefully constructed and imaginative fiction which gives the reader a unity of impression; but then they proceed to list over 11,000 stories written within a five-year period! What, indeed, are we to do with short fictions which do not meet a notional definition of the short story as a work of art? For there is in fact now no current term for a short fiction which is not a short story. So the compilers of the *Index* really have no choice but to include everything, as they themselves also indicate, that is more than two and less than 150 pages long. Evidently the careful definitions of the critics who refuse to call every tale a short story are not taken too seriously. Short story anthologists with reputations at stake go so far as to take excerpts from novels and include them in current story collections,[7] and no one seems to notice or mind.

We can, however, formulate a simple definition of the short story which will accept everything in the *Short Story Index*, insofar as excerpts from novels have not been allowed to creep in by mistake, and will reject such stories-after-the-fact as cuttings from memoirs: a short story is a complete narrative normally too short to be published by itself.[8] Thus a long short story such as Hemingway's *The Old Man and the Sea* is excluded but a novella-like piece usually reprinted in an anthology or collection like Henry James' "The Turn of the Screw" is included.

The division may seem arbitrary, and it may seem materialistic insofar as it depends on the history and conditions of printing: the size of a printer's sheet and the usual methods of folding it prevent a publisher from producing a book of less then 16 leaves or 32 pages, and the costs of marketing and distribution make 32 or even 64 pages problematical, 128 or 256 pages more likely. The 6000 to 8000 words, which was the usual limit in the heyday of the Victorian period and which is now rather longer than average, meant 20 to 25 pages of text. This is too little for separate publication. Thus our arbitrary definition reflects the conditions of the market with which short story writers have been confronted for 150 years and which has constituted for them a norm and a framework within which the genre has in fact developed and thrived.

No doubt this limitation of length has brought with it other limitations which tend to be observed: a limited cast of characters, a restricted time scheme, a single action or at least only a few separate actions, and a unity of technique and tone (but with some notable exceptions, like Salinger's "For Esmé with Love and Squalor") that the novel is rather less likely to maintain. Then too, a short story has no subplot – but this point is equally useless for a definition, since few novels have subplots either. There is no single ingredient of the many short story definitions other than its form of publication that cannot be claimed for countless novels as well.

The examination of how the narrative modes are used in both novels and short stories can add a few points as to how the two differ. Since the novel can afford a fuller exposition, because of a wider cast of characters and a more extended time scheme, it is a little more likely to use the static modes in the opening passages (see Appendix B). As to the special techniques of exposition discussed in Chapter VI, the novel and the short story can be clearly distinguished. 87% of the 600 short stories use either the technique of habituality or anteriority or both of them at the beginning, as opposed to only 51% of the 300 novels. The technique of the pronoun without a referent in the first paragraph is to be found in 13% of the stories, but only in 7% of the novels. Again, these differences reflect tendencies only, not absolute distinctions between the two genres.

The inner views which interior monologue and narrated monologue allow tend to be restricted to a single person in the short story, whereas the inner view shifts more readily in a longer narrative. But there are short stories, and they are not only the shorter ones, which give narrated monologue to more than one character, such as Lawrence's "The Horse Dealer's Daughter", Joyce's "The Boarding House" and Maugham's "The Force of Circumstance" and "The Outstation". So the attribution of inner views to several characters is no monopoly of the novel. It is also a tendency of the short story as opposed to the novel to end with some form of speech, which the novels examined here do to a lesser extent: 13% of the novels as opposed to 32% of the short stories. Why this should be so is hard to say.

The short story also cleaves to some of the conventions of closure discussed in Chapters VII and VIII as the novel does not. The story is more likely to end with a descriptive sentence (16% as opposed to 9%). The closing sentence of five words or less is used in 17% of our stories, but in only 8% of the novels. When the final sentence of the story is longer, it is three to four times as likely to be cast in a polysyndetic structure (11% as opposed to 3%).

On the other hand, it seems perfectly obvious that we could expect short stories to end more often with an epanalepsis, a repetition of something in its title or its exposition. For we are more likely to remember the beginning when we come to the end of a short story, whereas the novelist cannot expect to gain an effect by a verbal echo on page 400 of a sentence on the first page. For the novelist cannot assume, avid novel consumers to the contrary, that many of his readers will digest his work at a single sitting. Even if the reader did this, he would hardly remember at the end exactly how the first chapter began. And it is true that 8.3% of our 600 stories use epanalepsis, but over 5.3% of our 300 novels do so as well, and the figure for novels of the last forty years is 22%! So our logical expectations are not supported by the facts. Either the reader is assumed to have quite a good memory after all, or novelists think of the novel as an artful structure too, and construct their conclusions accordingly.

Short stories tend to ironic endings, which novels do not. Novels, by contrast, end in weddings: almost all of the classics of the English novel do, whereas a wedding at the end of the short story is a most unusual exception. Probably the short story does not permit the back and forth, the advances and the hindrances, usual to the development of a love affair leading to marriage.

Death, on the other hand, can come without long preparations, in fiction as in reality. Thus it is frequent at the end of the short story (16.6%), but even more so in novels (32%). Novels do, after all, tend to less open endings than do short stories: the *dubbio* is simply not a conclusion commensurate with the job the modern novel seems normally to set itself to do. For short stories pose questions, novels usually depict complex situations and answer questions, or at least pretend to. In contrast to the short story, then, the novel that ends with a question mark is the exception.

On balance, then, our examination of the narrative modes suggests some essential differences between the novel and the short story. But it brings us no closer to a watertight definition of the one genre that is inapplicable to the other – except for the usual form of publication.

Some slight contribution to a differentiation is also made by a list of subgenres based on modes and submodes. We noted in Chapter II that the subgenres are generally named according to the objects of description and, to a lesser extent, the kind of report. Most of these subgenres are valid for both the novel and the short story. It is true that the label may normally designate the one of the other but not both; thus we have in conventional parlance the "historical novel" but no "historical story". Yet so many stories by Poe, Hawthorne and Crane belong to this subgenre that it seems a happenstance of criticism that the term is not applied to short stories as well as to novels.

If we list the kinds of fiction which critics mention, we find that many of them are governed by the kind of person depicted in the story, with the kind of action second in importance, the time third, and the place last:

Table: Tradition subgenres of fiction

Kind of Fiction	description			report
	place	person	time	
Love story		*		*
Detective story, detective novel		*		*
Science fiction			*	*
Women's fiction		*		
Silver fork novel	*	*		
Novel of adolescence		*		
Story of initiation		*		*
Artist's novel (Künstlerroman)		*		
War novel, war story	*	*		*
Proletarian fiction (Arbeiterrroman)		*		
Political fiction				*
The western	*	*		*
Gothic novel, gothic tale	*	*	*	*
Novel of colonial life	*	*	*	
Novel of prairie life	*	*		

Kind of Fiction	description			report
	place	person	time	
Novel of adventure, adventure story				*
Novel of adultery				*
Subgenres usually applied to the novel only:				
Bildungsroman				*
Entwicklungsroman		*		*
Country house novel	*			
Discussion novel				*
Utopia			*	
Academic novel	*	*		
Subgenres usually applied to short forms only:				
Ghost story		*		*
Folk tale		*	*	
Local colour story	*			
Dialect story				
Horror story				
Story of suspense				

It is notable that only the last three terms cannot be marked on the chart: the dialect story is named after the kind of speech used, the story of horror and suspense on the kind of effect which the story is to have on the reader. A different category altogether, that of the literary value of the work, is involved in the terms "magazine story", "pulp fiction", "literature of use" (*Gebrauchs-literatur*), and, at least according to John Wain, "novelette".[9]

One would think that some genre terms would have been generated by the kinds of comment with which story beginnings and endings were once so often provided. For comment often gives the abstract label to the central meaning of the work. There is only the general term, "didactic fiction", which is a kind of subgenre, and the French *roman à these*. Beyond this catch-all label, however, one could imagine the "jealousy story", for instance, the "children-are-ungrateful tale" or the "contemplative-life-is-superior novel". But these seem not to exist. Instead, it is those ingredients of fiction which many readers think only peripheral, like the time and place of the action (presumably mere vehicles of the message which the story was meant to transport), which give us our traditional categories.

Short story and novel, then, overlap. In most of the sections of this study it was unnecessary to differentiate between them: the chief uses of the modes and submodes have proven to be identical. For both story and novel the categories offered by the idea of the narrative modes are tools which help us discover more exactly the forms and techniques of narrative.

Notes

Notes to the Preface

1 Terence Hawkes, *Structuralism and Semiotics* (London, 1977), esp. p. 61.
2 Malcolm Bradbury, *Possibilities: Essays on the State of the Novel* (London, 1973), p. 292.

Notes to Chapter I, "Theories of Narrative Modes" (pages 1 to 17)

1 Terence Hawkes, *Structuralism and Semiotics* (London, 1977), p. 87.
2 Susan Suleiman, "Ideological Dissent from Works of Fiction," *Neophilologus*, 60 (1976), 162–177.
3 Jeffrey J. Folks, "The Influence of Poetry on the Narrative Technique of Faulkner's Early Fiction," *Journal of Narrative Technique*, 9 (1979), 185.
4 Stephen M. Ross, " 'Voice' in Narrative Texts: The Example of *As I Lay Dying*," *PMLA*, 94 (1979), 300f.
5 George Watson, *The Story of the Novel* (London and Basingstoke, 1979), pp. 42–44.
6 Robert Petsch, *Wesen und Formen der Erzählkunst* (Halle/Saale, 1934), pp. 166–185.
7 R. Koskimies, *Theorie des Romans* (Helsinki, 1935), pp. 187–206.
8 Wolfgang Kayser, *Das sprachliche Kunstwerk*, 10th ed. (Bern and Munich, 1964), pp. 182–186.
9 Eberhard Lämmert, *Bauformen des Erzählens* (Stuttgart, 1955), pp. 86–89.
10 Lämmert, p. 88; W. Wolfgang Holdheim, "Description and Cliché," *Arcadia*, 13 (1978), special issue, p. 1. A similar observation is made by David Lodge in his *Working with Structuralism* (Boston, London & Henley, 1981), p. 39.
11 Uffe Hansen, "Segmentierung Narrativer Texte: Zum Problem der Erzählperspektive in der Fiktionsprosa," *Text & Kontext*, 3.2 (1975), 2–48.
12 Percy Lubbock, *The Craft of Fiction* (London, 1963), pp. 66f.
13 Jerome Thale, "The Imagination of Charles Dickens," *Nineteenth Century Fiction*, 22 (1967/68), pp. 127–143.
14 *English Composition and Rhetoric*, 1967, quoted in James L. Kinneavy, *A Theory of Discourse* (Englewood Cliffs, 1971), p. 28.
15 Kinneavy, p. 28.
16 Seymour Chatman, "The Structure of Fiction," *University of Kansas City Review*, 37 (1971), 190–214.
17 Seymour Chatman, "The Structure of Narrative Transmission," in *Style and Structure in Literature*, ed. R. Fowler (Oxford, 1975), pp. 213–257.
18 Chatman, "Structure of Narrative Transmission," p. 238.
19 Chatman, "Structure of Narrative Transmission," p. 239.

20 Norman Friedman, "Point of View in Fiction," *PMLA*, 70 (1955), 1160–1184.
21 Paul Hernadi, "Verbal Worlds Between Action and Vision: A Theory of the Modes of Poetic Discourse," *College English*, 33 (1971), 18–31.
22 Seymour Chatman, "New Ways of Analyzing Narrative Structure, with an Example from Joyce's *Dubliners*," *Language and Style*, 2 (1969), 3–36.
23 Gerard Genette, "Frontières du récit," in his *Figures II* (Paris, 1969), pp. 49–69.
24 Gerard Genette, "Boundaries of Narrative," *New Literary History*, 8 (1976/77), 1–13; *Narrative Discourse*, tr. Jane E. Lewin (Oxford, 1980).
25 Harald Weinrich, *Tempus* (Stuttgart, 1964).
26 Roman Jakobson, "Linguistics and Poetics," in *Style and Language*, ed. Thomas A. Sebeok (Bloomington, Ind., 1960), pp. 353–357.
27 Norman Page, "Trollope's Conversational Mode," *English Studies in Africa*, 15 (1972), 33–37.
28 David Lodge, *The Modes of Modern Writing* (London, 1977).
29 Josef Warren Beach, *The Twentieth Century Novel, Studies in Technique* (New York, 1932), p. 14.
30 John Dewey, "Thought and its Subject-Matter," in *Studies in Logical Theory* (Chicago, 1903), p. 3.
31 Ernst Leisi, "Der Erzählstandpunkt in der neueren englischen Prosa," in *Aufsätze* (Heidelberg, 1978), pp. 30f.
32 Lubomir Doležel, *Narrative Modes in Czech Literature* (Toronto and Buffalo, 1973), p. 18, fn. 5.
33 Mas'ud Zavarzadeh, *The Mythopoeic Reality: The Postwar American Nonfiction Novel* (Urbana, 1976), pp. 63–65.
34 Helmut Bonheim, "Topoi of the Canadian Short Story,'" *Dalhousie Review*, (1981), 659–669.
35 Franz Link, "'Tale,' 'Sketch,' 'Essay,' und 'Short Story,'" *Die Neueren Sprachen*, 6 (1957), 345–352.
36 Charles Morris, *Signs, Language and Behavior* (1946; rpt. New York, 1955), p. 125.
37 I am indebted here to a similar list of Waltraud Achten in *Psychoanalytische Literaturkritik* (Frankfurt am Main, 1981), pp. 18–19.

Notes to Chapter II, "Mode Chopping" (pages 18 to 36)

1 Cf. H. Bonheim, "Instrumentale Literaturkritik," *Poetica*, 6 (1974), 76–86; "Einige Werkzeuge der instrumentalen Literaturkritik," Anglistik und Englischunterricht, V: *Literatur an der Schule* (Trier, 1978), pp. 43–56.
2 Elizabeth Gülich and Wolfgang Raible, *Linguistische Textmodelle* (Munich, 1977).
3 Gülich and Raible, p. 314.
4 Ibid. The same sort of complaint is voiced by Götz Wienold, "Probleme der linguistischen Analyse des Romans," *Literaturwissenschaft und Linguistik*, ed. Jens Ihwe (Frankfurt, 1972), III, 329.
5 For the negative judgement see David Lodge, *The Modes of Modern Writing* (London, 1977), p. x; Lodge published *Working with Structuralism* in 1981.
6 Gülich and Raible have an excellent chapter surveying the problem of models.
7 An earlier version of this survey of mode markers appeared as "Mode Markers in the American Short Story," *Proceedings of the Fourth International Congress of Applied Linguistics* (Stuttgart, 1976), I, 541–550.
8 The terms are suggested by Dorrit Cohn in "Narrated Monologue: Definition of a Fictional Style," *Comparative Literature*, 18 (1966), 109.

9 See the footnotes to Chapters III and IV.

10 Wolf-Dieter Stempel, "Erzählung, Beschreibung und der historische Diskurs," *Geschichte – Ereignis und Erzählung*, ed. R. Kosellek and W.-D. Stempel (Munich, 1973), pp. 325–346; T. A. van Dijk, "Action, Action Description and Narrative," *New Literary History*, 6 (1974/75), 282.

11 Eberhard Lämmert, *Bauformen des Erzählens* (Stuttgart, 1955), p. 88.

12 Karl Kroeber, *Styles in Fictional Structure* (Princeton, 1971), p. 217.

13 Seymour Chatman, "New Ways of Analysing Narrative Structure, with an Example from Joyce's *Dubliners*," *Language and Style*, II (1969), 22.

14 Seymour Chatman, "The Structure of Fiction," *University of Kansas City Review*, 37 (1971), 207.

15 Chatman, "The Structure of Fiction," 213.

16 Gerard Genette, "Boundaries of Narrative," *New Literary History*, 8 (1976/77), 1–13.

17 For a recent discussion of the theory of description see John R. Searle, *Speech Acts: An Essay in the Philosophy of Language* (Cambridge, 1969, 1977), pp. 157–162.

18 Wolfgang Stegmüller, *Das ABC der modernen Logik und Semantik* (Berlin, 1969), I, 76: "Beschreibungen haben den Charakter erzählender Berichte, in denen entweder eigene Beobachtungen geschildert werden oder in denen über die Wahrnehmungen anderer referiert wird."

19 Robert Liddell, *A Treatise on the Novel* (London, 1947), p. 111.

20 Gerard Genette, "Boundaries of Narrative," 6.

21 Chatman, "New Ways of Analysing Narrative Structure," pp. 4 and 21.

22 Mas'ud Zavarzadeh, *The Mythopoeic Reality: The Postwar American Nonfiction Novel* (Urbana, 1976), pp. 63ff.

23 Over a dozen such figures are listed by Richard Lanham, *A Handlist of Rhetorical Terms* (Berkeley and Los Angeles, 1969), pp. 122f. Examples are given by Sister Miriam Joseph, *Rhetoric in Shakespeare's Time* (New York and Burlingame, 1962), pp. 309–312.

24 David Lodge has a brief survey of such attempts at definition in the opening pages of his *The Modes of Modern Writing* (London, 1977). Other recent studies include Jürgen Landwehr, *Text und Fiktion* (Munich, 1975); S. J. Schmidt, "Towards a Pragmatic Interpretation of Fictionality," in *Pragmatics of Language and Literature*, ed. Teun van Dijk (Amsterdam, 1976), pp. 161–178; Wiklef Hoops, "Fiktionalität als pragmatische Kategorie," *Poetica*, 11 (1979), 281–317.

25 Zavarzadeh, pp. 56f.

26 Hans Robert Jauss, *Literaturgeschichte als Provokation* (Frankfurt, 1970), p. 201.

27 Robert Petsch, *Wesen und Formen der Erzählkunst* (Halle/Saale, 1934), pp. 147f.; R. Koskimies, *Theorie des Romans* (Helsinki, 1935), p. 193.

28 Wolfgang Kayser, *Das sprachliche Kunstwerk* (1948; rpt. Munich, 1964), pp. 185f.

29 O. Schissel von Fleschenberg, "Die Technik des Bildeinsatzes," *Philologus*, 72 (1913), 83–114; E. C. Harlan, *The Description of Paintings as a Literary Device and its Application in Achilles Tatius*, Diss. Columbia 1965.

30 *Encyclopedia Britannica* (New York, 1959), *sub* "Apperception".

31 Robert Ulich in *The Encyclopedia of Philosophy* (New York, 1967), *sub* "Apperception".

32 Rudolph Eisler, *Kant-Lexikon* (Berlin, 1930), *sub* "Apperzeption".

33 Wilhelm Wundt, *Grundriss der Psychologie*, quoted by Ulich.

34 Ramond F. Howes, *Historical Studies of Rhetoric and Rhetoricians* (Ithaca, 1961), p. 88.

35 Fredric Jameson, *The Political Unconscious: Narrative as a Socially Symbolic Act* (London, 1981), pp. 29–32.
36 George Williamson, *The Senecan Amble* (London, 1951), Chapter III.
37 Searle, pp. 138f.
38 For a discussion of the concept of fabulation see Robert Scholes, *The Fabulators* (New York, 1967), *passim*, Manfred Pütz, *The Story of Identity: American Fiction of the Sixties*, American Studies/Amerika Studien, 54 (Stuttgart, 1979), Chapter II, and Raymond Olderman, *Beyond the Waste Land: A Study of the American Novel in the Nineteen-Sixties* (New Haven and London, 1972), pp. 1–29.
39 van Dijk, p. 284.

Notes to Chapter III, "The Modes in Concert" (pages 37 to 49)

1 Karl Kroeber, *Styles in Fictional Structure* (Princeton, 1971), p. 166.
2 J. F. Wallwork, *Language and Linguistics* (London, 1971), p. 140.
3 Seymour Chatman, "The Structure of Narrative Transmission", in *Style and Structure in Literature*, ed. Roger Fowler (Oxford, 1975), p. 239.
4 Percy Lubbock, *The Craft of Fiction* (London, 1921, 1963,) p. 66f.
5 Franz K. Stanzel, *Die typischen Erzählsituationen im Roman* (Vienna and Stuttgart, 1965).
6 Wayne Booth, *The Rhetoric of Fiction* (Chicago, 1961).
7 The concept of narrative/narrated time has been studied in great detail by Günther Müller, *Die Bedeutung der Zeit in der Erzählkunst* (Bonn, 1947) and "Erzählzeit und erzählte Zeit" in *Festschrift für P. Kluckhohn und H. Schneider* (Tübingen, 1948), pp. 195–212. The development of the concept is also surveyed by Eberhard Lämmert in his *Bauformen des Erzählens* (Stuttgart, 1955), pp. 257–258, footnote 12.
8 Eberhard Lämmert, *Bauformen des Erzählens* (Stuttgart, 1955), pp. 82–86.
9 Theodor Wolpers, "Kürze im Erzählen," *Anglia*, 89 (1971), 48–86.
10 Wolpers, 64.
11 Eckard Cwik, *Erzählmodi in der Short Story, 1820–1970*, unpubl. thesis, University of Cologne, 1975.
12 Käthe Friedemann, *Die Rolle des Erzählers in der Epik* (Leipzig, 1910), p. 157.
13 Marshall McLuhan, *Understanding Media* (New York, London, Sydney, Toronto, 1964), chapter 2; Dennis Duffy, *Marshall McLuhan* (Toronto, 1969), pp. 38f.
14 Wolfgang Iser, *Der implizite Leser* (Munich, 1972); *The Implied Reader: Patterns of Communication in Prose Fiction from Bunyan to Beckett* (Baltimore, 1974).
15 Franz K. Stanzel, "Die Komplementärgeschichte: Entwurf einer leserorientierten Romantheorie," *LiLi: Zeitschrift für Literaturwissenschaft und Linguistik*, Beiheft 6, ed. W. Haubrichs, 1977, pp. 240–259.
16 Recent German monographs on reader response theory and research include the introductory survey by Hannelore Link, *Rezeptionsforschung* (Stuttgart, 1976) and an extensive review of earlier work by Bernd Zimmermann, *Literaturrezeption im historischen Prozeß* (Munich, 1977). A theoretical framework as well as a number of examples discussed in detail (German writers influenced by their public as well as their predecessors) are offered by Gunter Grimm, *Rezeptionsgeschichte* (Munich, 1977). Also largely theoretical, despite the title, is Norbert Groeben, *Rezeptionsforschung als empirische Literaturwissenschaft* (Kronberg/Ts., 1977). An extensive empirical study (of what 228 lawyers and 309 pupils read and how they read) is reported by Werner Faulstich, *Domänen der Rezeptionsanalyse* (Kronberg/Ts., 1977). The development of this field of theory in Germany is

surveyed in English by Rien T. Segers, "Some Implications of 'Rezeptionsästhe-tik,'" *Yearbook of Comparative and General Literature*, 24 (1975), 15–23; see also chapter 5 of D. W. Fokkema and Elrud Kunne-Ibsch, *Theories of Literature in the Twentieth Century* (London, 1977), and Steven Mailloux, "Learning to Read: Interpretation and Reader-Response Criticism," *Studies in the Literary Imagination*, 12 (1979), 93–108; a recent collection of "classical" essays in the field, including an annotated bibliography, is *Reader-Response Criticism: From Formalism to Post-Structuralism*, ed. Jane P. Tompkins (Baltimore and London, 1980), which does not, however, do justice to the relevant German work of the 1970's.

17 In the bibliography to his book, Norbert Groeben cites 45 empirical as well as a mass of theoretical and speculative studies.

18 Norman Holland, *5 Readers Reading* (New Haven, 1975).

Notes to Chapter IV, "The Submodes of Speech" (pages 50 to 74)

1 Bernard Fehr, "Substitutionary Narration and Description: A Chapter in Stylistics," *English Studies*, 20 (1938), 97–107.

2 Paul Hernadi, "Dual Perspective: Free Indirect Discourse and Related Techniques," *Comparative Literature*, 24 (1972), 32–43.

3 Norman Page, *Speech in the English Novel* (London, 1973).

4 Judith C. Espinola, "The Nature, Function and Performance of Indirect Discourse in Prose Fiction," *Speech Monographs*, 41 (1974), 193, fn. 3.

5 Wayne Booth, *The Rhetoric of Fiction* (Chicago, 1961), pp. 155–159; and "Distance and Point of View: An Essay in Classification," *Essays in Criticism*, 11 (1961), 60–79.

6 Boris Uspensky, *A Poetics of Composition* (Berkeley and Los Angeles, 1973).

7 Page, p. 35.

8 E. Lorck, Die "Erlebte Rede": *Eine sprachliche Untersuchung* (Heidelberg, 1921).

9 Fehr, p. 97.

10 Quoted in Dorrit Cohn, "Narrated Monologue: Definition of a Fictional Style," *Comparative Literature*, 18 (1966), 100, fn. 9.

11 W. N. Vickery, "Three Examples of Narrated Speech in Pushkin's Poltava," *Slavic and East European Journal*, 8 (1964), 273; Ronald James Lethcoe, *Narrated Speech and Consciousness*, Diss. Wisconsin, 1969.

12 Robert Humphrey, *Stream of Consciousness in the Modern Novel* (Berkeley, 1965), p. 24.

13 Charles Bally, "Le Style indirect libre en français moderne," *Germanisch-Romanische Monatsschrift*, 4 (1912), 549–556 and 597–606.

14 Cohn, "Narrated Monologue" and *Transparent Minds:Narrative Modes for Presenting Consciousness in Fiction* (Princeton, 1978), chapter 3.

15 Roy Pascal, *The Dual Voice* (Manchester, 1977).

16 Page, pp. 34 and 35.

17 Page, p. 32.

18 V. N. Voloshinov, *Readings in Russian Poetics*, ed. L. Matejka and K. Pomorska (Cambridge, Mass., 1971), p. 173.

19 J. Pouillon, *Temps et roman* (Paris, 1946), p. 72.

20 Uspensky, p. 52.

21 Uspensky, p. 51, fn. 59.

22 Vivienne Mylne, "The Punctuation of Dialogue in Eighteenth Century French and English Fiction," *The Library*, sixth series, I (1979), 43–61.

23 Donald Ross, Jr., "Who's Talking? How Characters Become Narrators in Fiction," *Modern Language Notes*, 91 (1976), 1230.
24 Seymour Chatman, "The Structure of Narrative Transmission," in *Style and Structure in Literature*, ed. Roger Fowler (Oxford, 1975), p. 253; and Chatman, *Story and Discourse: Narrative Structure in Fiction and Film* (Ithaca and London, 1978), p. 199.
25 Mylne, cf. fn. 22.
26 Michael Gregory, "Old Bailey Speech in *A Tale of Two Cities*," *Review of English Literature*, 6 (1965), 46.
27 Gregory, p. 55.
28 S. Ullmann, *Style in the French Novel* (Cambridge, 1957).
29 Randolph Quirk, *et al.*, *A Grammar of Contemporary English* (London, 1972), section 3.26.
30 Page, p. 29.
31 Quirk, *et al.*, sections 11.74 and 11.75.
32 For the concept of *voice*, see Gerard Genette, *Narrative Discourse* (Oxford, 1980), pp. 31f, 186–189 and 212–262.
33 Erich Auerbach, *Mimesis* (New York, 1957), pp. 470–471.
34 See the separate list of relevant studies in the bibliography.
35 Gertrude L. Schuelke, "'Slipping' in Indirect Discourse," *American Speech*, 33 (1958), 90–98.
36 Graham Hough, "Narrative and Dialogue in Jane Austen," *Critical Quarterly*, 12 (1970), 214.
37 See Gregory, p. 55, and Dieter Beyerle, "Ein vernachlässigter Aspekt der erlebten Rede," *Archiv für das Studium der neueren Sprachen und Literaturen*, 208 (1972), 350–366.
38 Fehr, p. 98.
39 Wilhelm Bühler, *Die erlebte Rede im englischen Roman* (Leipzig, 1937), p. 153 and Beyerle, p. 360.
40 Hernadi, "Dual Perspective," p. 41.
41 Shari Benstock, "Who Killed Cock Robin? The Sources of Free Indirect Style in *Ulysses*." *Style*, 14 (1980), 264.
42 Fehr, p. 99.

Notes to Chapter V, "Inquits" (pages 75 to 90)

1 Dorrit Cohn, *Transparent Minds* (Princeton, 1978), pp. 63 and 98.
2 Donald Ross, Jr., "Who's Talking? How Characters Become Narrators in Fiction," *Modern Language Notes*, 91 (1976), 1230.
3 Ursula Oomen, "Systemtheorie der Texte," *Folia Linguistica*, 5 (1971), 12–34.
4 Gisela Junke, *Die Formen des Dialogs im frühen englischen Roman*, Diss. Cologne, 1975, p. 135.
5 The greater variety of inquit formula in the nineteenth as opposed to the eighteenth century has been studied by Jaroslav Peprnik, "Reporting Phrases in English Prose," *Brno Studies in English*, 8 (1969), 145–151.
6 Percy Lubbock, *The Craft of Fiction* (London, 1921), p. 62.
7 Barbara Kreifelts, *Eine statistische Stilanalyse zur Klärung von Autorenschaftsfragen*. Diss. Cologne, 1972.
8 The terminology is that of Martin Joos, *The Five Clocks* (New York, 1961).
9 Over sixty years ago it was observed that the anastrophe of the final inquit was no longer altogether acceptable, but it has not, in fact, yet quite died out. Cf. E. Kieckers, "Die Stellung der Verba des Sagens in Schaltesätzen im Griechischen

und in den verwandten Sprachen," *Indogermanische Forschungen*, 30 (1912), 179. The phenomenon of the anastrophe has been reexamined by William P. Bivens, III, "Parameters of Poetic Inversion in English," *Language and Style*, 12 (1979), 13–25.

10 Otto Jespersen, *Essentials of English Grammar* (London, 1933), p. 101. See also G. O. Curme, *A Grammar of the English Language in Three Volumes* (Boston, 1931), III, 348f.

11 Quoted by David H. Hirsch, "Speech Acts or Fluid Language," *Journal of Literary Semantics*, 5 (1976), 15.

Notes to Chapter VI, "Short Story Beginnings" (pages 91 to 117)

1 The "etic/emic" contrast goes back to Kenneth Pike. See Roland Harweg, *Pronomina und Textkonstitution* (Munich, 1968), pp. 152ff.

2 Eckard Cwik, *Erzählmodi in der short story, 1820–1970*, senior thesis, Cologne, 1975.

3 Seymour Chatman, "New Ways of Analysing Narrative Structure, with an Example from Joyce's *Dubliners*," *Language and Style*, 2 (1969), 4.

4 Genette, p. 118.

5 Percy Lubbock, *The Craft of Fiction* (London, 1963).

6 Bronislaw Malinowski, "The Problem of Meaning in Primitive Languages," (1923), in C. K. Ogden and I. A. Richards, *The Meaning of Meaning* (London, 1969), p. 315.

7 Roman Jakobson, "Linguistics and Poetics," in *Style in Language*, ed. Thomas A. Sebeok (Cambridge, Mass., 1960), pp. 350–377.

8 John R. Searle, *Speech Acts: An Essay in the Philosophy of Language* (Cambridge, 1969, 1977).

9 Richard Ohmann, "Instrumental Style: Notes on the Theory of Speech as Action," in *Current Trends in Stylistics*, ed. Braj B. Kachru and H. F. W. Stahlke (Edmonton and Champaign, 1972), pp. 115–141.

10 This summary is based on an examination of 300 English and American short stories which was conducted for me by Barbara Korte.

11 Dietrich Weber, *Theorie der analytischen Erzählung* (Munich, 1975).

Notes to Chapter VII, "How Stories End I: the Static Modes" (pages 118 to 134)

1 Edgar Allan Poe, "Hawthorne's Tales," in *The Works of Edgar Allan Poe*, eds. E. C. Stedman and G. E. Woodberry (New York and Pittsburgh, 1903), VII, 31.

2 Barbara H. Smith, *Poetic Closure* (Chicago, 1968), p. 102.

3 Dorrit Cohn, *Transparent Minds* (Princeton, 1978), p. 243.

4 William Labov and Joshua Waletzky, "Narrative Analysis: Oral Versions of Personal Experience," in *Essays on the Verbal and Visual Arts*, ed. June Helm (Seattle and London, 1967), pp. 39–41.

Notes to Chapter VIII, "How Stories End II: The Dynamic Modes (pages 135 to 164)

1 Barbara H. Smith, *Poetic Closure* (Chicago, 1968), p. 102.

2 Helmut Bonheim, "He Didn't Look Back: Literary Tradition and the Canadian Short Story." *Queen's Quarterly*, forthcoming.

3 Frank Kermode, *The Sense of an Ending* (Oxford University Press, 1966).

4 Frank Kermode, "Sensing Endings,' *Nineteenth Century Fiction* 33 (1978), 149.

5 Martin Joos, *The Five Clocks* (New York, 1961), p. 11.

6 William Labov and Joshua Waletzky, "Narrative Analysis: Oral Versions of Personal Experience," in *Essays on the Verbal and Visual Arts*, Proceedings of the 1966 Annual Spring Meeting of the American Ethnological Society, ed. June Helm (Seattle and London, 1967), 12–44.

7 Boris Uspensky, *A Poetics of Composition* (Berkeley and Los Angeles, 1973), pp. 125 seq.

8 Paul Goetsch, *Die Short Story* (Tübingen, 1978), p. 46.

9 Hershel Parker and Henry Binder, "Exigencies of Complication and Publication: *Billy Budd, Sailor* and *Pudd'nhead Wilson*," *Nineteenth Century Fiction*, 33 (1978), 131.

10 Eckard Cwik, *Erzählmodi in der Short Story, 1820–1970*, unpubl. thesis, University of Cologne, 1975, pp. 113f.

11 The convention of the *dubbio* is discussed at length by Thomas Frederick Crane, *Italian Social Customs of the Sixteenth Century and their Influence on the Literatures of Europe* (New Haven, 1920), especially chapter XI.

12 Kermode, "Sensing Endings," 156.

13 Helmut Bonheim, "Topoi of the Canadian Short Story," *Dalhousie Review*, 60 (1981), p. 668.

14 The term is that of Raymond Federman: *Surfiction: Fiction Now ... and Tomorrow* (Chicago, 1975).

15 See Chapter II, note 38.

Notes to the Conclusion, "Novel and Short Story" (pages 165 to 169)

1 Two of the variants have been reprinted in Alfred Weber and Walter F. Greiner, *Short-Story-Theorien* (1573–1973), (Kronberg, 1977), pp. 45–48, 67. The vexed question whether the short story has characteristics to which the novel cannot lay claim is given a thorough review by Mary Louise Pratt, "The Short Story: The Long and the Short of it", *Poetics*, 10 (1981), 175–194.

2 H. L. Terrie, Jr., "Henry James and the 'Explosive Principle'," *Nineteenth Century Fiction*, 15 (1960/61), 283–299; Paul Goetsch, "Arten der Situationsverknüpfung," in his *Studien und Materialien zur Short Story* (= Schule u. Forschung 15), (Frankfurt, 1977), 40–43.

3 Klaus Doderer, "Die angelsächsische *short story* und die deutsche Kurzgeschichte," *Die neueren Sprachen*, 2 (1953), 417–424.

4 J. Berg Esenwein, "What is a Short-Story," in *What is the Short Story?*, eds. Eugene Current-Garcia and Walton R. Patrick (Glenview, Illinois, 1961), pp. 51–57.

5 See, for instance, the 113 excerpts from short story theorizing which are reprinted by Weber and Greiner.

6 *Short Story Index: An Index to 60,000 Stories in 4,320 Collections*, ed. Dorothy E. Cook and Isabel S. Monro (New York, 1953). The *Supplement 1964–1968* by Estelle A. Fiddell lists 11,301 stories in 793 collections.

7 For instance the "stories" by Duncan and Moodie in *Stories from Ontario*, selected by Germaine Warkentin (Toronto, 1974).

8 The same idea has recently been advanced by Pratt (see footnote 1, above), p. 186.

9 John Wain quoted by Greiner and Weber, p. 197.

BIBLIOGRAPHY A

Short story collections and anthologies

1. *Author collections*

Atwood, Margaret. *Dancing Girls and Other Stories*. Toronto: McClelland and Stewart, 1978.
Faulkner, William. *The Portable Faulkner*. New York: Viking, 1949.
Gallant, Mavis. *The End of the World and Other Stories*. Toronto: McClelland and Stewart, 1974.
Gordimer, Nadine. *Livingstone's Companions*. Harmondsworth: Penguin, 1975.
Hawthorne, Nathaniel. *Twice-Told Tales and Other Short Stories*. 1837; rpt. New York: Washington Square Press, 1960.
Hemingway, Ernest. *Hemingway: The Viking Portable Library*. New York: Viking, 1944.
Joyce, James. *The Portable James Joyce*. New York: Viking, 1947.
Laurence, Margaret. *The Tomorrow-Tamer and Other Stories*. 1963; rpt. Toronto: McClelland and Stewart, 1970.
Lawrence, D. H. *The Complete Short Stories of D. H. Lawrence*. Vol. 1. New York: Viking, 1961.
——. *The Complete Short Stories of D. H. Lawrence*. Vol. 2. New York: Viking, 1961.
Leacock, Stephen. *Sunshine Sketches of a Little Town*. 1931; rpt. Toronto: McClelland and Stewart, 1960.
——. *Arcadian Adventures with the Idle Rich*. 1914; rpt. Toronto: McClelland and Stewart, 1969.
Mansfield, Katherine. *The Garden Party*. New York: Modern Library, 1922.
Munro, Alice. *Something I've Been Meaning to Tell You: Thirteen Stories*. Scarborough, Ontario: New American Library, 1975.
Poe, Edgar Allan. *Great Tales and Poems*. New York: Pocket Library, 1956.
Raddall, Thomas H. *At the Tide's Turn and Other Stories*. Toronto: McClelland and Stewart, 1959.
Richler, Mordecai. *The Street*. Toronto: McClelland and Stewart, 1969; rpt. Harmondsworth: Penguin, 1977.
Roberts, Charles G. D. *The Last Barrier and Other Stories*. 1958; rpt. Toronto: McClelland and Stewart, 1970.
Ross, Sinclair. *The Lamp at Noon and Other Stories*. Toronto: McClelland and Stewart, 1968.
Salinger, J. D. *Nine Stories*. 1954; rpt. New York: New American Library, 1960.
Scott, Duncan Campbell. *In the Village of Viger and Other Stories*. Toronto: McClelland and Stewart, 1973.

Wiebe, Rudy. *Where Is the Voice Coming From?* Toronto: McClelland and Stewart, 1974.
Wilson, Ethel. *Mrs. Golightly and Other Stories.* Toronto: Macmillan, 1961.

2. Anthologies

Blaise, Clark and John Metcalf, eds. *'79 Best Canadian Stories.* Ontario: Oberon Press, 1979.
Cochrane, James, ed. *The Penguin Book of American Short Stories.* Harmondsworth: Penguin, 1972.
Crane, Milton, ed. *50 Great Short Stories.* New York: Bantam Books, 1959.
Dolley, Christopher, ed. *The Penguin Book of English Short Stories.* Harmondsworth: Penguin, 1967.
——. *The Second Penguin Book of English Short Stories.* Harmondsworth: Penguin, 1972.
Grant, Douglas, ed. *American Short Stories.* London: Oxford Univ. Press, 1965.
Lucas, Alec, ed. *Great Canadian Short Stories: An Anthology.* New York: Dell, 1971.
Peterson, Spiro, ed. *The Counterfeit Lady Unveiled and Other Criminal Fiction of Seventeenth-Century England.* Garden City, New York: Doubleday, 1961.
Stephens, Donald, ed. *Contemporary Voices: The Short Story in Canada.* Scarborough, Ontario: Prentice-Hall, 1972.
Stevens, John, ed. *Modern Canadian Stories.* 1975; rpt. Toronto: McClelland and Stewart, 1978.
Warkentin, Germaine, ed. *Stories from Ontario.* Toronto: Macmillan of Canada, 1974.
Warren, Robert Penn, ed. *Short Story Masterpieces.* 1954; rpt. New York: Dell, 1960.
Weaver, Robert, ed. *Canadian Short Stories.* Toronto: Oxford Univ. Press, 1966.
——. *Canadian Short Stories: Second Series.* Toronto: Oxford Univ. Press, 1968.
——. *Canadian Short Stories: Third Series.* Toronto: Oxford Univ. Press, 1978.
Wilson, Richard, ed. *English Short Stories: An Anthology.* 1921; rpt. London: Dent, 1966.
Wolfe, Morris, and Douglas Daymond, eds. *Toronto Short Stories.* Toronto: Doubleday, 1977.

BIBLIOGRAPHY B

Literature on speech in fiction, especially narrated monologue (erlebte Rede, style indirect libre)

Bally, Charles. "Le style indirect libre en français moderne." *Germanisch-Romanische Monatsschrift*, 4 (1912), 549–56 and 597–606.

Banfield, Ann. "Narrative Style and the Grammar of Direct and Indirect Speech." *Foundations of Language: International Journal of Language and Philosophy*, 10 (1973), 1–39.

——. "Where Epistemology, Style and Grammar Meet Literary History: The Development of Represented Speech and Thought." *New Literary History*, 9 (1978), 415–54.

——. "The Formal Coherence of Represented Speech and Thought." *PTL*, 3 (1978), 289–314.

Benstock, Shari. "Who Killed Cock Robin? The Sources of Free Indirect Style in *Ulysses*." Style, 14 (1980), 259–273.

Bickerton, Derek. "James Joyce and the Development of Interior Monologue." *Essays in Criticism*, 18 (1968), 32–46.

——. "Modes of Interior Monologue. A Formal Description." *Modern Language Quarterly*, 28 (1967), 229–39.

Bühler, Wilhelm. *Die "erlebte Rede" im englischen Roman*. Zürich / Leipzig: Niehans, 1937.

Cohen, Marcel. "Le style indirect libre et l'imparfait en français apres 1850." *Grammaire et Style*. 1450–1950. Paris: Ed. Sociales, 1954, pp. 99–107.

Cohn, Dorrit. "Narrated Monologue: Definition of a Fictional Style." *Comparative Literature*, 18 (1966), 97–112.

——. *Transparent Minds: Narrative Modes for Presenting Consciousness in Fiction*. Princeton: Princeton Univ. Press, 1978, chapter 3.

Dillon, George L. and Frederick Kirchoff. "On the Form and Function of Free Indirect Style." *PTL*, 1 (1976), 431–440.

Doležel, Lubomir. "Represented Discourse in Modern Czech Narrative Prose." In his *Narrative Modes in Czech Literature*. Toronto and Buffalo: Univ. of Toronto Press, 1973, pp. 15–55.

Dujardin, Edouard. *Le Monologue Intérieur*. Paris: Messein, 1931.

Espinola, Judith C. "The Nature, Function and Performance of Indirect Discourse in Prose Fiction." *Speech Monographs*, 41 (1974), 193–204.

Fehr, Bernard. "Substitutionary Narration and Description: A Chapter in Stylistics." *English Studies*, 20 (1938), 97–107.

Goldstein, K. "Die pathologischen Tatsachen in ihrer Bedeutung für das Problem der Sprache." Kongress deutscher Gesellschaft für Psychologie, 12, 1932.

Gregory, Michael. "Old Bailey Speech in *A Tale of Two Cities*." *Review of English Literature*, 6 (1965), 42–55.

Guiraud, Pierre. "Modern Linguistics Looks at Rhetoric: Free Indirect Style." *Yearbook of Comparative Criticism*, 3 (1971), 77–89.

Heinerman, Theodor. "Die Arten der reproduzierten Rede." *Forschungen zur Romanischen Philologie*, 2 (1931), 3–50.

Hernadi, Paul. "Dual Perspective: Free Indirect Discourse and Related Techniques." *Comparative Literature*, 24 (1972), 32–43.

——. "Verbal Worlds Between Action and Vision: A Theory of the Modes of Poetic Discourse." *College English*, 33 (1971), 18–31.

Hough, Graham. "Narrative and Dialogue in Jane Austen." *Critical Quarterly*, 12 (1970), 201–29.

Jones, C. "Varieties of Speech Presentation in Conrad's *The Secret Agent*." *Lingua*, 20 (1968), 162–76.

Kalepky, Theodor. "Zum 'style indirect libre' ('verschleierte Rede')." *Germanisch-Romanische Monatsschrift*, 5 (1913), 608–19.

Lerch, Eugen. "Die stilistische Bedeutung des Imperfektums der Rede ('style indirect libre')." *Germanisch-Romanische Monatsschrift*, 6 (1914), 470–89.

Lethcoe, Ronald James. *Narrated Speech and Consciousness*. Diss. Wisconsin 1969.

Lips, Marguerite. *Le Style Indirect Libre*. Paris: Payot, 1926.

Lorck, Etienne. *Die "Erlebte Rede": Eine sprachliche Untersuchung*. Heidelberg: Carl Winter Universitätsverlag, 1921.

Mc Hale, Brian. "Free Indirect Discourse: A Survey of Recent Accounts." *PTL*, 3 (1978), 249–287.

Miller, Nobert. "Erlebte und verschleierte Rede." *Akzente*, 5 (1958), 213–26.

Page, Norman. *Speech in the English Novel*. London: Longman, 1973, esp. pp. 24–50.

——. "Categories of Speech in Persuasion." *Modern Language Review*, 64 (1969), 734–41.

——. "Trollope's Conversational Mode." *English Studies in Africa*, 15 (1972), 33–37.

Pascal, Roy. *The Dual Voice*. Manchester: Manchester Univ. Press, 1977.

Ron, Moshe. "Free Indirect Discourse, Mimetic Language Games and the Subject of Fiction." *Poetics Today*, 2.2. (1981), 17–39.

Ryan, Marie-Laure. "When 'Je' is 'Un Autre': Fiction, Quotation, and the Performative Analysis." *Poetics Today*, 2.2 (1981), 127–155.

Schuelke, Gertrude L. "'Slipping' in Indirect Discourse." *American Speech*, 33 (1958), 90–98.

Sørensen, Knud. "Subjective Narration in *Bleak House*." *English Studies*, 40 (1959), 431–39.

Stanzel, Franz. "Episches Präteritum, erlebte Rede, historisches Präsens." *Deutsche Vierteljahresschrift*, 33 (1959), 1–12.

Steinberg, Günter. *Erlebte Rede. Ihre Eigenart und ihre Formen in neuerer deutscher, französischer und englischer Erzählliteratur*. Göppingen: Kümmerle, 1971.

Storz, Gerhard. "De quelques interprétations récentes du style indirect libre." *Recherches Anglaises et Américaines*, 7 (1974), 40–74.

Strauch, Gérard. "Contribution à l'étude sémantique des verbes introducteurs du discours indirect." *RANAM* 5 (1972), 226–242.

Ullmann, Stephen. "Reported Speech and Internal Monologue in Flaubert." In his *Style in the French Novel*. Cambridge: Cambridge Univ. Press, 1957.

Vickery, W. N. "Three Examples of Narrated Speech in Pushkin's Poltava." *Slavic and East European Journal*, 8 (1964), pp. 273–283.

Vygotsky, L. S. *Thought and Language*, ed. & tr. E. Hanfmann and G. Vakar. Cambridge, Mass., M. I. T. Press, 1962.

Walzel, Oskar. "Von erlebter Rede." *Das Wortkunstwerk: Mittel seiner Erforschung.*
    Leipzig: Quelle & Meyer, 1926, pp. 207–230.
Watson, J. *Psychology from the Standpoint of a Behaviorist.* Philadelphia: Lippincott,
    1919.
Williams, Raymond. "Talking to Ourselves." *The Cambridge Review*, CII (1981),
    160–164.

BIBLIOGRAPHY C

Other works consulted

Achten, Waltraud. *Psychoanalytische Literaturkritik: Eine Untersuchung am Beispiel der amerikanischen Zeitschrift "Literature and Psychology"*. Frankfurt am Main: Lang, 1981.

Allen, Walter. "Narrative Distance, Tone, and Character." In: *The Theory of the Novel*. Ed. J. Halperin. New York: Oxford Univ. Press, 1974, pp. 323–337.

Auerbach, Erich. *Mimesis*. New York: Doubleday Anchor Books, 1957.

Backus, Joseph M. "'He Came into her Line of Vision Walking Backward': Non-sequential Sequence Signals in Short Story Openings.' *Language Learning*, 15 (1965), 67–83.

Beach, Joseph Warren. *The Twentieth Century Novel: Studies in Technique*. New York/London: The Century Co., 1932.

Behagel, Otto. *Deutsche Syntax: Eine geschichtliche Darstellung*. Vol. IV. Heidelberg: Carl Winter Universitätsverlag, 1932

Bekes, P. "Poetologie des Titels." *Poetica*, 11 (1979), 394–426.

Bellos, David M. "The Narrative Absolute Tense." *Language and Style*, 13 (1980), 77–84.

Benjamin, James. "Performatives as a Rhetorical Construct." *Philosophy and Rhetoric*, 9 (1976), 84–95.

Beyerle, Dieter. "Ein vernachlässigter Aspekt der erlebten Rede." *Archiv für das Studium der neueren Sprachen und Literaturen*, 208 (1972), 350–366.

Bivens, William P., III. "Parameters of Poetic Inversion in English." *Language and Style*. 12 (1979), 13–25.

Blanchard, Marc Eli. *Description: Sign, Self, Desire*. Mouton: The Hague, 1980.

Bonheim, Helmut. "Instrumentale Literaturkritik." *Poetica*, 6 (1974), 76–86.

——. "Theory of Narrative Modes." *Semiotica*, 14:4 (1975), 329–344.

——. "Mode Markers in the American Short Story." *Proceedings of the Fourth International Congress of Applied Linguistics*. Ed. Gerhard Nickel. Stuttgart: Hochschulverlag, 1976. Vol. I, pp. 541–550.

——. "Einige Werkzeuge der instrumentalen Literaturkritik." *Anglistik und Englischunterricht: Literatur in der Schule*, 5 (1978), 43–56.

——. "He Didn't Look Back: Literary Tradition and the Canadian Short Story." *Queen's Quarterly*, forthcoming.

——. "Topoi of the Canadian Short Story." *Dalhousie Review*, 60 (1981), 659–669.

Booth, Wayne C. "Distance and Point-of-View: An Essay in Classification." *Essays in Criticism*, 11 (1961), 60–79.

——. *The Rhetoric of Fiction*. Chicago: Chicago Univ. Press, 1961.

Bowling, Lawrence Edward. "What Is the Stream of Consciousness Technique?" *PMLA*, 65 (1950), 333–345.

Bradbury, Malcolm. *Possibilities: Essays on the State of the Novel.* London: Oxford University Press, 1973.

Bruffee, Kenneth. "Getting Started." *Language and Style*, 13 (1980), Special Number, 52–60.

Bullough, Edward. "Psychical Distance." In: Melvin Rader, ed., *A Modern Book of Esthetics.* New York: Holt, Rinehart and Winston, 4th ed., 1973, pp. 368–384.

Campbell, Bruce G. "Towards a Workable Taxonomy of Illocutionary Forces, and its Implication to Works of Imaginative Literature." *Language and Style*, 8 (1975), 3–20.

Campbell, Paul N. "Poetic-Rhetorical, Philosophical, and Scientific Discourse." *Philosophy and Rhetoric*, 6 (1973), 1–29.

Chatman, Seymour. "New Ways of Analysing Narrative Structure. With an Example from Joyce's *Dubliners.*" *Language and Style*, 2 (1969), 3–36.

——. "The Structure of Fiction." *University of Kansas City Review*, 37 (1971), 190–214.

——. "The Structure of Narrative Transmission." *Style and Structure in Literature*, ed. Roger Fowler. Oxford: Basil Blackwell, 1975, pp. 213–257.

——. *Story and Discourse: Narrative Structure in Fiction and Film.* Ithaca: Cornell University Press, 1978.

——. "Analgorithm." *James Joyce Quarterly*, 18 (1981), 293–299.

Cohn, Dorrit. *Transparent Minds: Narrative Modes for Presenting Consciousness in Fiction.* Princeton, N.J.: Princeton Univ. Press, 1978.

Cook, Dorothy E. and Isabel S. Monro, eds. *Short Story Index: An Index to 60,000 Stories in 4320 Collections.* New York: H. W. Wilson, 1953. *Short Story Index Supplement 1964–1968.* Ed. Estelle A. Fiddell.

Crane, Thomas Frederick. *Italian Social Customs of the Sixteenth Century and their Influence on the Literature of Europe.* New Haven: Yale Univ. Press, 1920, esp. ch. XI.

Curme, George Oliver. *A Grammar of the English Language in Three Volumes.* Boston: Heath, 1931–1953. Vol. III. pp. 348–349.

Cwik, Eckard. *Erzählmodi in der short story, 1820–1970.* Diss. Cologne 1975.

Dewey, John. "Thought and its Subject-Matter." In: *Studies in Logical Theory.* Chicago: Univ. of Chicago Press, 1903.

van Dijk, Teun A. "Action, Action Description and Narrative." *New Literary History*, 6 (1974/75), 273–294.

Doderer, Klaus. "Die angelsächsische short story und die deutsche Kurzgeschichte." *Die Neueren Sprachen*, 2 (1953), 417–424.

Dolezel, Lubomir. *Narrative Modes in Czech Literature.* Toronto: Univ. of Toronto Press, 1973.

——. "A Scheme of Narrative Time." In: *Semiotics of Art: Prague School Contributions.* Ed. Ladislav Matejka and I. R. Titunik. Cambridge, Mass.: The MIT Press, 1976, pp. 209–217.

——. "Extensional and Intensional Narrative Worlds." *Poetics*, 8 (1979), 193–211.

Duffy, Dennis. *Marshall McLuhan.* Toronto: McClelland and Stewart, 1969.

Eisler, Rudolph. *Kant-Lexikon.* Berlin: Pan-Verlag Kurt Metzler, 1930.

Engelsing, Rolf. "Das Thema 'Lesergeschichte'." *Jahrbuch für internationale Germanistik* XII/1 (1980), 168–178.

Esenwein, J. Berg. "What Is a Short-Story?" In: *What Is the Short Story?* Eds. Eugene Current-Garcia and Walton R. Patrick. Glenview, Ill.: Scott, Foresman, 1961, pp. 51–57.

Fairley, Irene R. "Experimental Approaches to Language in Literature: Reader Responses to Poems." *Style*, 13 (1979), 335–364.

Faulstich, Werner. *Domänen der Rezeptionsanalyse*. Kronberg/Ts: Athenäum, 1977.
Federman, Raymond, ed. *Surfiction: Fiction Now . . . and Tomorrow*. Chicago: The Swallow Press, 1975.
Fokkema, D. W. and Elrud Kunne-Ibsch. *Theories of Literature in the Twentieth Century*. London: C. Hurst, 1977.
Folks, Jeffrey J. "The Influence of Poetry on the Narrative Technique of Faulkner's Early Fiction." *Journal of Narrative Technique*, 9 (1979), 184–190.
Fowler, Roger. *Linguistics and the Novel*. London: Methuen, 1977.
Friedemann, Käthe. *Die Rolle des Erzählers in der Epik*. Leipzig, 1910; rpt. Darmstadt: Wissenschaftliche Buchgemeinschaft, 1965.
Friedman, Norman. "Point of View in Fiction: The Development of a Critical Concept." *PMLA*, 70 (1955), 1160–1184.
Füger, Wilhelm. "Zur Tiefenstruktur des Narrativen." *Poetica*, 5 (1972), 268–292.
Geismar, Maxwell. "The American Short Story Today." *Studies on the Left*, 4 (1964), 21–27.
Gelley, Alexander. "The Represented World: Toward a Phenomenological Theory of Description in the Novel." *Journal of Aesthetics and Art Criticism*, 37 (1979), 415–422.
Genette, Gerard. "Frontières du récit." In his *Figures II: Essais*. Paris: Les Editions du Seuil, 1969, pp. 49–69.
——. "Boundaries of Narrative." *New Literary History*, 8 (1976/77), 1–13.
——. *Narrative Discourse: An Essay in Method*. Oxford: Basil Blackwell; Ithaca: Cornell University Press, 1980.
Gibson, Walker. "Authors, Speakers, Readers, and Mock Readers." *College English*, 11 (1950), 265–269.
Goetsch, Paul. "Arten der Situationsverknüpfung." In his *Studien und Materialien zur Short Story* (= Schule und Forschung 15). Frankfurt: Diesterweg, 1977, pp. 40–63.
——. *Die Short Story*. Tübingen: Deutsches Institut für Fernstudien an der Universität Tübingen, 1978.
Grabes, Herbert. "Fiktion-Realismus-Ästhetik: Woran erkennt der Leser Literatur?" In: *Text – Leser – Bedeutung: Untersuchungen zur Interaktion von Text und Leser*. Ed. H. Grabes. Grossen-Linden: Hoffmann, 1977, pp. 61–81.
Grimm, Gunter. *Rezeptionsgeschichte*. Munich: Wilhelm Fink, 1977.
Groeben, Norbert. *Rezeptionsforschung als empirische Literaturwissenschaft*. Kronberg/Ts.: Athenäum, 1977.
Gülich, Elisabeth and Wolfgang Raible. *Linguistische Textmodelle: Grundlagen und Möglichkeiten*. Munich: Wilhelm Fink, 1977.
Gunter, Richard. "Structure and Style in Poems: a Paradox.' In: *Style in English*. Ed. John Albert Nist. Indianapolis: The Bobbs-Merrill Company, 1969, pp. 50–57.
Hansen, Uffe. "Segmentierung narrativer Texte: zum Problem der Erzählperspektive in der Fiktionsprosa." *Text & Kontext*, 3.2. (1975), 3–48.
Harland, Richard. "Referential Distance and the Presentation of Experience in the Novel." *Southern Review*, XIII (1980), 130–149.
Harweg, Roland. *Pronomina und Textkonstitution*. Munich: Wilhelm Fink, 1968, pp. 152–167, 316–323.
Hatcher, Anna Granville. "*Voir* as a Modern Novelistic Device." *Philological Quarterly*, 23 (1944), 354–374.
Hirsch, David H. "Speech Acts or Fluid Language." *Journal of Literary Semantics*, 5 (1976), 15–31.
Hoffmann, Gerhard. *Raum, Situation, erzählte Wirklichkeit. Poetologische und historische Studien zum englischen und amerikanischen Roman*. Stuttgart: Metzlersche Verlagsbuchhandlung, 1978.

Holdcroft, David. "Forms of Indirect Communication: An Outline." *Philosophy and Rhetoric*, 9 (1976), 147–161.
——. *Words and Deeds: Problems in the Theory of Speech Acts*. Oxford: Clarendon Press, 1978.
Holdheim, W. Wolfgang. "Description and Cliché." *Arcadia*, 13 (1978), 1–9.
Holland, Norman. *5 Readers Reading*. New Haven: Yale Univ. Press, 1975.
Hoops, Wiklef. "Fiktionalität als pragmatische Kategorie." *Poetica*, 11 (1979), 281–317.
Howes, Raymond F. *Historical Studies of Rhetoric and Rhetoricians*. Ithaca: Cornell Univ. Press, 1961.
Humphrey, Robert. *Stream of Consciousness in the Modern Novel*. Berkeley: Univ. of California Press, 1965.
Iser, Wolfgang. *Der implizite Leser: Kommunikationsformen des Romans von Bunyan bis Beckett*. Munich: Wilhelm Fink, 1972.
——. *The Implied Reader. Patterns of Communication in Prose Fiction from Bunyan to Beckett*. Baltimore: John Hopkins Univ. Press, 1973.
Jakobson, Roman. "Linguistics and Poetics." *Style in Language*. Ed. Thomas A. Sebeok. Bloomington, Ind.: The Technology Press of Mass. Inst. of Technology, 1960, pp. 353–357.
Jameson, Fredric. *The Political Unconscious: Narrative as a Socially Symbolic Act*. London: Methuen, 1981.
Jauss, Hans Robert. *Literaturgeschichte als Provokation*. Frankfurt am Main: Suhrkamp, 1970.
Jespersen, Otto. *Essentials of English Grammar*. London: Allen & Unwin, 1933.
Jolles, André. *Einfache Formen*. Tübingen: Niemeyer, 1930; rpt. 1974.
Joos, Martin. *The Five Clocks*. New York: Harcourt, Brace & World, 1961.
Joseph, Miriam (Sister). *Rhetoric in Shakespeare's Time*. New York: Harcourt, Brace & World, 1962.
Junke, Gisela. *Die Formen des Dialogs im frühen englischen Roman*. Diss. Cologne 1975.
Jüttner, Siegfried. "Im Namen des Lesers." *GRM*, 29 (1979), 1–26.
Kaufmann, Gerhard. *Die indirekte Rede und mit ihr konkurrierende Formen der Redeerwähnung* (= Heutiges Deutsch III/1). München: Hueber, 1976.
Kayser, Wolfgang. *Das sprachliche Kunstwerk*. 10th ed. Bern and Munich: Francke, 1964.
Kermode, Frank. *The Sense of an Ending*. New York: Oxford Univ. Press, 1966.
——. "Sensing Endings." *Nineteenth Century Fiction*, 33 (1978), 144–158.
Kieckers, E. "Die Stellung der Verba des Sagens in Schaltesätzen im Griechischen und in den verwandten Sprachen." *Indogermanische Forschungen*, 30 (1912), 145–185.
——. "Zur oratio recta in den indogermanischen Sprachen I." *Indogermanische Forschungen*, 35 (1915), 1–93.
——. "Zur oratio recta in den indogermanischen Sprachen II." *Indogermanische Forschungen*, 36 (1916), 1–70.
Kinneavy, James L. *A Theory of Discourse*. Englewood Cliffs, N.Y.: Prentice-Hall, 1971.
Koskimies, R. *Theorie des Romans*. Helsinki: Druckerei der finnischen Literaturgesellschaft, 1935.
Kreifelts, Barbara. *Eine statistische Stilanalyse zur Klärung von Autorenschaftsfragen, durchgeführt am Beispiel von Green's "Groatsworth of Wit"*. Diss. Cologne 1972.

Kroeber, Karl. *Styles in Fictional Structure*. Princeton N.J.: Princeton Univ. Press, 1971.

Labov, William and Joshua Waletzky. "Narrative Analysis: Oral Versions of Personal Experience." *Essays on the Verbal and Visual Arts*, Proceedings of the 1966 Annual Spring Meeting of the American Ethnological Society, ed. June Helm. Seattle and London: distributed by the University of Washington Press, 1967. German version as "Erzählanalyse: Mündliche Versionen persönlicher Erfahrung." *Literaturwissenschaft und Linguistik*, ed. Jens Ihwe. Frankfurt: Athenäum, 1973, II, 78–126.

Lämmert, Eberhard. *Bauformen des Erzählens*. Stuttgart: Metzlersche Verlagsbuchhandlung und Karl Ernst Poeschel Verlag, 1955.

Landwehr, Jürgen. *Text und Fiktion*. Munich: Wilhelm Fink, 1975.

Lanham, Richard. *A Handlist of Rhetorical Terms*. Berkeley: Univ. of California Press, 1969.

Leisi, Ernst. "Der Erzählstandpunkt in der neueren englischen Prosa." *Aufsätze*. Heidelberg: Carl Winter Universitätsverlag, 1978, pp. 21–33.

Liddell, Robert. *A Treatise on the Novel*. London: Cape, 1947.

Link, Franz. "'Tale', 'Sketch', 'Essay' und 'Short Story'". *Die Neueren Sprachen*, 6 (1957), 345–352.

Link, Hannelore. *Rezeptionsforschung. Eine Einführung in Methoden und Probleme*. Stuttgart: Kohlhammer, 1976.

Lodge, David. *The Modes of Modern Writing*. London: Arnold, 1977.

——. *Working with Structuralism*. Boston, London and Henley: Routledge and Kegan Paul, 1981.

Lubbers, Klaus. *Typologie der Short Story*. Darmstadt: Wissenschaftliche Buchgemeinschaft, 1977.

Lubbock, Percy. *The Craft of Fiction*. 1921; rpt. London: Cape, 1926.

Maas, Utz, and Dieter Wunderlich. *Pragmatik und sprachliches Handeln*. Athenäum-Skripten Linguistik. Frankfurt: Athenäum, 1972.

McGuire, R. R. "Speech Acts, Communicative Competence and the Paradox of Authority." *Philosophy and Rhetoric*, 10 (1977), 30–45.

McLuhan, Marshall. *Understanding Media: The Extensions of Man*. New York: McGraw Hill; London: Routledge and Kegan Paul, 1964.

Mailloux, Steven. "Learning to Read: Interpretation and Reader-Response Criticism." *Studies in the Literary Imagination*, 12 (1979), 93–108.

Malinowski, Bronislaw. "The Problem of Meaning in Primitive Languages." 1923; rpt. in: *The Meaning of Meaning*. Eds. C. K. Ogden and I. A. Richards. London: Routledge and Kegan Paul, 1969, pp. 296–336.

Miller, Norbert. ed. *Romananfänge: Versuch zu einer Poetik des Romans*. Berlin: Literarisches Colloquium, 1965.

Morris, Charles. *Signs, Language and Behavior*. 1946; rpt. New York: George Braziller, 1955.

Müller, Günther. *Die Bedeutung der Zeit in der Erzählkunst*. Bonn: Universitätsverlag, 1947.

——. "Erzählzeit und erzählte Zeit." In: *Festschrift für P. Kluckhohn und Hermann Schneider*, 1948. Rpt. in *Morphologische Poetik*. Darmstadt: Wiss. Buchgesellschaft, 1968, pp. 269–86.

Mylne, Vivienne. "The Punctuation of Dialogue in Eighteenth-Century French and English Fiction." *The Library*, Sixth Series, I (1979), 43–61.

Ohmann, Richard. "Instrumental Style: Notes on the Theory of Speech as Action." *Current Trends in Stylistics*. Ed. Braj B. Kachru and Herbert F. W. Stahlke. Edmonton, Alberta and Champaign, Ill.: Ling. Research Inc., 1972, pp. 115–141.

Olderman, Raymond M. *Beyond the Waste Land.* New Haven: Yale Univ. Press, 1972.

Oomen, Ursula. "Systemtheorie der Texte." *Folia Linguistica*, 5 (1971), 12–34.

Ostbomk, Willi. *Modes of Narrative bei Mordecai Richler.* Cologne, senior thesis, 1978.

Parker, Hershel and Henry Binder. "Exigencies of Complication and Publication: *Billy Budd, Sailor* and *Pudd'nhead Wilson.*" *Nineteenth-Century Fiction*, 33 (1978), 131–143.

Partee, Barbara Hall. "The Semantics of Belief-Sentences." *Approaches to Natural Language.* Ed. K. J. J. Hintikka et al. Dordrecht/Boston: Reidel Publ. Comp., 1973, pp. 309–336.

Peprnik, Jaroslav. "Reporting Phrases in English Prose." *Brno Studies in English*, 8 (1969), 145–151.

Petsch, Robert. *Wesen und Formen der Erzählkunst.* Halle/Saale: Niemeyer, 1934.

Poe, Edgar Allan. "Hawthorne's Tales." *The Works of Edgar Allan Poe.* Ed. E. C. Stedman and G. C. Woodberry. New York and Pittsburgh: Colonial Co., 1903. Vol. VII, pp. 19–38.

Pouillon, Jean. *Temps et roman.* Paris: Gallimard, 1946.

Pratt, Mary Louise. "The Short Story: The Long and the Short of it." *Poetics*, 10 (1981), 175–194.

Pütz, Manfred. *The Story of Identity: American Fiction of the Sixties* (= American Studies/Amerika Studien 54). Stuttgart: Metzlersche Verlagsbuchhandlung, 1979.

Quirk, Randolph et el. *A Grammar of Contemporary English.* London: Longman, 1972.

Raible, Wolfgang. "Literatur and Natur. Beobachtungen zur literarischen Landschaft." *Poetica*, 11 (1979), 105–123.

Richter, D. H. *Fable's End. Completeness and Closure in Rhetorical Fiction.* (Chicago: University of Chicago Press, 1975).

Rose, Ellen Cronan. "Feminine Endings – And Beginnings: Margaret Drabble's *The Waterfall.*" *Contemporary Literature*, 21 (1980), 81–99.

Ross, Donald Jr. "Who's Talking? How Characters Become Narrators in Fiction." *Modern Language Notes*, 91 (1976), 1222–1242.

Ross, Stephen M. "'Voice' In Narrative Texts: The Example of *As I Lay Dying.*" *PMLA*, 94 (1979), 300–310.

Ruthrof, H. G. "Narrative Language." *Language and Style*, 10 (1977), 42–51.

Said, Edward W. *Beginnings: Intention and Method.* New York: Basic Books, 1975.

Sanders, Robert E. "In Defense of Speech Acts." *Philosophy and Rhetoric*, 9 (1976), 112–115.

Schiffer, Paul S., "'Homing, upstream': Fictional Closure and the End of *Ulysses.*" *James Joyce Quarterly*, 16 (1979), 283–298.

Schlissel von Fleschenberg, O. "Die Technik des Bildeinsatzes." *Philologus*, 72 (1913), 83–114.

Schmid, Wolf. *Der Textaufbau in den Erzählungen Dostoevskijs* (= Beihefte zu *Poetica*, 10). Munich: Wilhelm Fink, 1973.

Schmidt, Siegfried J. "Towards a Pragmatic Interpretation of Fictionality." *Pragmatics of Language and Literature.* Ed. Teun van Dijk. Amsterdam: North-Holland Publishing Company, 1976, pp. 161–178.

Scholes, Robert. *The Fabulators.* New York: Oxford Univ. Press, 1967.

Schuhmann, Kuno. "Englische Romananfänge im 19. Jahrhundert." In *Romanan-*

fänge: Versuch zu einer Poetik des Romans. Ed. Nobert Miller. Berlin: Literarisches Colloquium, 1965, pp. 185–205.

Searle, John R. *Speech Acts: An Essay in the Philosophy of Language.* 1969; rpt. Cambridge: Cambridge Univ. Press, 1977.

——. "The Logical Status of Fictional Discourse." *New Literary History,* 6 (1974/75), 319–332.

Segers, Rien T. "Some Implications of 'Rezeptionsästhetik'." *Yearbook of Comparative and General Literature,* 24 (1975), 15–23.

Shiner, Roger A. "Freedom of Speech-Acts." *Philosophy and Rhetoric,* 3 (1970), 40–50.

Shirley, Edward S. "Reply to Professor Sanders." *Philosophy and Rhetoric,* 9 (1976), 175–180.

——. "The Impossibility of a Speech Act Theory of Meaning." *Philosophy and Rhetoric,* 8 (1975), 114–122.

Smith, Barbara H. *Poetic Closure.* Chicago: Univ. of Chicago Press, 1968.

Spitzer, Leo. "Milieu and Ambiance." In: *Essays in Historical Semantics.* New York: S. F. Vanni, 1948, pp. 179–225.

Stanzel, Franz K. *Die typischen Erzählsituationen im Roman.* Vienna and Stuttgart: Braumüller, 1965.

——. "Die Komplementärgeschichte: Entwurf einer leserorientierten Romantheorie." *LiLi: Zeitschrift für Literaturwissenschaft und Linguistik,* Beiheft 6. Ed. W. Haubrichs, 1977, 240–259.

——. "Second Thoughts on *Narrative Situations in the Novel*: Towards a 'Grammar of Fiction'." *Novel: A Forum on Fiction,* 11 (1978), 247–264.

——. *Theorie des Erzählens.* Göttingen: Vandenhoeck & Ruprecht, 1979.

Stegmüller, Wolfgang. *Das ABC der modernen Logik und Semantik.* Berlin: Springer, 1974.

Steinmann, Martin Jr. "The Old Novel and the New." In *From Jane Austen to Conrad.* Ed. Robert C. Rathburn and Martin Steinmann. Minneapolis: Univ. of Minnesota Press, 1958.

Stempel, Wolf-Dieter. "Erzählung, Beschreibung und der historische Diskurs." In *Geschichte – Ereignis und Erzählung* (= Poetik und Hermeneutik, V). Ed. R. Kosellek and W.-D. Stempel. Munich: Wilhelm Fink, 1973, pp. 325–346.

Suleiman, Susan. "Ideological Dissent from Works of Fiction." *Neophilologus,* 60 (1976), 162–177.

Terrie, Henry L. Jr. "Henry James and the 'Explosive Principle'." *Nineteenth-Century Fiction,* 15 (1960/61), 283–299.

Thale, Jerome. "The Imagination of Charles Dickens." *Nineteenth-Century Fiction,* 22 (1967/68), 127–143.

Tompkins, Jane P., ed. *Reader-Response Criticism: From Formalism to Post-Structuralism.* Baltimore: Johns Hopkins Press, 1980.

Torgovnik, Marianna. "James's Sense of an Ending: The Role Played in its Development by the Popular Conventional Epilogue." *Studies in the Novel,* 10 (1978), 183–198.

——. *Closure in the Novel.* Princeton: Princeton University Press, 1981.

Ulich, Robert. "Apperception." *The Encyclopedia of Philosophy.* New York: Macmillan, 1967.

Ullmann, Stephen. *Style in the French Novel.* Cambridge: Cambridge Univ. Press, 1957.

Uspensky, Boris. *A Poetics of Composition: The Structure of Artistic Text and Typology of Compositional Form.* Trans. V. Zavarin and S. Wittig. Berkeley and Los Angeles: Univ. of California Press, 1973.

Voloshinov, V. N. "Reported Speech." In *Readings in Russian Poetics: Formalist and Structuralist Views*. Ed. Ladislav Matejka and K. Pomorska. Cambridge, Mass.: The MIT Press, 1971.

Wallwork, Jean F. *Language and Linguistics*. London: Heinemann, 1971.

Watson, George. *The Story of the Novel*. London and Basingstoke: Macmillan, 1979.

Weber, Alfred and Walter F. Greiner. *Short-Story-Theorien (1573–1973)*. Kronberg/ Ts.: Athenäum, 1977.

Weber, Dietrich. *Theorie der analytischen Erzählung*. Munich: C. H. Beck, 1975.

Weinrich, Harald. *Tempus. Besprochene und erzählte Welt*. Stuttgart: Kohlhammer, 1964. 2nd rev. ed. 1971.

Weisman, Herman. "An Investigation of Methods and Techniques in the Dramatization of Fiction." *Speech Monographs*, 19 (1952), 48–59.

Wicker, Brian. *The Story-Shaped World*. London: Athlone Press, 1975.

Wienold, Götz. "Probleme der linguistischen Analyse des Romans." *Literaturwissenschaft und Linguistik: Ergebnisse und Perspektiven*. Ed. Jens Ihwe. Frankfurt/ Main: Athenäum, 1972. Vol. III, pp. 322–344.

Williamson, George. *The Senecan Amble*. London: Faber & Faber, 1951.

Wolpers, Theodor. "Kürze im Erzählen." *Anglia*, 89 (1971), 48–86.

Wunderlich, Dieter. "Bemerkungen zu den verba dicendi." *Die Muttersprache*, 79 (1969), 97–107.

Zavarzadeh, Mas'ud. *The Mythopoeic Reality: The Postwar American Nonfiction Novel*. Urbana: Univ. of Ill. Press, 1976.

Zimmermann, Bernd. *Literaturrezeption im historischen Prozeß*. Munich: Beck, 1977.

Statistical Survey of Narrative Modes in the Short Story

	Anglo-American						Canadian		Anglo-American and Canadian together	
	pre-1900		post-1900		together					
Short story beginnings										
metanarrative	13	12%	2	1%	15	5%	13	4.3%	28	5%
comment	15	13%	7	4%	22	7%	10	3.3%	32	5%
description	40	36%	64	34%	104	35%	124	41.3%	228	38%
report	35	31%	92	49%	127	42%	113	38%	240	40%
speech	9	8%	23	12%	32	11%	36	12%	68	11%
uncertain							4	1%	4	1%
sum	112	100%	188	100%	300	100%	300	100%	600	100%
Short story endings										
metanarrative	11	10%	2	1%	13	4%	9	3%	22	4%
comment	27	24%	25	13%	52	17%	42	14%	94	16%
description	20	18%	24	13%	44	15%	49	16%	93	15.5%
report	29	26%	57	30%	86	29%	96	32%	182	30%
speech	21	19%	72	38%	93	31%	97	32%	190	32%
uncertain	4	4%	8	4%	12	4%	7	2%	19	3%
sum	112	100%	188	100%	300	100%	300	100%	600	100%

APPENDIX B:

Devices in Beginnings and Endings

	SHORT STORIES			NOVELS						
	Anglo-American	Canadian	together	16/17th cent.	18th cent.	19th cent.	1900–1940	1941–1980	Canadian	together
BEGINNINGS										
Anteriority	203 67,66%	212 70,6%	415 69,16%	15 30%	28 56%	30 60%	30 60%	27 54%	10 20%	140 46,69%
Habituality	185 61,66%	224 74,66%	409 68,16%	3 6%	5 10%	12 24%	18 36%	11 22%	5 10%	54 18%
Anteriority + Habituality	132 44%	169 56,33%	301 50,16%	1 2%	4 8%	10 20%	14 28%	8 16%	3 6%	40 13,34%
neither Ant. nor Hab.	43 14,33%	33 11%	76 12,66%	33 66%	21 42%	18 36%	16 32%	20 40%	38 76%	146 48,67%
referentless 3rd per. pronoun	38 12,66%	38 12,66%	76 12,66%	0 0%	1 2%	1 2%	5 10%	8 16%	6 12%	21 7%
MODES — metanarrative	15 5%	13 4,3%	28 5%	2 4%	7 14%	9 18%	2 4%	4 8%	3 6%	27 9%
comment	22 7%	10 3,3%	32 5%	6 12%	6 12%	5 10%	2 4%	0 0%	0 0%	19 6,34%
description	104 35%	124 41,3%	228 38%	14 28%	10 20%	18 36%	21 42%	9 18%	5 10%	77 25,67%
report	127 42%	113 38%	240 40%	25 50%	14 28%	14 28%	18 36%	26 52%	37 74%	134 44,34%
speech	32 11%	36 12%	68 11%	0 0%	13 26%	4 8%	2 4%	7 14%	5 10%	34 11,34%
Beginning in Present Tense	72 24%	75 25%	147 24,5%	10 20%	14 28%	21 42%	9 18%	13 26%	15 30%	82 27,34%
ENDINGS										
Brevity	43 14,33%	59 19,66%	102 17%	0 0%	0 0%	6 12%	5 10%	6 12%	6 12%	23 7,67%
Conjunctions	52 17,33%	68 22,66%	120 20%	13 26%	11 22%	9 18%	4 8%	7 14%	12 24%	56 18,67%
Question	11 3,66%	22 7,33%	33 5,5%	1 2%	0 0%	2 4%	2 4%	1 2%	0 0%	6 2%
Negation	47 15,66%	72 24%	119 19,83%	14 28%	16 32%	16 32%	10 20%	9 18%	8 16%	73 24,3%
Death	50 16,6%	50 16,6%	100 16,6%	20 40%	12 24%	17 34%	18 36%	17 34%	17 34%	96 32%
Epanalepsis	27 9%	23 7,6%	50 8,3%	2 4%	0 0%	1 2%	3 4%	11 22%	0 0%	16 5,34%
MODES — metanarrative	13 4%	9 3%	22 4%	19 38%	6 12%	7 14%	0 0%	1 2%	2 4%	35 11,67%
comment	52 17%	42 14%	94 16%	9 18%	5 10%	9 18%	4 8%	1 2%	5 10%	33 11%
description	44 15%	49 16%	93 15,5%	0 0%	2 4%	3 6%	8 16%	9 18%	5 10%	27 9%
report	86 29%	96 32%	182 30%	16 32%	22 44%	15 30%	16 32%	23 46%	17 34%	109 36,34%
speech	93 31%	97 32%	190 32%	1 2%	11 22%	10 20%	20 40%	12 24%	16 32%	70 23,34%
polysyndetic/asyndetic	39 13%	26 8,6%	65 10,83%	2 4%	0 0%	1 2%	1 2%	0 0%	4 8%	8 2,67%
Sum	n = 300	n = 300	n = 600	n = 50	n = 50	n = 50	n = 50	n = 50	n = 50	n = 300

Index

(Note: page numbers in italics indicate substantial discussion.)

Index